The IDG Books *Creating Cool* Series Advantage

We at IDG Books Worldwide created *Creating Cool Web Pages with Word for Windows 95* to meet your growing need for quick access to the most complete and accurate computer information available. Our books work the way you do: They focus on accomplishing specific tasks — not learning random functions. Our books are not long-winded manuals or dry reference tomes. In each book, expert authors tell you exactly what you can do with new technology and software and how to evaluate its usefulness for your needs. Easy to follow information, comprehensive coverage, and convenient access in language and design — it's all here.

The authors of IDG books are uniquely qualified to give you expert advice as well as to provide insightful tips and techniques not found anywhere else. Our authors maintain close contact with end users through feedback from articles, training sessions, e-mail exchanges, user group participation, and consulting work. Because our authors know the realities of daily computer use and are directly linked to the reader, our books have a strategic advantage.

Our experienced authors know how to approach a topic in the most efficient manner, and we know that you, the reader, will benefit from a "one-on-one" relationship with the author. Our research shows that readers make computer book purchases because they want expert advice. Because readers want to benefit from the author's experience, the author's voice is always present in an IDG book.

In addition, the author is free to include or recommend useful software in an IDG book. The software that accompanies each book is not intended to be casual filler but is linked to the content, theme, or procedures of the book. We know that you will benefit from the included software.

You will find what you need in this book whether you read it from cover to cover, section by section, or simply one topic at a time. As a computer user, you deserve a comprehensive resource of answers. We at IDG Books Worldwide are proud to deliver that resource with *Creating Cool Web Pages with Word for Windows 95*.

Brenda McLaughlin
Senior Vice President and Group Publisher

Internet: YouTellUs@IDGBooks.com

Creating Cool™ Web Pages
with Word for Windows® 95

by Ron Wodaski

Creating Cool™ Web Pages with Word for Windows® 95

by Ron Wodaski

IDG Books Worldwide, Inc.
An International Data Group Company

Foster City, CA ♦ Chicago, IL ♦ Indianapolis, IN ♦ Braintree, MA ♦ Southlake, TX

Creating Cool™ Web Pages with Word for Windows® 95

Published by
IDG Books Worldwide, Inc.
An International Data Group Company
919 E. Hillsdale Blvd.
Suite 400
Foster City, CA 94404

Library of Congress Catalog Card No.: 96-75769

ISBN: 1-56884-880-3

Printed in the United States of America

10 9 8 7 6 5 4 3 2 1

1O/SW/QU/ZW/IN

Distributed in the United States by IDG Books Worldwide, Inc.

Distributed by Macmillan Canada for Canada; by Computer and Technical Books for the Caribbean Basin; by Contemporanea de Ediciones for Venezuela; by Distribuidora Cuspide for Argentina; by CITEC for Brazil; by Ediciones ZETA S.C.R. Ltda. for Peru; by Editorial Limusa SA for Mexico; by Transworld Publishers Limited in the United Kingdom and Europe; by Al-Maiman Publishers & Distributors for Saudi Arabia; by Simron Pty. Ltd. for South Africa; by IDG Communications (HK) Ltd. for Hong Kong; by Toppan Company Ltd. for Japan; by Addison Wesley Publishing Company for Korea; by Longman Singapore Publishers Ltd. for Singapore, Malaysia, Thailand, and Indonesia; by Unalis Corporation for Taiwan; by WS Computer Publishing Company, Inc. for the Philippines; by WoodsLane Pty. Ltd. for Australia; by WoodsLane Enterprises Ltd. for New Zealand.

For general information on IDG Books Worldwide's books in the U.S., please call our Consumer Customer Service department at 800-762-2974. For reseller information, including discounts and premium sales, please call our Reseller Customer Service department at 800-434-3422.

For information on where to purchase IDG Books Worldwide's books outside the U.S., contact IDG Books Worldwide at 415-655-3021 or fax 415-655-3295.

For information on translations, contact Marc Jeffrey Mikulich, Director, Foreign & Subsidiary Rights, at IDG Books Worldwide, 415-655-3018 or fax 415-655-3295.

For sales inquiries and special prices for bulk quantities, write to the address above or call IDG Books Worldwide at 415-655-3200.

For information on using IDG Books Worldwide's books in the classroom, or ordering examination copies, contact the Education Office at 800-434-2086 or fax 817-251-8174.

For authorization to photocopy items for corporate, personal, or educational use, please contact Copyright Clearance Center, 222 Rosewood Drive, Danvers, MA 01923, or fax 508-750-4470.

 is a trademark under exclusive license to IDG Books Worldwide, Inc., from International Data Group, Inc.

About the Author

Ron Wodaski lives on the quiet shores of Puget Sound, north of Seattle. A former freelance correspondent for National Public Radio, Ron turned to personal computers more than 15 years ago. He has worked at every level of the computer industry, from programmer to MIS director. He has also worked with many languages, from dBASE to Visual Basic to C++, and he was working with the Internet long before it became popular.

"My goal was to get to know every corner of the computer industry," Ron says, "and as a writer that has been my greatest asset." He has written for many magazines, including *Multimedia World, Technique, CD-ROM World,* and others. Several of his books have made the best-seller lists. You can visit Ron's home page at http://www.olympus.net/biz/mmad.

Dedication

This book is dedicated to my family, who make all things possible.

Credits

Senior Vice President and Group Publisher
Brenda McLaughlin

Acquisitions Manager
Gregory Croy

Acquisitions Editor
Ellen L. Camm

Marketing Manager
Melisa M. Duffy

Managing Editor
Andy Cummings

Editorial Assistant
Timothy J. Borek

Production Director
Beth Jenkins

Production Assistant
Jacalyn L. Pennywell

Supervisor of Project Coordination
Cindy L. Phipps

Supervisor of Page Layout
Kathie S. Schnorr

Supervisor of Graphics and Design
Shelley Lea

Reprint/Blueline Coordination
Tony Augsburger
Todd Klemme
Theresa Sánchez-Baker

Blueline Coordinator
Patricia R. Reynolds

Media/Archive Coordination
Leslie Popplewell
Melissa Stauffer
Jason Marcuson

Development Editors
Gregory R. Robertson
Pat O'Brien

Technical Reviewer
Beth Slick

Associate Project Coordinator
Debbie Sharpe

Project Coordination Assistant
Regina Snyder

Graphics Coordination
Gina Scott
Angela F. Hunckler

Production Page Layout
Cameron Booker
Linda M. Boyer
Dominique DeFelice
Maridee V. Ennis
Drew R. Moore
Mark C. Owens
Kate Snell

Proofreaders
Susan Christopherson
Joel Draper
Christine Meloy Beck
Dwight Ramsey
Carl Saff
Robert Springer

Indexer
Steve Rath

Book Design
Theresa Sánchez-Baker

Cover Design
three 8 creative group

Acknowledgments

First and foremost, I owe a huge debt of gratitude to my wife, **Donna Brown**, whose assistance has been invaluable in completing this book. Through thick and thin, she has made everything possible. In addition to the many large and small ways in which she has assisted me, Donna also read every single word and made helpful suggestions. This would not be the book it is without her help.

I am also grateful to the thoroughly professional staff at PC Press and IDG Books, including my development editor, **Greg Robertson**, and my acquisitions editor, **Greg Croy**. They are both outstanding professionals.

I also want to thank my kids, who put up with me while I wrote this book: **Chanel**, **Chris**, and **Justen**. Justen also provided help with the numerous images in the book, including format conversions and file management.

A big thank you to all the folks at the Bayview Restaurant (including **CJ**, **Cricket**, **Janet**, **Shellie**, **Lisa**, and many others), who put up with me while I pounded the keyboard on my laptop for hours at a time, forgetful of the time while I enjoyed writing under their watchful eyes. Thanks, too, for the restaurant's splendid view of Puget Sound.

Thanks also to the many visitors to the MSWORD forum on CompuServe, who offered questions and suggestions to help round out the book. And thanks to you, dear reader, for your confidence in purchasing this book! I welcome all suggestions at ronw@olympus.net.

(The Publisher would like to give special thanks to **Patrick J. McGovern**, without whom this book would not have been possible.)

Contents at a Glance

Introduction: Word: Whiz-Bang Wonder of the Web 1

Chapter 1: Instant Internet: Create a Home Page 9

Chapter 2: Instant Internet: Converting Existing Documents 55

Chapter 3: Instant Internet: Creating Cool Web Pages
from Scratch 103

Chapter 4: Mastering the Internet: Images and Image Maps ... 139

Chapter 5: Mastering the Internet: Multimedia 189

Chapter 6: Mastering the Internet: Forms and Feedback 219

Chapter 7: Mastering the Internet: Advanced Web Tricks 261

Appendix A: A Catalog of the CD-ROM 281

Appendix B: HTML and Internet Assistant 295

Glossary: The Words of the Web 311

Index 323

Disk License Agreement 338

Disk Installation Instructions 339

Reader Response Card .... Back of Book

Introduction: Word: Whiz-Bang Wonder of the Web 1

Templates Let You Create Web Pages Instantly 3
Convert Existing Documents for the Web 4
Create Custom Web Pages 4
The Keys to Easy Web Pages 4
What You Need to Know 4
Version Differences to Know About 5
How This Book Is Organized 5
    Conventions Used in This Book 5
Getting Started 6
    Step 1: Download Internet Assistant 6
    Step 2: Install Internet Assistant 7
Feedback 8

Chapter 1: Instant Internet: Create a Home Page 9

Working with Templates 10
Asking the Right Questions 10
    What is Internet Assistant? 13
    What is HTML? 13
    What is the Web? 14
    What do I need to surf the Web? 16
    What do I need to create Web pages? 17
    What can I do with my Web pages? 19
        If you have (or plan to own) your Web server 19
        If your company already has a Web server 19
        If you already have your own Internet provider 20
        If you don't have access to a Web server 21
Getting Started 21
    Accessing templates from the CD-ROM 21
    Setting up the tutorial 23
        Automatic setup 23
        Manual setup 24

Tutorial 1: Using the Templates 26
   Creating a new document 26
   Customizing your document 28
   Replacing template images 29
   Replacing template text 43
   Completing the page 46
   Bonus: Adding a table border 50
   Installing templates to a hard disk 50

Chapter 2: Instant Internet: Converting Existing Documents 55

Setting Up the Tutorial 56
   Automatic setup 56
   Manual setup 57
Tutorial 2: Converting a Word Document for the Web 57
   Starting the conversion 59
   Web-legal styles 62
      Headings 62
      Lists 63
      Miscellaneous 69
Tutorial 2: Begin Again 74
   Adding a graphic 76
   Adjusting paragraph spacing 78
   Setting background color 79
   Making layout changes 81
   Adding a list 84
   Adding Web features 85
Automating Conversion 88
   Word styles and Internet Assistant 89
   Working in the Registry 93
      Navigating in the Registry 94
      Registry entries 96
      Adding entries to the Registry 99
   Using macros 101

**Chapter 3: Instant Internet: Creating Cool Web Pages
from Scratch 103**

Setting Up the Tutorial 103
   Automatic setup 104
   Manual setup 104
Tutorial 3A: Creating a Web Page from Scratch 105
   Step 1: Start with a plan for the page 105
   Step 2: Choosing a strategy 106
   The nature of the tutorial 108

Step 3: Creating the Web page 109
   Adding hyperlinks 114
   What is a bookmark? 119
   How do I create bookmarks? 119
      How do I manage bookmarks? 120
      How do I link to a bookmark? 121
   Bookmarks 122
   Minor Topics 123
   The end of the page 124
Tutorial 3B: Fancy Tables 126
   Table headers 129
   Table cells 131
   Table Enhancements 133

Chapter 4: Mastering the Internet: Images and Image Maps ... 139

Setting Up the Tutorial 140
   Automatic setup 140
   Manual setup 141
Tutorial 4A: Background Images 142
   Background (and other) colors 143
   Background pictures 145
      Repeating textures 148
      Lines and columns 158
   Watermarks 161
   Page samples 162
Tutorial 4B: Images on the Page 163
Image Tricks and Tips 165
   Interlacing 165
   Transparency 167
   Sizing 171
   Hyperlinks 172
Tutorial 4C: Image Maps 173
   Server-based image maps 174
   The conventions 180
   NCSA 181
      CERN 182
   Client- (browser-) based maps 183
   How does a MAP file work? 185
Clip Art Collections 185

Chapter 5: Mastering the Internet: Multimedia 189

Setting Up the Tutorial 189
   Automatic setup 190
   Manual setup 190

Tutorial 5A: Adding Video 192
    Video variations 194
    Animations 198
    Video to the max 200
Tutorial 5B: Adding Audio 202
    Clickable audio 203
    Background audio 210
    Real Audio 211
    VDOLive video 212
The Future of Web Multimedia 213
    VRML 214
    Shockwave 216
CD Bonus: Creating Video clips with Adobe Premiere 218
CD Bonus: Creating Audio Files with Sound Forge 218

Chapter 6: Mastering the Internet: Forms and Feedback 219

Setting Up the Tutorial 219
    Automatic setup 220
    Manual setup 220
What is a Form? 221
Creating a Sample Form 224
    Defining form boundaries 225
        Text box 227
    Adding form controls 229
        Selection list 231
        Checkbox 233
        Radio Button Group 234
        Multiline Text Box 235
        Submit button 239
        Reset button 240
    Editing form elements 242
Submitting a Form 242
    Mailto and Forms 243
    Scripts and forms 249
Creating Elegant Forms 252
    Creating a feedback form 252
    Creating an order form 258

Chapter 7: Mastering the Internet: Advanced Web Tricks 261

Setting Up the Tutorial 261
    Automatic setup 262
    Manual setup 262
Tutorial 7A: Adding HTML Markup 263
    What is markup? 264
    Free-standing markup 266
        No Break 270
        Soft line breaks 272

Plain Text 272
Other tags 274
Embedded markup 274
Tutorial 7B: Embedding Objects in a Page 277
What is embedding? 277
Embedding objects 278
Embedding support on the Web 280
CD-ROM Bonus Techniques 280

Appendix A: A Catalog of the CD-ROM **281**

Late-Breaking News 281
Internet Assistant 2.0 281
Installing Internet Assistant from the CD-ROM 282
Detailed method for installing Internet Assistant via download 282
Step 1: Word for Windows 7.0 and Windows 95 282
Step 2: Download Internet Assistant 2.0 282
Step 3: Install Internet Assistant 2.0 285
Internet Explorer 2.0 288
Templates 288
Graphics 289
Software for the Book 290
Automatic Setup software 290
Files for manual setup 292
The Magic Parser 292
Third-Party Software 293
SnapShot/32 293
MapTHIS! 294

Appendix B: HTML and Internet Assistant **295**

HTML Tags and Word for Windows/Internet Assistant 295
Form Tags and Word for Windows/Internet Assistant 303
Word versus HTML 308
File Woes, and How to Avoid Them 308
Special Symbols 309

Glossary: The Words of the Web **311**

Index **323**

Disk License Agreement **338**

Disk Installation Instructions **339**

Reader Response Card ....**Back of Book**

Word: Whiz-Bang Wonder of the Web

Introduction

When I sat down to write this book, I wanted to know one thing:

What is the simplest way to create Web pages?

Not only did I find the method I was looking for, I found a way to make it even simpler. The key to creating Web pages easily is combining Microsoft's Word for Windows and Internet Assistant. Otherwise, you are stuck creating Web pages with HTML (HyperText Markup Language). Figure I-1 shows what it is like to create a Web page using raw HTML. The codes for HTML, the codes for images, the codes for text alignment — all these things are mixed right in with the text for the page. It takes time, effort, and unwavering determination to create a Web page this way.

Now look at Figure I-2. This is how you create a Web page in Word. Big difference! There are almost no HTML codes visible. The text and pictures look like text and pictures. What you see is what you get. What could be simpler?

To create Web pages with Word, all you need to do is install Internet Assistant. You can install it from the CD-ROM, or you can download it from Microsoft's Web page (see "Getting Started," later in this introduction, to learn how you can do it).

In minutes, you can begin to create your own Web pages, ready to place on the Internet.

HTML code   Text for Web page

```
SAMPLE FROM TEMPLATE COMPLETED.HTM - NOTEPAD          _ □ X
FILE   EDIT   SEARCH   HELP

<HTML>

<HEAD>

<TITLE>The Vortex</TITLE>

<META NAME="GENERATOR" CONTENT="Internet Assistant for Microsoft Word 2.0z Beta">
</HEAD>

<BODY bgcolor="#ffffff">
<CENTER>
<IMG SRC="vortex.gif"><BR>
</CENTER>
<P>
<CENTER>
<I><FONT SIZE=2>The online newsletter that has no boundaries.</FONT></I>
</CENTER>
<HR>
<TABLE BORDER="0" cellpadding=8>
<TR><TD COLSPAN=2>

<CENTER>
<H1>The Nature of Reality: What Is It, Anyway? <br>
<I><FONT SIZE=2>by William Roberts, Esq.</FONT></I>
</H1>
</CENTER>


</TD></TR>
<TR><TD>
<CENTER>
<IMG SRC="image2.gif" ALIGN="TOP"> <BR>
</CENTER>
<TD>
<font size=6><i>R</i></font>eality is often presumed to be tangible, but, as this
example shows, that isn't always the case.
It has often been said that reality is the physical world that we contact through
our senses.  Unfortunately, our senses are prone to error.
<P>
You might suppose that this could be easily remedied by the use of various <A
HREF="webpage.htm" >scientific devices</A>.  Indeed, the course of modern science
has been away from the flawed sensory apparatus of our own bodies, and toward the
powerful, carefully-constructed instruments of the scientist.
```

Figure I-1: Creating a Web page with raw HTML.

Figure I-2: Creating a Web page with Word and Internet Assistant.

Templates Let You Create Web Pages Instantly

As easy as Internet Assistant is, I've found a way to make it even easier to get started creating Web pages. I have included dozens and dozens of Web page templates on the CD-ROM that comes with this book. These are real, Word for Windows templates that you can install and use just like the templates that come with Word itself. The templates tell you everything you need to know to create great-looking Web pages. The templates include superb page designs, reserved locations for graphics, tables, bulleted lists, newsletters, brochures, catalogs — in short, anything and everything you could ever hope to do with a Web page.

Convert Existing Documents for the Web

This means that you'll be creating Web pages instantly. If your time is important, that's great news. But I'm sure that you'll have your own ideas, too. This book also shows you how to publish your existing documents on the Web, such as press releases, company newsletters, or product information. Whatever you have, you can put it on the Net with Word for Windows.

Create Custom Web Pages

Internet Assistant makes it easy to get your information on the Web fast. However, it's also a powerful Web development tool, packed with features. You also learn how to create your own Web pages from scratch. That means that you can create unique, interesting Web pages of your very own.

The Keys to Easy Web Pages

This book includes your keys to success on the Internet:

➡ Work with the word processor you already know: Word for Windows.

➡ Get started instantly by using hundreds of included templates.

➡ Learn how to convert your existing documents for the Web.

➡ Learn how to create custom Web pages that reflect your reasons for being on the Web.

The best part is that you don't need to buy fancy or expensive new software to use these keys. You don't need to learn a whole new word processor. You just start with the word processor you already know — Word for Windows — and add Internet Assistant. And thanks to Microsoft's commitment to the Internet, Internet Assistant is a free add-on for Word.

What You Need to Know

Your starting point is your knowledge of Word for Windows and Windows 95. I show you everything else you need to know to create cool Web pages. You don't need to be an expert with Word to create Web pages. If you can create headings and apply styles, you can use Internet Assistant and Word to create great Web pages.

Version Differences to Know About

You need Windows 95 installed, with Word for Windows version 7.0. Version 7.0 is a 32-bit version of Word designed for Windows 95. The latest version of Internet Assistant (2.0 or later) is also a 32-bit application, and it works only with Word 7.0.

How This Book Is Organized

This book is organized around the creation of actual Web pages. You won't find a whole lot of theory, but you will find tons and tons of practical advice. You want to be sitting at your computer for most of the time you spend with the book because you'll be building cool Web pages as soon as you start with Chapter 1.

I strongly believe that the best way to learn any skill is to use that skill. You're going to practice Web-page building throughout this book. You won't have to wade through long-winded explanations; you just roll up your sleeves and create Web pages. There is no better way to get started on the Web.

The typical Web site has a collection of pages, not just a single home page. You see how to create a mix of pages as we move from chapter to chapter. You are going to create a complete set of home pages for a fictitious company called WebStarr. You learn about creating specific kinds of Web pages, such as a table of contents, product information pages, pages for different parts of your company, and so on. If you are building personal Web pages, you can apply the same ideas to your own work.

By the time you finish this book, you'll know not just how to build Web pages, but how to make them look great and work effectively.

Conventions Used in This Book

Stuff you type appears in bold, like this: **something you actually type.**

When you select menus and their options, the selections are indicated in small caps, with an arrow between them. For example, TOOLS⇨OPTIONS means that you click the Tools menu and then select the Options menu item.

Menu options, button names, styles, and dialog box names are indicated by initial caps on their names, such as Background and Links dialog box, Reset button, the style Definition List, DL, and so on.

Filenames, names of Web sites (URLs), and directories appear in a special typeface, like the following one, which lets visitors sign a White House guest book:

```
http://www.whitehouse.gov/White_House/html/Guest_Book.html
```

HTML-formatted text appears in the same special typeface, like this:

```
<HTML>
<TITLE>Creating Cool Web Pages with Word for Windows 95</TITLE>
<IMG SRC="intro.gif" ALT="Creating Cool Web Pages">
```

I use *three* icons in this book:

 Tip icons point out expert advice on tricks and techniques. They typically offer practical steps you can apply to your own Web pages.

 Caution icons let you know of any dangers that are lurking in the software. This includes bugs, methods for working around bugs, and powerful features that can have unexpected results.

 Note icons point out details that may deserve special attention in the long term.

Getting Started

If you already have a Web browser, you can install Internet Assistant (IA) in two easy steps. If you don't have a browser, turn to Appendix A for more information.

Step 1: Download Internet Assistant

Go to Microsoft's Web page for free Word stuff at

```
http://www.microsoft.com/msoffice/freestuf/msword
```

Click the Internet Assistant hyperlink (see Figure I-3), and follow instructions for downloading. You wind up with an .exe file on your local hard disk.

Hyperlink to download Internet Assistant

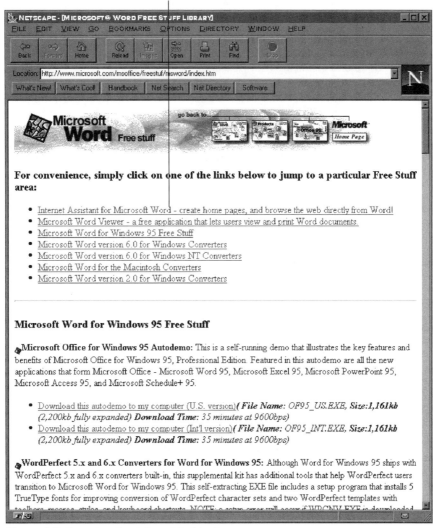

Figure I-3: Downloading Internet Assistant.

Step 2: Install Internet Assistant

To install Internet Assistant, double-click the icon for the .exe file you downloaded in Step 1 and then follow the on-screen instructions. To verify installation, open Word for Windows. You should see a new icon at the left of the Formatting toolbar — it is the Internet Assistant Browse Mode icon, and it looks like a small pair of glasses (see Figure I-4).

Figure I-4: *The Internet Assistant icon.*

Need more information? I have provided a detailed description of how to download and install Internet Assistant in Appendix A.

Don't have a browser yet? You can install the browser from the CD-ROM that comes with this book (see Appendix A).

Don't have an Internet connection? You can install Internet Assistant from the CD-ROM. However, you should follow up and download the latest version from Microsoft's Web pages.

After you have Internet Assistant installed, head for Chapter 1 to get started creating your very own Web pages.

Feedback

I'd love to hear from you, so I have created a home page (using Word for Windows and Internet Assistant, naturally!) that you can visit. The URL is

```
http://www.olympus.net/biz/mmad/coolpage
```

This is a complete Web site featuring the fictitious company WebStarr. It features many more Web page tricks in addition to the ones included in this book.

You can also send me e-mail at `ronw@olympus.net`, and I'll be happy to exchange ideas with you. If you have ideas for future editions of the book, I'd love to hear them.

Instant Internet: Create a Home Page

In This Chapter

Internet Assistant features and facts

The World Wide Web (Web for short), and how you can learn to master it

How to create a new document by using a template

How to replace template images with custom images

How to replace template text with custom text

How to access templates from the CD-ROM, or copy them to your hard disk

Bonus: Adding a border to a table

As you learn from the introduction to this book (you *did* read the introduction, right?), the CD-ROM that comes with the book includes a very valuable resource: hundreds of Word **templates** that you can use to create your own **Web pages**. In this chapter, you learn how to use these templates to create custom **Web** documents.

Along the way, there will be plenty of territory to cover. This is not a quick journey that shows you just the highlights and then leaves you to figure out the rest. I move at a leisurely pace. You have plenty of opportunities to learn the tricks of the Web-page trade along the way. After all, the little tricks are what make your Web pages a better place to visit!

Working with Templates

The **templates** that come with this book were created with Microsoft Word for Windows 95 (Version 7.0) and Internet Assistant. If you aren't familiar with Word's templates, they are a special kind of Word document that you can use over and over as patterns for new documents. For example, Figure 1-1 shows a typical template. It contains three images that are **placeholders** — you replace them with your own graphics. The template also contains placeholder text that you can replace with your own text. Figure 1-2 shows one example of a Web page created from that template. With different graphics and text, you could create a very different Web page.

Normal Word documents use the DOC file extension. Templates use the DOT file extension. For example, MYHTML.DOT is a valid template filename. Most of the time, you don't need to worry about template names — you can choose templates by looking at a preview that shows what the template looks like.

Every template on the CD-ROM includes the following:

➡ A preview of the template, viewable when you create a new file

➡ Graphic images that guide you in placing your own images

➡ Bullets, text blocks, **hyperlinks,** and plenty of suggestions to help you design and lay out your Web page

I designed these templates to do two important jobs. The first is the obvious one: to give you a quick, simple way to create Web pages. The other is not as obvious, but very valuable: The templates will help you become a better Web page author. Nestled in among the images and technical talk are practical suggestions that can make the difference between an average Web page and one that has some zing.

Asking the Right Questions

Putting your Web pages into action requires that you know some basic facts about the Internet. This section helps you understand how the various pieces of the Internet fit together. The process begins with creating a Web page with Internet Assistant, using Word for Windows 95. It ends when either you or your network manager copies the files onto a Web server. What happens in between? The following questions fill in the details.

If you are anxious to get started with Internet Assistant and Word for Windows, skip ahead to the "Getting Started" section. You can return here at any time to get the background information about the Internet.

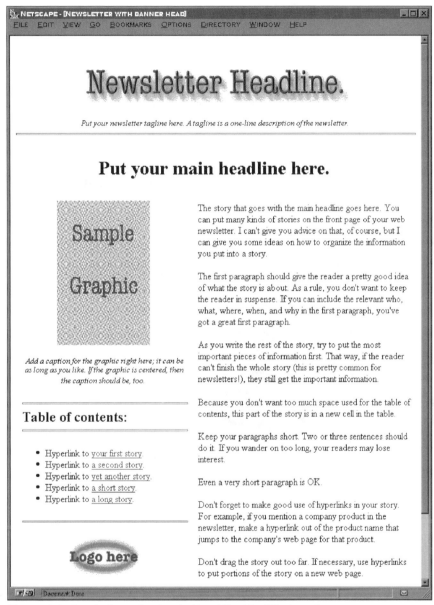

Figure 1-1: A typical template loaded into Word for Windows 7.

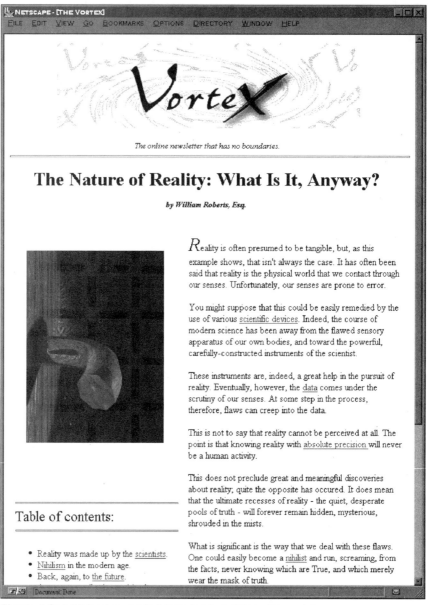

Figure 1-2: A Web page created from the template in Figure 1-1.

What is Internet Assistant?

Internet Assistant is a Word for Windows add-on program from Microsoft. It is free. You can download it from Microsoft's **Internet site**; see the introduction for fast download instructions.

Internet Assistant is a sophisticated program, adding a huge amount of functionality to Word. Internet Assistant's features fall into four general categories:

➡ New tools, mostly on the Formatting toolbar

➡ New menu selections

➡ Automatic conversion to and from the standard Web file format, **HTML**

➡ Removal of features not supported by HTML

What is HTML?

HTML (HyperText Markup Language) is a language used on the Web to create Web pages. Because you will be working with Word and Internet Assistant, you are not required to learn HTML. In the latter chapters of this book, however, I suggest ways you can use HTML to add very cool features to your Web pages.

Here's a sample of what HTML looks like:

```
<body>
<h1>This is a headline</h1>
This is some text that will appear in a normal typeface. However,
you can also use HTML to create <b>bold</b> and <I>italic</I>
text.
<P>
That's a paragraph separator above, which adds white space
between paragraphs.<br>
You can also use the BR command to add a line break without extra
white space<br>
between lines.
</body>
```

Figure 1-3 shows what this page would look like on the Web.

As you can see, HTML commands are embedded right in the text of your document. Word for Windows, on the other hand is a WYSIWYG (*what you see is what you get*) word processor. When Internet Assistant saves your Web

Headline

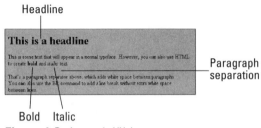

Paragraph separation

Bold   Italic

Figure 1-3: A sample Web page viewed in the Netscape browser.

pages, it converts Word's internal, fancy-schmancy text storage techniques into HTML code. When you are working in Word with Internet Assistant, you won't have to look at the HTML codes — you can simply create your document the same way you always have, and then save it as an HTML file. Later, you copy the HTML file to a **Web server**, where anyone on the Web can access it.

Because Word came along before HTML became popular, Word does not support all HTML features. That's why Internet Assistant removes many Word buttons and menu selections when you work on an HTML file — if the feature isn't visible, you won't be tempted to use it. To further complicate the picture, HTML is growing so fast that no one product supports all the features of HTML. See the sidebar "HTML wars" for details. You can find out exactly which HTML features Word supports in Appendix B.

The bottom line is simple: If you want to create Web pages without fuss and bother, Internet Assistant lets you do that. You don't have to get involved with HTML unless you want to.

If you *do* want to learn about HTML, you get the help you need later in the book. You can also turn to some of the excellent reference books described at the end of this book.

I don't think of this book as a reference, although you certainly can use it that way. I prefer to think of this project as an adventure. I've gotten a tremendous kick out of creating Web pages, and I want to infect you with the same enthusiasm.

What is the Web?

"Web" is short for World Wide Web. The **Internet** has been around almost as long as computers, but the Web is a recent invention. It came about because of the need to add graphics to the Internet.

The heart of the Web is something called **protocol**. Before the Web came along, the protocol of choice was **FTP** (File Transfer Protocol). FTP enabled anyone to log into a distant computer and copy files back and forth.

HTML wars

When HTML was first created, it was a very simple thing. It supported a very small set of word processing features — lists, bold text, italic text, and so on. This was fine at first. But as more and more people began to use HTML, the demand for features increased dramatically.

A group of people (referred to as a standards committee) is trying to add new features to HTML in an orderly way. This standardization would allow all the companies and individuals using HTML on the Web to focus on a single HTML standard. After a lot of effort, they finally agreed on the HTML 2.0 standard. Before they ever printed the standard, however, the race was already on to create HTML 3.0.

You see, various companies didn't want to wait for agreement on a new HTML standard. With all the companies involved, it took a long time to agree on a single standard. The result: Some companies decided to create their own version of HTML. Netscape and Microsoft, for example, each introduced HTML features that are not part of any standard. Both are large companies, and both will probably succeed in getting their ideas accepted.

What does this mean for you? Your HTML files will be read by various people using various Web browsers. Not everyone will be able to see everything you put into your Web pages. Some browsers, for example, don't support tables. The Netscape browser doesn't support Microsoft's marquee command, and the Microsoft browser, Internet Explorer, doesn't support some Netscape commands.

If you want your work to be seen by the largest number of Web surfers, stay away from HTML features that aren't widely supported. I point out any features supported in Word that aren't part of the accepted standards.

Another good idea: Tell everyone which browser to use to view your Web pages. These days, just about everyone has access to multiple browsers. A little message at the top of your first page does the trick, such as "This site best when viewed with Internet Explorer 2.0."

Copying files is cool if you've never done it before, but something much better was needed for graphics. It wouldn't be convenient to use FTP for graphics — you would have to download graphics, and then view them later with a viewer program. Something better was needed.

The answer was HTTP (HyperText Transfer Protocol). HTML was the engine chosen to drive HTTP. This gave the world a language that was easy to use and that allowed viewing of graphics online.

Figure 1-4: A Web browser allows you to surf the Web.

You use a Web browser to do the viewing. All Web browsers understand HTML. The HTML file is transferred to the browser, and the browser then downloads all the image (or other) files mentioned in the HTML file. The browser then puts all of this on your screen (see Figure 1-4). The key feature of HTML is that it allows **hyperlinks** — **hot** text and hot graphics that jump to a new Web page, download a file, send mail, and so on. Hyperlinks are what make it possible to surf the Web, jumping from Web page to Web page. Each hyperlink points to a URL (Uniform Resource Locator). See the sidebar, "What the heck is a URL?" for more information.

And that's what makes the Web a Web: the ability to move about with complete freedom. With Word and Internet Assistant, you can be part of the Web without having to learn the innermost secrets of HTML.

What do I need to surf the Web?

You don't need a whole lot to surf the Web. All you need are the following:

➡ A modem or a high-speed (**ISDN**, **T-1**, and so on) phone connection

➡ An **Internet provider**

➡ A Web browser

Most likely, you'll be accessing the Web with a modem; I highly recommend a 28.8 Kbps (kilobits per second) modem. 14.4 modems are acceptable, but noticeably slower. Those who are lucky enough to have high-speed connections such as ISDN already know that it takes a lot of money and skill to get them and use them. If you aren't familiar with the hardware, software, and installation requirements for high-speed modems, contact your Internet provider or Web administrator for details on what is available in your area.

Look for the cost and complexity of ISDN connections to go down by the end of 1996 — that may be a good time to look into high-speed access to the Web. Contact your regional phone company (Bell South, U.S. West, and so on) for information.

As far as Internet providers go, huge numbers of them are seeking your business. If your company already provides access to the Internet via your LAN or WAN, you are ready to go. Otherwise, the primary choice you have to make is whether to go with a local provider or a national provider. Local providers are often less expensive but may not offer full service. National providers often cost more, but some (not all) provide a full set of features. If you are creating Web pages, you want to connect with a provider who can give you the most space for Web pages at the lowest cost, as well as support for **CGI** scripts and **forms**. The best solution is a local provider who really knows the Web and can provide a full set of features at a reasonable cost — you'll get personal service that the national providers can't match.

As for browsers, more than 30 commercial browsers are on the market, with more being added every month. And there are hundreds of homemade browsers, too. If you want to stay with the mainstream, I recommend two major choices:

➡ **Netscape Navigator 2.0**: Netscape is the industry standard browser. Versions of Netscape are used by 75 percent of the people surfing the Web. Netscape is also a leader in the development of cool browser features.

➡ **Microsoft Internet Explorer**: Microsoft has made a strong effort to compete with Netscape's browser. Best of all, Internet Explorer is free for the download. I have included a copy of Internet Explorer on the CD-ROM, or you can download the latest version from Microsoft's Web site (`http://www.msn.com`). Like Netscape's browsers, Internet Explorer supports many of the newest features of HTML.

I use both browsers. Each has advantages and disadvantages. I strongly suggest you keep both of them handy on your hard disk — most sites support one or the other browser's special features.

What do I need to create Web pages?

Relax — you have everything you *need* now. Assuming you have Word for Windows, the combination of Internet Assistant and this book completes your tool kit.

You can add some hot tools to expand your capabilities. An image editor is a good start, especially one that supports Web features such as transparency and interlacing (Photoshop is an example).

If you decide to learn the inner workings of HTML, you probably will want to look at other titles in the *Creating Cool* series of books, including the classic that started it all: *Creating Cool Web Pages with HTML,* 2nd Edition, by Dave Taylor, IDG Books Worldwide, Inc.

What the heck is a URL?

A **URL** (Uniform Resource Locator) is like a phone number: It uniquely identifies a place on the Web. URLs come in a wide variety of formats, but all they do is enable you to get somewhere on the Web. The correct pronunciation of URL is to spell it out: *You Are El.* Don't be caught making the mistake of saying "Earle."

For example, here's a URL for a page on the Web:

```
http://www.olympus.net/biz/mmad/index.htm
```

Let's break this down into its component parts:

Component	Description
`http://`	This is the protocol for the Web site. Other protocols include FTP, Gopher, and so on. Web pages are almost always accessed with the http protocol.
`www.olympus.net/`	This is the **domain name** on a **Web server**. Every domain name is unique, and every domain name points to a specific **server** somewhere on the Web. The last part of the name, NET, tells you what kind of Web site you have reached. COM, for example, refers to a commercial site, and EDU refers to an educational institution. NET is, well, a network.
`/biz/mmad/`	This is a path on the Web server. It's just like a directory (or folder) path on any other computer.
`index.htm`	This is the name of a file on the Web server. This is the actual Web page. When you create Web pages with Word and Internet Assistant, you must place them on a Web server to be accessed on the Web.

There are also some strange sorts of URLs out there. For example, some international Web sites append a country code to the domain name. Ninety-nine percent of the time, you find URLs that look very similar to the example here.

Every Web page has a unique URL. To find URLs, you can use search tools. However, as more and more companies and individuals provide the URL for their home pages in traditional media — everything from TV ads to newspaper columns include URLs these days — it becomes easier and easier to see more URLs than you can ever visit.

If you are serious about Web publishing, you probably want to start a collection of browsers — each browser is likely to handle your Web pages just a bit differently (sometimes a *lot* differently). By trying your Web pages in many different browsers, you know just how compatible your Web pages are.

What can I do with my Web pages?

Your Web pages should have one destination: the Web itself. There are several ways to put your pages on the Web. In all cases, the idea is to put your files on a Web server. This server has a direct connection to the Internet, and anyone who knows the URL for your files can find them. That URL can come from a hyperlink on another Web page, or you can put the URL on a brochure, in an ad, on your business card, and so forth.

If you have (or plan to own) your Web server

This is the ideal situation; it gives you total control over your Web site. However, it takes a great deal of time and effort to manage a Web server — even a small one. Before you launch yourself onto a personal Web server, keep in mind that the costs of phone lines (especially high-speed phone connections) can be surprisingly high. In addition, ask yourself if you have the time, energy, and resources to learn all the details of maintaining a Web server.

If your company already has a Web server

If your company has a Web server, and if you are creating Web pages for your company, the process of getting your pages on the Web is probably already well-defined. You simply need to plug into the existing process. In most cases, there is an individual who manages the Web server. This person is called the Webmaster, and he or she is responsible for everything that happens on the server. The Webmaster will either have you copy your Web pages to a network location that serves as a waiting area, or have you copy your files directly to the server.

If your company uses a waiting area, you usually have to wait until your files are later copied to the server. You may have to wait five minutes or several days. You need to follow the procedures set up by your Webmaster; contact him or her for full details.

If you are allowed to copy files directly to the server, you need to be very careful about your work. In effect, you are putting files "live" onto the Web. If any bugs or mistakes exist, users find them fast! Always check your files on your local machine to make sure that every link is correct.

It's likely that users will access your Web files by using your company's URL. For example, here's a URL for an IBM Web page dealing with the ThinkPad notebook computer line:

```
http://www.pc.ibm.com/thinkpad/tppromo.html
```

The first part of the URL, `http://www.pc.ibm.com`, is the domain name for IBM's personal computer Web site. The directory `/thinkpad` identifies the notebook computer line, and the file `tppromo.html` is a file that describes a particular promotion for the notebook line.

The Web server at even a small company probably has many different directories. You need to know exactly where to copy your files, and the Webmaster usually provides that information and everything else you need to know to put your files on a Web server. In some cases, you do not copy your files to the actual destination directories, but to a holding directory. The Webmaster then copies the files for you.

If you already have your own Internet provider

If you deal directly with an Internet provider, the chances are good that you can easily create your own Web site. Most providers give you a small amount of hard disk space on the Web server and a URL to your own home directory. For example, my Internet provider's URL is

```
http://www.olympus.net
```

My URL is

```
http://www.olympus.net/biz/mmad
```

This means that my directory, `/mmad`, is a subdirectory of the general business directory, `/biz`. In general, you get more hard disk space (and pay more money) for a business-level Internet connection. If you plan on only a few personal Web pages, a personal Web account may be all you need. Depending on how much hard disk space you require, and how many visitors "hit" each page, a business Web site might cost anywhere from 10 percent to 500 percent more than a single-user Web site.

How you copy files to your provider's Web server varies with the provider. If the Web server runs Windows NT, there's a good chance you can simply use a Windows 95 dial-up connection to link to the server. You can then simply use Windows drag and drop to copy your files. This method is extremely convenient.

In many cases, you need to use special tools to copy files to the server. In the worst case, you have to e-mail your files to the provider and wait until they show up on the server. If you are looking for a provider, ask how you upload your Web pages to the server. The more flexible the methods you can use, the easier your job is.

If you don't have access to a Web server

The cost of a personal Web page on a Web server is no longer very high. You can pay as little as $10 a month for a personal page on a Web server. You will probably be limited to half a megabyte or so of disk space. Many providers include a small home page as part of your basic fee.

If you need business-level support, you'll probably pay significantly more money. This may range from $20 to $75 per month, depending on how much disk space you use, how many people visit your Web pages, and exactly what services you require from the Webmaster. You can also spend hundreds or even thousands of dollars a month for a really sophisticated Web site.

Whatever your needs are, I recommend that you ask friends and business associates which providers do the best job. It's a simple fact that some providers do a better job than others. Testing the waters can save you some grief down the line. Don't just look at the price; the level of service, reliability, and access to assistance make a difference.

Getting Started

This book shows you, step by step, how to create Web pages. The CD-ROM contains a tremendous amount of resource material that fits into that process. Before you start each tutorial, you transfer some of the material from the CD-ROM to your hard disk. This tutorial is no exception; read on for instructions.

Accessing templates from the CD-ROM

There are two ways to use the templates: copy them from the CD-ROM to your hard disk, or set up Word to use the Workgroup Template folder. The next section tells you how to access the templates you need for the tutorials in this book from your CD-ROM. Later in this chapter, you learn how (and when) to copy templates to your hard disk for fast, easy access.

Throughout this book, I use the word *folder* instead of *directory*. If you are a long-time Windows user and think in terms of directories allow me to reassure you that if you know directories, you know folders, and vice versa. There is simply no difference between the two. It's just that, when Windows 95 hit the market, all of a sudden we started talking about folders. Just like the Mac!

File Locations tab

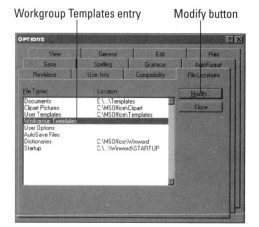

Figure 1-5: The Options dialog box.

Workgroup Templates entry   Modify button

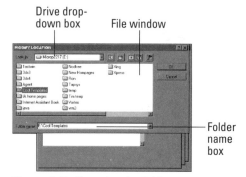

Figure 1-6: Setting file locations in Word.

Drive drop-
down box   File window

Folder
name
box

Figure 1-7: Changing the folder
path for Workgroup Templates.

For the tutorial in this chapter, you use the templates directly from the CD-ROM. Before you start, make sure that the CD-ROM that came with this book is loaded into your CD-ROM drive. To tell Word for Windows where to find the templates, select TOOLS⇨ OPTIONS. This action displays the dialog box shown in Figure 1-5. The exact location of the File Locations tab may be different on your machine. Wherever the File Locations tab is, click it to make it the active tab, as shown in Figure 1-6.

NOTE If you are already using your Workgroup Template folder for templates on a network, you can still use the templates. See the section "Installing templates to hard disk," later in this chapter for detailed information.

Click the Workgroup Templates entry under File Types, and then click the Modify button. This opens the dialog box shown in Figure 1-7. At the top of the dialog box, click the Drive drop-down list box and select your CD-ROM drive. This selection displays the folders on the CD-ROM in the file window of the dialog box. Click the Cool Templates folder and verify that the folder name appears in the Folder name box (refer to Figure 1-7). Click the OK button.

NOTE The folders you see will be different from those shown in Figure 1-7. The CD-ROM was not complete at the time this chapter was written.

From now on, Word looks for templates on your CD-ROM drive when you choose FILE⇨NEW.

Setting up the tutorial

Most of tutorials included in this book require files that are included on the CD-ROM that comes with the book. For each tutorial, you have two choices about how to copy those files to your hard disk. You can use automatic setup, which uses an installation program from the CD-ROM, or you can manually copy the files yourself. The next section describes how to use automatic setup, and the following section describes manual setup for the tutorial.

You have the choice of automatic or manual setup for each tutorial. If you choose to use automatic setup, see Appendix A for information about how to install the automatic setup program.

Automatic setup

If you haven't already installed the software for automatic setup of the tutorials, turn to Appendix A and do so now. Otherwise, if you choose not to use automatic setup, see the next section, "Manual setup," which tells you how to copy the necessary files for this tutorial. IF YOU DIDN'T USE AUTOMATIC SETUP EARLIER, YOU CAN FIND COMPLETE INSTRUCTIONS FOR STARTING, RUNNING, AND USING THE AUTOMATIC SETUP PROGRAM IN CHAPTER 1.

To run automatic setup, click the Start button, then Programs, and then click the Autopage program. You can also click the Autopage icon in the folder `c:\My Programs\Autopage` (see the icon shown after this paragraph). After the program loads, you need to identify which drive letter to use for your CD-ROM drive. The automatic setup program tries to determine the correct drive letter itself. If you have more than one CD-ROM drive, you need to select the drive that holds the CD-ROM from this book by using the CD-ROM Drive drop-down list (see Figure 1-8)

Click the Chapter 1 Files radio button to display the files for this chapter (see Figure 1-8).

> [AUTOPAGE]

Next, select the correct drive to copy files to, using the Destination Drive drop-down box (see Figure 1-8). Unless your `My Documents` folder is on a drive other than drive C, accept the default value of drive C. Now select the chapter files to copy. You can select any one chapter for copying, or you can indicate that you want to copy all tutorial files for all chapters. To select Chapter 1 files for copying, click the radio button marked Chapter 1 Files (see Figure 1-9). To select all tutorial files for copying, click the radio button marked Copy All Files Now. Messages and the list of files to be copied appear in the large box at the right of the radio buttons. If you elect to copy all files now, you can skip over the instructions for tutorial setup in future chapters, but you will use several megabytes of hard disk space.

Select Chapter
radio buttons

CD-ROM drive
drop-down box

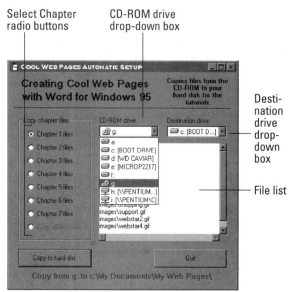

Destination drive drop-down box

File list

Figure 1-8: Automatic setup for Chapter 1 tutorial.

Click here for Chapter 1 files

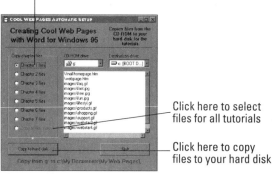

Click here to select files for all tutorials

Click here to copy files to your hard disk

Figure 1-9: Selecting automatic setup options.

To actually copy the files for the tutorial to your hard disk, click the Copy to Hard Disk button (see Figure 1-9). The files are copied to the My Web Pages subfolder of the My Documents folder. If you installed Microsoft Office to your C drive, the following is usually the folder:

`c:\My Documents\My Web Pages`

 This is the same folder you will use for all of the tutorials. From time to time, you may notice that one or more additional subfolders is created in the My Web Pages folder; this is normal, and all is explained during each tutorial. See the following section on manual setup for the names of the folders that are created.

After you have copied the necessary files, skip ahead to the start of the tutorial. If you choose not to use the automatic setup, read the next section to find out how to copy the necessary files manually.

Manual setup

Before you start the tutorial, create a new folder, called My Web Pages, on your hard disk. I recommend that you create it as a subfolder of the My Documents folder. The My Documents folder was created when you installed Word 7 or Microsoft Office, usually on drive C: (C:\My Documents).

TIP To create a new folder, select FILE⇨NEW⇨FOLDER in an existing folder. After you create the folder, it has the default name "new folder" selected. Type the name **My Web Pages**.

You'll be saving all your work in the My Web Pages folder. In addition, you need subfolders of My Web Pages for various files. Create the following subfolders: images, videos, audio, maps, vrml, and java.

Why all these folders? You don't use all of them in this chapter, but you do use them all as you work through the tutorials in this book. More importantly, these folders reflect the kind of folder/directory structure you'll use on your own Web page projects. The basic idea: Put your Web pages in one folder, and put images and other support files in subfolders. You learn more about folder/directory structure, and how to use it to your advantage, in Chapter 3.

Figure 1-10 shows the way your folders should look. I refer to these various folders over and over again throughout the tutorials.

The tutorial in this chapter uses image files from the CD-ROM. They are located in the folder \tutorial\chap01. Before you continue, copy the image files from this folder to the My Web Pages\images folder you created earlier. Copy the following files (just click and drag): faq.gif, fast.jpg, free.jpg, fun.jpg, lifestyl.gif, products.gif, shopping.gif, support.gif, Webstar2.gif, and Webstar4.gif.

When you install Word for Windows, you select which graphic **filters** to install with it. The most common image formats for Web pages are GIF and JPEG (pronounced "jiff" and "**jay**-peg"). It doesn't matter whether you installed filters for GIF and JPEG; Internet Assistant installs them for you during its own installation. You can verify this for yourself. Click INSERT⇨PICTURE, and then click the Filetype drop-down box (see Figure 1-11). You find entries for both GIF and JPEG. Figure 1-11 shows the entry for the JPEG format.

You are now ready to begin the tutorial.

Folder name

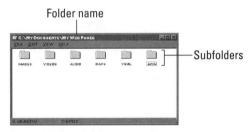

Subfolders

Figure 1-10: Folders set up for the tutorial.

File type drop-down box

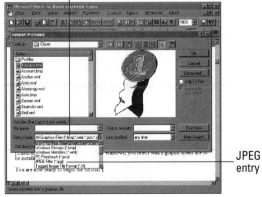

JPEG entry

Figure 1-11: Checking support for GIF and JPEG graphic files.

Tutorial 1: Using the Templates

The templates are now available for you to use in Word for Windows. You can use the Cool Templates the same way you use any Word template. For example, to create a new HTML document using one of the Corporate Looks templates, start Word for Windows 7. The Word opening window shown in Figure 1-12 appears on-screen. Your copy of Word may look somewhat different, depending on which toolbars are visible. If you have already installed Internet Assistant, you see its icon at the left of the Formatting toolbar (see Figure 1-12).

If you don't see the Internet Assistant icon, you need to install Internet Assistant. See the Introduction for quick instructions or Appendix A for detailed instructions.

Internet Assistant makes many changes to your menus and toolbars. You see some of these changes in this chapter, and I explore the changes in detail in Chapter 2.

Internet Assistant Icon

Figure 1-12: The Word for Windows opening screen.

Creating a new document

Preview window   Corporate Look tab

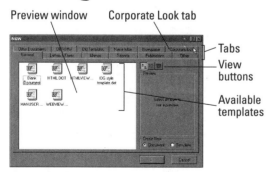

Tabs

View buttons

Available templates

Figure 1-13: The New dialog box.

To create a new HTML document, choose FILE⇨NEW. This displays the New dialog box, shown in Figure 1-13. The tabs at the top of the dialog box show the various template folders available to you, and the middle of the dialog box shows you the templates available in the current folder. Click the Corporate Look tab at the top of the dialog box to display the templates in that folder. Figure 1-14 shows the result.

NOTE If you do not see icons as shown in Figure 1-13, click the left-most button in the group of view buttons just below the tabs. These buttons control the appearance of the list of templates. From left to right, these are Large icons, List, and Details.

 You should see more than the two templates shown in Figure 1-13; I created the illustration while I was writing the book, before all the Corporate Looks templates were created.

Click the template named `Headline and Buttons.dot` to highlight it. Notice that a preview of the template appears in the Preview Window. All the templates provided with the book contain previews.

Preview

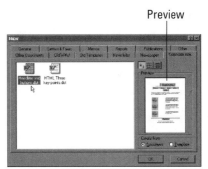

Figure 1-14: Viewing the templates in the Corporate Look folder.

To create a new document using the selected template, click the OK button in the dialog box. The new document should look like Figure 1-15. Notice that it contains simple graphics as placeholders; you replace these with your own graphics or with graphics from the CD-ROM.

Placeholder graphics

Internet Assistant tools

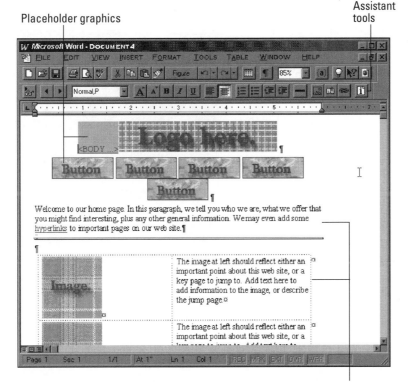

Figure 1-15: A newly created document.

Placeholder text

Ignore the text to the left of the top image for now. It indicates that Internet Assistant has set a custom background color for this page.

Note that the contents of the Standard and Formatting toolbars have changed. A number of the usual Word tools are missing, and Internet Assistant has added quite a few tools of its own. *Don't be concerned about the missing tools!* They come back when you edit a regular document. You only see the new tools when you are editing a Web page. Chapter 8 contains a complete reference to Internet Assistant menu selections and tools.

 If you do not see both the Standard and Format toolbars, select VIEW⇨ TOOLBARS to make them visible (see Figure 1-16).

Customizing your document

The text and graphics in the template are simply there to guide you in the placement of your own words and images. In this section, you learn how to replace the placeholders with meaningful content.

The background color of this template is white. You can change this color to any color you choose — or omit a background color altogether. To change the background color, choose FORMAT⇨BACKGROUND⇨ LINKS. This choice displays the dialog box shown in Figure 1-17.

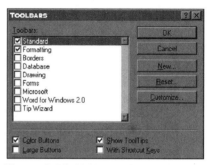

Figure 1-16: Making toolbars visible.

Background Image box   Color drop-down box

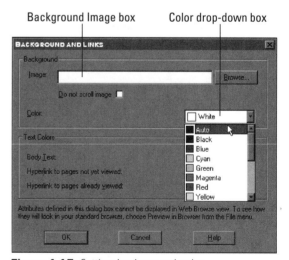

Figure 1-17: Setting background color.

 This is an example of a menu selection that is available only for HTML files. You may notice that your menus have changed a lot from the normal Word menus. Don't worry about this difference — when you edit regular Word documents, all the usual menus and tools come back.

The top half of the Background and Links dialog box enables you to set either a background image or a background color. (See Chapter 2 for an example that uses a background image.) To set a background color, click the Color drop-down list box, as shown in Figure 1-17, and select the color you want to use. This example uses the color white. If you do not want to select a color, pick Auto instead of a color. This selection enables the browser to use its default color (usually, but not always, gray).

You can also set colors for body text and hyperlinks in this dialog box. If you choose a dark background color, for example, you should set a light color for the body text.

The colors you set in this dialog box are not displayed while you are working in Word for Windows. These colors are features that are supported in most Web browsers, but they are not supported visually in Word.

I return to Word in a moment, but first I explore some facts about images on Web pages.

Replacing template images

One of the keys to getting the most out of the templates is to replace the images I put into the templates with your own images. Pictures can be a powerful accent to your Internet message. Table 1-1 lists several ways to obtain or create great images.

Table 1-1	Sources for Images
Source	**Description**
Clip art collections	There are now a wide variety of sources for clip art. Although many clip art collections are intended for desktop publishing, most translate well for use on the Internet (see Figure 1-18). The key thing to look for is bit-mapped images. Clip art that supports PCX, BMP, TIF, or other bit-mapped image formats work great on the Web. Avoid artwork that supports only the EPS or AI formats, which are intended strictly for print publishing.
Company artwork	If you work for a medium-sized or large company, there's a good chance that the public relations, marketing, or sales departments have a great many images that you can use. Best of all, these images are directly related to your company's mission and products. If the images are not already available in electronic form, you can use a scanner to get the job done yourself. If your company has slides, consider having the slides put onto a Photo CD — the cost is small compared to the benefits.

(continued)

Table 1-1	Sources for Images
Source	**Description**
Scanned images	If you or your company have access to a scanner, you can digitize all kinds of images — signatures, company logos, hand-drawn artwork, public-domain images, and so on. If you are handy with a paint program such as Photoshop, you can enhance or clean up the images after you scan them.
Scanned photos	If you already have a scanner, you may want to experiment with scanning photos. For example, you can take along a 35mm camera to any event, get prints back from a photofinishing shop in an hour, and then scan the prints and be ready to upload to the Net the very same day. Several companies now offer scanners designed specifically for scanning photographs. The units are smaller than conventional full-page scanners, but they are perfect for Web-page images. Do not confuse these units with conventional hand-scanners — you feed the photo into a slot for scanning. This gives much better results than hand-scanning.
Photo CD	Just about any photo shop can assist you in putting your photos on CD-ROM. Kodak's Photo CD offers very high image quality, and they are very convenient — the cover of the CD-ROM jewel case shows a thumbnail of very image on the CD. If image quality is important, you can usually get a better image via Photo CD than you can get with your own scanner.
Original images	If you have any artistic talent at all, you can use a variety of image programs to create stunning graphics for your Web pages. Examples include Web 3D from Asymetrix, Adobe Photoshop, Fractal Design Painter, and many other packages. The images in this chapter, for example, were created in Painter and polished in Photoshop. You can find more details about these and other software packages in Chapter 4.

Figure 1-18 shows a variety of clip art images. I have included several samples of clip art libraries on the CD-ROM that comes with this book, as well as a number of original images I created myself. See Appendix A for information.

Figure 1-19 shows an example of a scanned photo that would be perfect for a Web page. If you don't have a scanner, a Photo CD makes a great way to digitize photos. In fact, the quality of Photo CD images is often better than what you can do yourself, even with a good scanner.

Figure 1-18: Examples of images from clip art libraries

Figure 1-19: An example of a scanned photo as a Web page image

However you generate images for your Web pages, here are some simple rules that make your images work effectively:

➥ Don't overload a page with images. Images take time to download. The more images you have, the longer it takes users to view your page.

➥ Avoid too many large images. The larger the images, the longer it takes to download.

➥ The physical size of an image doesn't totally determine the file size of the image. The GIF and JPEG image formats, often used with Web documents, use image compression to automatically reduce file size. If you use images with large areas of a single color, you can reduce the file size and still use large images. The company logo in this chapter is an example of a file that uses a large area of white space.

➥ Use the right tools to prepare your images for the Web. Interlacing and transparency, two important image treatments used on the Web, are not supported by all image editors. See Chapter 4 for details.

NOTE The custom Web images shown in this chapter were created with Fractal Design Painter. You learn about using Painter and other image tools in Chapter 4.

About WebStarr, Inc.

I created the company called WebStarr, Inc. out of thin air, but I used my extensive experience in business to create a company that has a lot in common with companies in the real world.

WebStarr is named after its premiere product, a Web browser called WebStarr. The company offers several different versions of WebStarr, as well as other Internet-related software products. WebStarr, Inc. is divided into two key divisions — Products and Support. The Products division writes and markets WebStarr software products. The Support division provides support by phone and on the Web.

The WebStarr Web site provides access to these two divisions. The Products division uses the Web to put out information about WebStarr software, and the Support division is using the Web to provide information about using the products.

WebStarr, Inc., also provides access to other kinds of information on its Web site. In this chapter, as you work through the tutorial, you are creating a home page for WebStarr, Inc. You can use these same procedures to create a home page for yourself, your company, or for others.

Let's return to the tutorial in Word. Replace an image in the current template with a custom image by following these steps:

Selected image

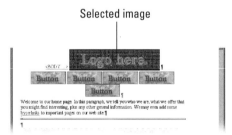

Figure 1-21: Selecting an image.

Bookmark tool

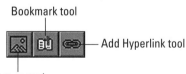

Add Hyperlink tool

Picture tool

Figure 1-22: Some of the new tools on the Formatting toolbar.

1. To continue, click the image at top center (the one with the text `Logo here` in it). After you click it, the image appears highlighted, as shown in Figure 1-21. To load a new image, use one of the tools on the modified toolbar. Figure 1-22 shows some of the new buttons that Internet Assistant has added to the Formatting toolbar.

2. Use the Picture tool to change to a new image. With the `Logo here` image selected, click the Picture tool. Normally, this action opens the Picture dialog box, but that's not what you see this time. Instead, you see the dialog box shown in Figure 1-20. The sidebar "Save your work!" explains the reasons behind the appearance of this dialog box.

3. To continue, click the Save Document Now button. In the Save As dialog box, change to the My Web Pages folder you created earlier. Type the filename **homepage.htm** and click the Save button.

4. After you save the file, you finally see the Picture dialog box (see Figure 1-23). Three tabs are at the top; the Picture tab is active. The filename of the current image is highlighted as the Image Source (mlogo1.jpg). Click the Browse button to search for a replacement image. This action opens the Insert Picture dialog, shown in Figure 1-24.

Browse button

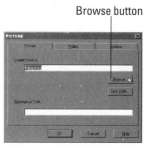

Figure 1-23: The Picture dialog box.

Preview

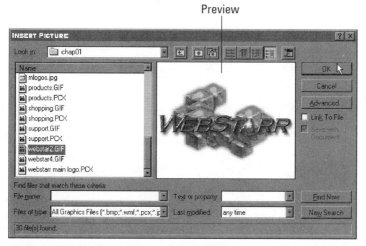

Figure 1-24: The Insert Picture dialog box.

5. The image you will use was copied to your hard disk earlier, into the My Web Pages\images folder. The filename is Webstar2.gif. When you click the image, you can see a preview of the image in the Insert Picture dialog box (refer to Figure 1-24). This image is a company logo for a fictitious company I invented for this tutorial. When you have the correct file highlighted, click OK. This takes you back to the Picture dialog box. The filename Webstar2.gif is now shown as the Image Source.

6. Not all Web browsers support graphics, so it's a good idea to include the alternate text "WebStarr logo" in the text box at the bottom of the Picture dialog box. Click OK to finish. Figure 1-25 shows one possible result: no picture, just the alternate text. (If you don't specify alternate text, you see the text Image not loaded instead of the image itself.)

Don't be alarmed if this happens to you! This is normal. Because Word saves the file as HTML, not in standard Word for Windows format, Word may not see the picture until you close and then reopen the file.

You can also view the picture in your Web browser, by choosing FILE⇨PREVIEW IN BROWSER. Save your work first, however, or you will see the dialog box shown in Figure 1-26. Word only converts the file to HTML when you save, and your Web browser can read only HTML files.

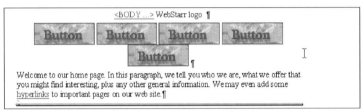

Figure 1-25: Where's the picture? See text for explanation.

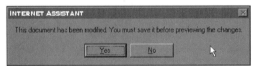

Figure 1-26: You see this warning if you try to preview an unsaved file.

TIP If you haven't yet set up a default browser, you see a dialog box that enables you to specify which browser to use. Simply change to the folder that contains the browser you like best, such as Internet Explorer or Netscape. To see all the features of Internet Assistant, your browser should support tables. Version 2 or later of either Internet Explorer or Netscape is suitable.

Figure 1-27 shows what the page looks like in the Netscape browser. It may look different in another browser, but it should be substantially similar.

This idea, that your work will look different in different browsers, is a very important concept. Each browser interprets the HTML code that Internet Assistant creates a little differently. Always check your work in several different browsers to make sure that nothing unexpected occurs.

In order to see the WebStarr company logo in Word, close the file by selecting FILE⇨CLOSE and then reopen it by choosing FILE⇨OPEN. Figure 1-28 shows the file with the image now visible in Word.

You could use other types of images besides a company logo at the top of this Web page. For example, if this template were used to create a personal Web page, you could put a picture of yourself, your cat, or even the view outside your bedroom window. You could also use an image with a different shape — for example, you could use a short, wide image instead of the blocky image shown here.

Figure 1-27: The appearance of the page in the Netscape browser.

Remember that Word and Internet Assistant may not display an image right away — you may see that dreaded `Image not Loaded` message instead of a picture. To view the image, you must close and then reopen the file. If you are adding several images, you do not have to close and reopen the file to show the images until you have added *all* of the images. For example, the next task is to change the images in the five buttons below the company logo. You can change the images for the buttons, one after the other, and then close and reopen the file to view the result.

Figure 1-28: The reopened file displays the inserted image.

The five buttons for WebStarr are the following:

➡ **Products.** Clicking this button jumps to a Web page that lists the various products that the company sells. Filename: `products.gif`.

➡ **Support.** This button jumps to a page that provides access to WebStarr support services. Filename: `support.gif`.

➡ **Shopping.** Using this Web page enables the visitor to shop for WebStarr products. Filename: `shopping.gif`.

➡ **FAQs.** This page provides a list of Frequently Asked Questions (FAQs) and their answers. Filename: `faq.gif`.

➡ **Lifestyle.** A good Web site should be more than informative — it should be fun, too. WebStarr, Inc. uses the Lifestyle Web page to add humor and links to other Web sites. Filename: `lifestyl.gif`.

The images for these buttons (whose filenames are in the preceding bulleted list) are also among the files you copied to the `My Web Pages\images` folder. Let's change the first button, and learn about a few additional tricks when using Internet Assistant. Before you begin, however, remember to save your work (press Ctrl+S or click FILE➪SAVE).

The overall process is the same one we used to load the company logo. Click the first button on the left to select it, and click the Picture button on the Formatting toolbar. Use the Browse button in the Picture dialog box to locate the `products.gif` file (see Figure 1-29). Click OK to load it, which redisplays the Picture dialog box. Use "Products" as the alternate text.

Figure 1-29: Adding the image for the Products button.

Three tabs are at the top of the Picture dialog box: Picture, Video, and Options. Click the Options tab to change the dialog box, as shown in Figure 1-30. This tab gives you the opportunity to change a number of options for the image: Size, Border, and Alignment with Text. Table 1-2 lists the options and what each one does.

Size entries   Options tab

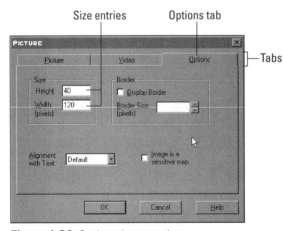

Figure 1-30: Setting picture options.

A Web page displays more neatly in a browser if you add size information to your Web pages. Add the height and width, in pixels, to the boxes in the Size area of the dialog box. In this case, the button image is 120 pixels wide and 40 pixels high (see Figure 1-30). When you are finished, click the OK button.

Save your work!

It's a good idea to save your work before you click any buttons or make any menu selections. If you don't, you see warnings like the one shown in Figure 1-20. Word saves Web pages in the HTML format, not the standard Word for Windows format. If you don't save your work, Word can become confused about the relationships between the file and the images (and other HTML links) in your document. Saving the document ensures that the result matches your expectations.

If you are certain that the task at hand won't cause a problem, you can click the Continue Without Saving button. However, I strongly recommend that you make it a habit to click the Save Document Now button. Word presents the standard Save or Save As dialog box, and you can save the file to the appropriate folder.

Note that the dialog box in Figure 1-20 refers to "relative links." HTML documents make frequent use of *relative links*. This means that, instead of supplying the full path to an image or HTML file, you normally supply a short form of the path. For example, the typical Web site puts HTML files in one folder and images in a subfolder. To link to an HTML file, you only supply the filename, not the path. To link to an image, you supply the *relative path*. For example, if you want to refer to an image whose filename is IMAGE.GIF, located in the subfolder `pictures`, you use a relative path, as follows:

```
pictures/image.gif
```

For comparison, an absolute path might look like this:

```
c:/My Documents/My Web Pages/pictures/image.gif
```

This path shows the location of the image file relative to the current folder (that's the folder where the current HTML file is located). Notice that I used the *forward* slash (/) instead of the backslash (\). Many Web servers require the forward slash, and nearly all Web browsers support it, so make it a habit to use the forward slash.

Relative paths allow for flexible management of your Web site. For more information about how to arrange files in folders, see the sidebar "Arrange your Web site," later in this chapter, and also see Chapter 7.

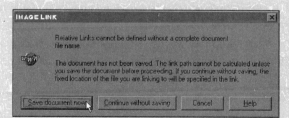

Figure 1-20: You see this warning if you forget to save a file.

Table 1-2	Picture Options Tab
Option	What It Does
Size	This isn't for changing the size of an image! It's simply for specifying the *actual size* of the image, in pixels. Many Web browsers use the size information to organize the page for viewing. You learn more about this subject in Chapter 4.
Border	You can add a border to your images by specifying the border width.
Alignment with Text	You can align pictures to the left of text, to the right, in the middle, and more. (See Chapter 4.)

 To find the size of an image, load it into an image editor. Most image editors either display the image size directly or allow you to find the size with a menu selection. Version 3.0 of SnapShot/32, an image editor and screen capture program included on the CD-ROM, shows the image size. You can drag your Web images into SnapShot/32 to find their width and height.

The result should look like Figure 1-31. Notice that the new image does not have a border around it, but that the other buttons do. Although you can add a border to an image, the border you see around the placeholder buttons isn't that kind of border. It signifies a hyperlink to another Web document. You learn about hyperlinks shortly.

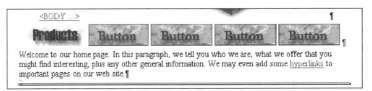

Figure 1-31: One of the button images has been replaced.

 Web browsers also put a border around images when they are used for hyperlinks to other Web pages. For this reason, I advise against using borders around your images unless you make them look different from hyperlinked image borders. This can be difficult, because today's browsers enable the user to select different colors for borders, and different browsers display different border widths. The best course of action is to avoid using borders for your images, unless you are certain it will not be confused with the border added by a browser.

At this point, the Products button isn't really a button at all — it's just another image. To turn it into a button that jumps to the Products Web page, we need to add a hyperlink. Click the Products image to highlight it, and then click the Add Hyperlink button. This action opens the Hyperlink dialog box shown in Figure 1-32.

Selected image   Bookmark hyperlink   File/URL hyperlink

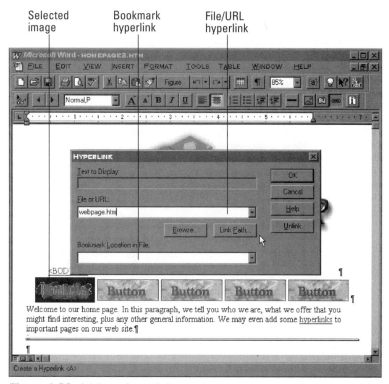

Figure 1-32: Adding a hyperlink to a picture.

The dialog box allows two kinds of hyperlinks for a picture: to a file or URL (middle of the Hyperlink dialog box) or to a bookmark location in the current file (bottom of the Hyperlink dialog box). For this example, the link is to an external file. Enter the filename **Webpage.htm** in the File or URL text box, as shown in Figure 1-32. This file doesn't exist yet. Click OK to add the hyperlink. Now look at the Products button. It should have a border around it, as shown in Figure 1-33. This border indicates that this isn't just a picture; it is an active button that takes you to a different Web page.

Webpage.htm is a stand-in file. We use it each time we add a hyperlink to a file that doesn't exist yet. It's a good idea to use a standard file to stand in for files that you will create later. This prevents file not found error messages and serves as a reminder that you have yet to create the necessary file.

If you want a challenge, you can create your own Webpage.htm file (see the sidebar "Creating Webpage.htm"), or you can copy it from the CD-ROM. This file is located at \tutorial\Webpage.htm. Copy it to the My Web Pages folder, where you saved homepage.htm.

Figure 1-33: Adding a hyperlink also adds a border to your image.

Figure 1-34: The appearance of the Webpage.htm file.

If you choose to copy `Webpage.htm` from the CD-ROM, Figure 1-34 shows what happens later, when you click the Products button in your browser. I describe how to do this shortly.

To add the other four buttons, repeat the steps you used to add the Products button, including adding the size information (which is the same for the four remaining buttons). The filenames, alternate text, and hyperlinks are shown in Table 1-3.

Creating `Webpage.htm`

You can create your own version of `Webpage.htm` by following these steps:

1. Create a new file by choosing FILE⇨NEW, using the blank HTML file template, `html.dot`.

2. Add the following text, using the indicated styles:

   Sample Web Page (style: Heading 1, H1)

   This page is just a placeholder. (style: Heading 4, H4)

   Click your browser's **back** button to return to the previous page. (style: Normal, P)

3. Add a horizontal rule below the first line.

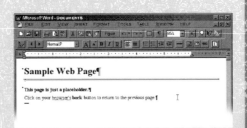

Figure 1-35: Creating a simple placeholder page.

The result should look like Figure 1-35. Save it as `Webpage.htm` in the same folder where you saved `homepage.htm`. placeholder page.

Table 1-3		Adding Other Buttons	
Button Name	**Filename**	**Alternate Text**	**Hyperlink**
Support	`support.gif`	Support	`Webpage.htm`
Shopping	`shopping.gif`	Shopping	`Webpage.htm`
FAQs	`faq.gif`	Frequently asked questions	`Webpage.htm`
Lifestyle	`lifestyl.gif`	Lifestyle Page	`Webpage.htm`

After you have added all five buttons, your Word window should look like the one shown in Figure 1-36. Be sure to save your work now.

Figure 1-36: The Web page with all five buttons replaced.

 If you accidentally delete one of the original template buttons, you can easily add a new button. Place the cursor where you want to add the button, then click the Picture icon on the toolbar. You can then continue just as if you were replacing a template picture.

 You may have noticed that funny little mark at the end of each paragraph. This mark is called (oddly enough) a paragraph mark. You can force Word to display paragraphs by selecting TOOLS⇨OPTIONS. Click the View tab of the dialog box shown in Figure 1-37, and then make sure that a check mark appears next to Paragraph Marks in the Non-Printing Characters section of the dialog box. I find that paragraph marks assist in understanding the layout of the page. They are especially helpful in finding extra blank lines.

To check your work, preview it in the browser (choose FILE⇨PREVIEW IN BROWSER). The results should look like Figure 1-38, which shows the appearance of the top portion of the page in Netscape. Notice that a border goes around each of the images, indicating that they are hyperlinks. Click any one of them to display the `Webpage.htm` file (it should look like Figure 1-35).

Notice that the cursor changes to a small hand with a pointing finger when it passes over the image with a hyperlink. The exact appearance of the hand may vary from one browser to the next; Figure 1-39 shows the appearance of the hand in Netscape and in Internet Explorer. A pointing hand also indicates hyperlinks found in text.

Click here to toggle display
of paragraph marks

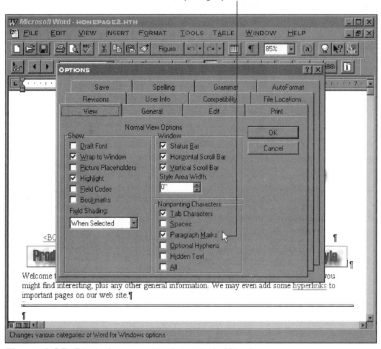

Figure 1-37: Displaying paragraph marks in Word.

Figure 1-38: All five buttons added, including
hyperlinks, as shown in Netscape.

Figure 1-39: A pointing hand
indicates a hyperlink. Left,
Netscape's hand; right,
Internet Explorer.

Replacing template text

I've covered a lot of territory so far. Adding images to a Web page adds a great deal of power and flexibility. It's time to turn your attention to the art of adding text to a Web page. You have noticed by now that there is already some text in the template. I added text at various locations to create a pleasing combination of text and images.

In many cases, the text is more than just empty filler. I have added tips and tricks throughout the templates. Sometimes, you find hints that guide you toward a great-looking page layout. Other times, you find jokes, quotations, or general advice about creating outstanding Web pages. Keep an eye out for the diamonds!

Figure 1-40 shows the next step: Select the text in the paragraph immediately below the buttons. Do not select the whole paragraph! Notice that the paragraph marker is not selected in Figure 1-40.

Selected text

Figure 1-40: *Selecting text in a template.*

I suggest that you make it a habit to read my template text before you delete it — it often has suggestions you'll find useful, such as the following:

Welcome to our home page. In this paragraph, we tell you who we are, what we offer that you might find interesting, plus any other general information. We may even add some **hyperlinks** to important pages on our Web site.

The text is more than filler; it is giving you ideas for what to say on this part of your Web page. It also includes a text hyperlink, indicated by the bold, underlined text. You learn how to add a special kind of hyperlink later in this section.

Underlining is an Internet convention to draw attention to text with hyperlinks. For this reason, you should avoid underlining text that is not a hyperlink. In practical terms, this means that you should avoid underlining at all costs.

After you have the text selected, press the Delete key to remove the text. Add the following text in place of the text you deleted (see Figure 1-41):

Welcome to the **WebStarr** home page. You can access everything you need to know about our company right here. If you can't find what you need, send mail to `help@Webstarr.com`.

Replacement text

Figure 1-41: Adding replacement text to your Web page.

Two special points are of interest in this text. First, I used bold to emphasize the company name, WebStarr. When working in print media, such as a newsletter, it's usually a good idea to avoid using bold text. Although I don't recommend overuse of bold on a Web page, it's okay to use bold to emphasize key words.

Second, I added an e-mail address at the end of the paragraph. Although it would be adequate to provide just the address, many Web browsers support sending e-mail directly from the browser. You use a hyperlink to set up this capability.

To add a text hyperlink, first select the text involved (see Figure 1-42). Only select the actual text (`help@Webstarr.com`), not the period at the end of the sentence. As a general rule, when creating a hyperlink, you should not include punctuation before or after text.

Selected text

Figure 1-42: Selecting text for a hyperlink.

Now click the Add Hyperlink button in the Formatting toolbar. This action displays the dialog box shown in Figure 1-43.

The Add Formatting button looks like two links in a chain.

TIP The dialog box looks almost exactly like the Hyperlink dialog box you used when you added a hyperlink to an image. The difference is that the Text to Display box now has text in it. In fact, it contains the very text you selected a moment ago. Type the following into the File or URL box: **mailto:help@Webstarr.com.**

When we added a hyperlink to the button images, we used a filename (`Webpage.htm`). This kind of entry is different. It is a command to the browser that requests it to send mail to a specific e-mail address. Click OK to close the dialog box. Figure 1-44 shows what the new text hyperlink looks like. As with any other hyperlink, the text appears underlined.

Let's see how this hyperlink behaves in a browser. First, save your work. Then choose FILE⇨PREVIEW IN BROWSER to view your Web page in your browser. Click the text hyperlink. The exact results vary with your browser, but you should see your mail program appear, with the To: address already filled in with `help@Webstarr.com`. Figure 1-45 shows the result in the Netscape browser, and Figure 1-46 shows the result in the Internet Explorer.

Type entry here

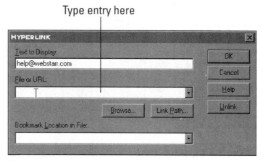

Figure 1-43: Adding a text hyperlink.

Hyperlink

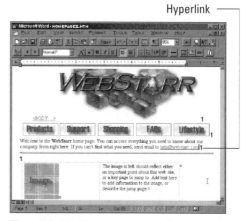

Figure 1-44: The appearance of a new text hyperlink.

Mail to address automatically added

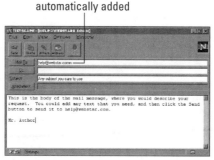

Figure 1-45: Sending mail with Netscape 2.0.

Completing the page

Mail to address
automatically added

Figure 1-46: Sending mail with Internet Explorer.

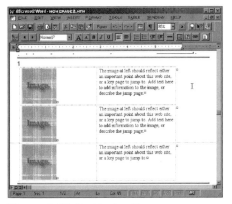

Figure 1-47: Positioning the page.

Setting text alignment

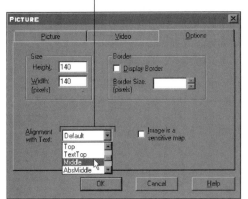

Figure 1-48: Specifying options.

The top portion, or header, of the Web page is finished, and it's time to move down to the middle section of the page. Use the arrow keys or the mouse to move down the page until you can see the middle portion, shown in Figure 1-47.

There are three images and three blocks of text. The dotted lines indicate that this is a Word for Windows table. The Internet doesn't support all of Word's table features, but we can still create a sharp-looking page. Let's start by selecting the top image and replacing it with an image that says something about WebStarr's flagship product. Follow almost exactly the same steps you used to replace the other images in the template:

1. Click the Picture button on the Formatting toolbar.

2. In the Picture dialog box, locate the file to add: fast.jpg.

3. Add the alternate text: **Fast!**

4. Click the Options tab at the top of the Picture dialog box and add the image width and height: 140 wide, 140 high.

5. Still in the Options tab, set the Alignment with Text to Middle (see Figure 1-48). This choice centers the image in the table cell. Click OK to save these settings.

The result is shown in Figure 1-49. The image uses the basic themes in the company logo (gold cubes and blue text) to dramatize a WebStarr feature: speed.

To edit the text at the right of the new image, select it. As in the earlier example, be very careful not to select the marker at the end of the text. Replace the text with the following:

WebStarr, our flag-
ship product, is the fastest
Web browser on the market.
You'll find yourself wondering
how you did without it!

When you compare browsers,
you need to compare more than
features. All the best browsers
support the key features. Only
WebStarr offers you blinding
speed, too.

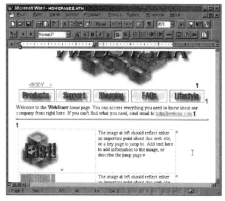

Figure 1-49: A new image loaded onto the page.

Now change the second image to `fun.jpg`, and add the size, appropriate alternate text, and set Alignment with Text to Middle. Then add the following text in the cell to the right of the new image:

A good Web browser should be easy to use, but a
great Web browser should be fun to use. **WebStarr**
is the only browser that is so easy to use you'll never have to
think about navigating around the Web. Think of where you
want to go, and **WebStarr** will find it for you. It's that easy!

WebStarr puts the fun back into Web surfing.

Finally, change the third image to `free.jpg`. Add the following text in the cell to the right of the new image:

Here's the best part: **WebStarr** is free. That's right,
you can download the personal edition of WebStarr
right from the Internet and get started right away.

If you want more power, you can download **WebStarr Pro**, a
version that includes full support for HTML 5, Perl 6, and a host
of other advanced features.

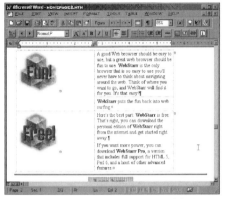

Figure 1-50: Two more images added.

Figure 1-51: The bottom portion of the Web page.

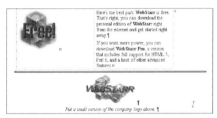

Figure 1-52: Adding a small logo at the bottom of the page.

Figure 1-53: Adding addresses to the page.

Figure 1-50 shows the result.

All that remains is to make changes to the bottom portion of the page (see Figure 1-51). You'll add a smaller version of the WebStarr logo, and add physical and e-mail addresses.

Replace the small template image shown in Figure 1-51 with the file `\tutorial\chap01\Webstar4.gif`. This is a miniature version of the company logo from the top of the page. Figure 1-52 shows what your Web page should look like with the small logo.

Change the text below the image to a fake address, as follows:

PO Box 999
West Hampshiretown, ME 01923

Select the address text and make it bold and italicized. Then add a line of plain text, also centered, with an e-mail address: `sales@Webstarr.com`. Figure 1-53 shows the result you are trying to achieve.

Treat this e-mail address the same as you treated the e-mail address at the top of the page: with a hyperlink. Select the address, click the Add Hyperlink button, and type **mailto: sales@Webstarr.com** in the File or URL text box (see Figure 1-54). Figure 1-55 shows the appearance of the finished bottom portion of the page. Save your work now.

To check your work, preview it in your browser (select FILE⇨PREVIEW IN BROWSER). Figure 1-56 shows the page in the Netscape browser. Notice that the hyperlinked text at the bottom also causes the cursor to change to a pointing hand.

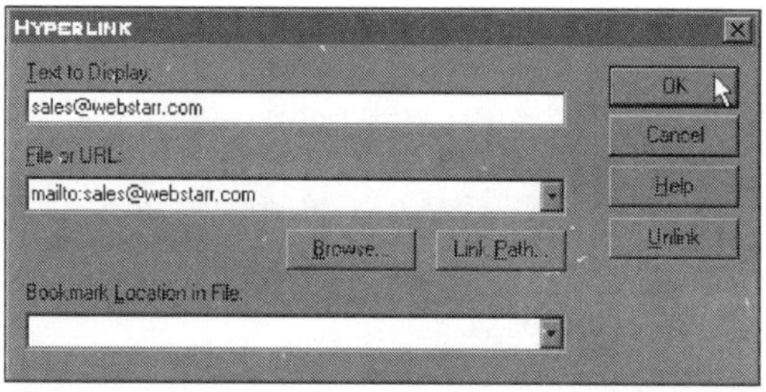

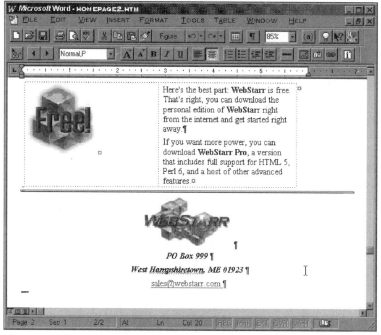

Figure 1-54: Adding a hyperlink.

Figure 1-55: The bottom portion of the completed page.

The pointing hand

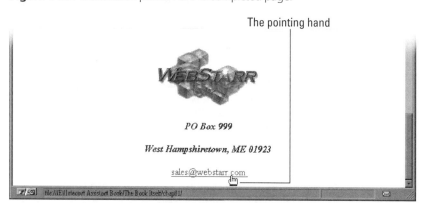

Figure 1-56: The page in the Netscape browser, with hyperlink text.

Bonus: Adding a table border

The conversion of the template into a real Web page is complete. However, you can also modify the template a bit to change the appearance to suit your own tastes. For example, you could add a border around the table that contains the Fast!, Fun!, and Free! images. Simply select the entire table by clicking and dragging (refer to Figure 1-57), and choose TABLE⇨BORDERS. This action brings up the dialog box shown in Figure 1-57.

Click the Grid icon, set the line size (the default of 1 is usually best), and click the OK button. Save your work and preview it in your browser. Figure 1-58 shows the result in the Word document, and Figure 1-59 shows what the border looks like in the Internet Explorer browser.

Installing templates to a hard disk

Earlier in this chapter, you learn how to use the templates from your CD-ROM drive. If space on your hard disk is tight, it makes sense to use the templates right from the CD-ROM. However, you can also install the templates to your hard disk for faster access. You also might want to use that CD-ROM drive for something besides templates! In this section, I show you how to install the Corporate Looks templates to your hard drive.

To begin, double-click the My Computer icon on your Windows 95 desktop. The appearance of this icon may vary, especially if you installed the Plus! pack for Windows 95. The icon is usually found at the top left of your desktop. Figure 1-60 shows a typical group of icons for the basic features of Windows 95. When you double-click the My Computer icon, you see a list of your computer's disk drives, among other things (see Figure 1-61).

Follow these steps to install the templates you need for the tutorials in this book:

1. Double-click the icon for the drive where you installed Word for Windows or Microsoft Office. (The usual location is your C drive.) This action displays the folders on your drive; double-click the MS Office folder, and then double-click the Templates folder to open it.

2. Double-click the icon for your CD-ROM drive. You can tell which drive is your CD-ROM drive by the icon used to represent it (see Figure 1-61; my CD-ROM drive is F). Double-click the folder icon for the Cool Templates folder. Rearrange your desktop so that you can clearly see the contents of the Templates and Cool Templates folders (see Figure 1-62). The MS Office Templates folder shows several template files and several template subfolders. The Cool Templates folder shows subfolders, each one of which contains a number of templates. Figure 1-62 shows approximately what your desktop should look like.

Grid icon

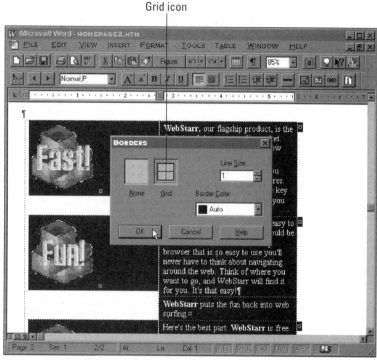

Figure 1-57: Adding a border to the table.

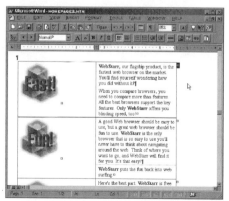

Figure 1-58: The appearance
of the table border in Word.

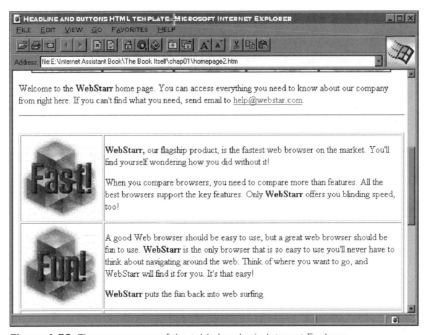

Figure 1-59: The appearance of the table border in Internet Explorer.

My Computer icon

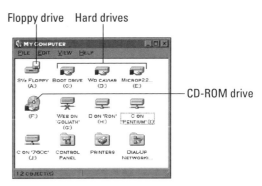

Floppy drive   Hard drives

CD-ROM drive

Figure 1-61: The result of double-clicking the My Computer icon.

Figure 1-60: Typical Windows 95 icons.

Hard drive   CD-ROM drive

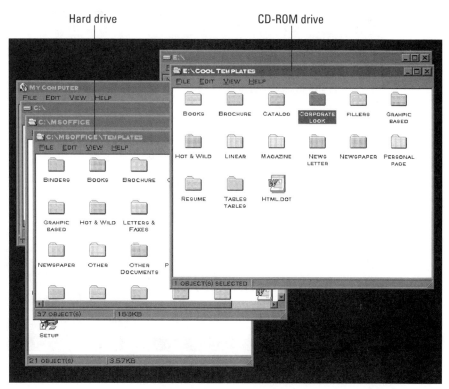

Figure 1-62: Desktop with template folders open and ready for installation.

3. The Cool Templates folder contains quite a few subfolders. Find the folder named Corporate Looks. Right-click and drag it into the MS Office Templates folder. When you release the mouse button, you see the pop-up menu (called a *context menu* in Windows 95) shown in Figure 1-63. Select the Copy option. This choice copies the Corporate Looks folder, as well as the templates and graphics it contains, to your hard drive. The Corporate Looks folder contains all the templates you use in the tutorials in this book.

You can install the other subfolders in the Cool Templates folder in the same way when you are ready to use them. All you have to do is drag a folder from the Cool Templates folder on the CD-ROM into the MS Office Templates folder.

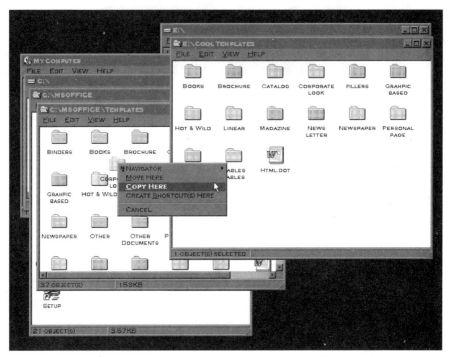

Figure 1-63: Copying a template folder to your hard drive.

Instant Internet: Converting Existing Documents

In This Chapter

Convert your existing Word styles to **Web-legal** styles

Use Web styles effectively

Work with **lists**

Use tables to arrange text on the Web page

Determine which Word features translate to the Web

Bonus: Use the Windows 95 Registry to automate conversions

One of the advantages of using Word for Windows to create Web pages is that any of your existing Word documents can be converted into a Web page. Each Word document that you convert will present unique challenges and opportunities. My goal in this chapter is to introduce you to the tools you need to handle any situation. In this chapter, you learn how to make this process as painless as possible.

Not every Word document can be instantly converted into a Web page. Many of Word's **styles** and features are fine for word processing, but don't translate to the Web. I've included a comprehensive guide in this chapter that tells you which Word features apply to the Web and which do not. I've also included information on how to use the Windows 95 **Registry** to automate parts of the conversion process. After you know which Word features apply to the Web, you can also take steps to standardize your documents so that they convert more easily to the Web.

Setting Up the Tutorial

This chapter shows you, step by step, how to convert a Word document into a Web page. Before starting the tutorial, you will set up the tutorial by copying files used in the tutorial from the CD-ROM to your hard disk. You may choose to run automatic setup or to set up the files manually.

Automatic setup

If you haven't already installed the software for automatic setup of the tutorials, turn to Appendix A and do so now. Otherwise, if you choose not to use automatic setup, see the next section, "Manual setup," which tells you how to manually copy the necessary files for this tutorial. If you didn't use automatic setup earlier, you can find complete instructions for starting, running, and using the automatic setup program in Chapter 1.

To run automatic setup, click the Start button, then Programs, and then click the Autopage icon, shown here. The Autopage icon is for the automatic tutorial setup program.

Click here for Chapter 2 files

Figure 2-1: Automatic setup for the Chapter 2 tutorial.

Click the Chapter 2 Files radio button to display the files for this chapter (see Figure 2-1).

To copy the files for the tutorial to your hard disk, click the Copy To Hard Disk button. Automatic setup copies the files to the My Web Pages subfolder of the My Documents folder. If you installed Microsoft Office on your C drive, the folder is usually the following:

> c:\My Documents\My Web Pages

NOTE This is the same folder you have been using for all the tutorials. From time to time, you may notice that one or more additional subfolders is created in the My Web Pages folder; this is normal, and all is explained during each tutorial.

After you have copied the necessary files, skip ahead to the start of the tutorial. If you choose not to use the automatic setup, read the next section to find out how to copy the necessary files manually.

Manual setup

Before you start the tutorial, open the folder My Web Pages on your hard disk. If you have already completed the tutorial in Chapter 1, you created it as a subfolder of the My Documents folder (usually C:\My Documents).

The tutorial in this chapter uses six image files from the CD-ROM. They are located in the folder \tutorial\chap02. Before you continue, copy the image file

```
Webstar3.gif
```

from the \tutorial\chap02 folder on the CD-ROM to the My Web Pages\ images folder you created earlier on your hard disk (see Chapter 1 for complete details). Copy the document file

```
Pressrel.doc
```

from the \tutorial\chap02 folder on the CD-ROM to the My Web Pages folder.

You are now ready to begin the tutorial.

Tutorial 2: Converting a Word Document for the Web

The task for this chapter is to convert an existing press release document into an **HTML** document (that is, a Web page). As in Chapter 1, we use the fictitious company WebStarr, Inc. as the basis for the exercise. In this example, the existing document is a WebStarr press release announcing a new version of the WebStarr Pro browser — a product called WebStarr Pro ElitE. Figure 2-2 shows what the existing press release looks like. Figure 2-3 shows what the Web page version will look like when we are finished with the conversion.

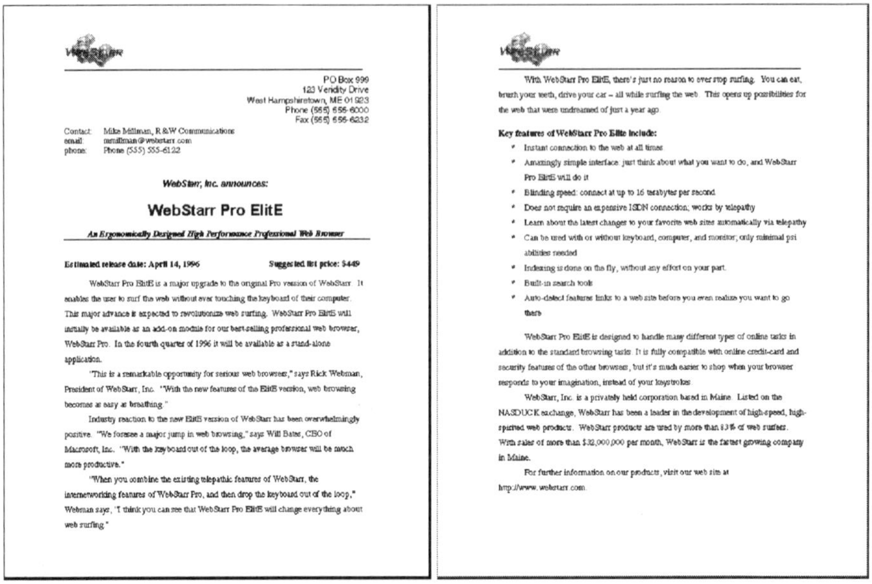

PO Box 999
123 Veridity Drive
West Hampshiretown, ME 01923
Phone (555) 555-6000
Fax (555) 555-6232

Contact: Mike Millman, R&W Communications
email: mmillman@webstarr.com
phone: Phone (555) 555-6122

WebStarr, Inc. announces:

WebStarr Pro ElitE

An Ergonomically Designed High Performance Professional Web Browser

Estimated release date: April 14, 1996 **Suggested list price: $449**

WebStarr Pro ElitE is a major upgrade to the original Pro version of WebStarr. It enables the user to surf the web without ever touching the keyboard of their computer. This major advance is expected to revolutionize web surfing. WebStarr Pro ElitE will initially be available as an add-on module for our best-selling professional web browser, WebStarr Pro. In the fourth quarter of 1996 it will be available as a stand-alone application.

"This is a remarkable opportunity for serious web browsers," says Rick Webman, President of WebStarr, Inc. "With the new features of the ElitE version, web browsing becomes as easy as breathing."

Industry reaction to the new ElitE version of WebStarr has been overwhelmingly positive. "We foresee a major jump in web browsing," says Will Bates, CEO of Macrosoft, Inc. "With the keyboard out of the loop, the average browser will be much more productive."

"When you combine the existing telepathic features of WebStarr, the internetworking features of WebStarr Pro, and then drop the keyboard out of the loop," Webman says, "I think you can see that WebStarr Pro ElitE will change everything about web surfing."

With WebStarr Pro ElitE, there's just no reason to ever stop surfing. You can eat, brush your teeth, drive your car – all while surfing the web. This opens up possibilities for the web that were undreamed of just a year ago.

Key features of WebStarr Pro Elite include:

- Instant connection to the web at all times
- Amazingly simple interface: just think about what you want to do, and WebStarr Pro ElitE will do it
- Blinding speed: connect at up to 16 terabytes per second
- Does not require an expensive ISDN connection; works by telepathy
- Learn about the latest changes to your favorite web sites automatically via telepathy
- Can be used with or without keyboard, computer, and monitor; only minimal psi abilities needed
- Indexing is done on the fly, without any effort on your part
- Built-in search tools
- Auto-detect features links to a web site before you even realize you want to go there

WebStarr Pro ElitE is designed to handle many different types of online tasks in addition to the standard browsing tasks. It is fully compatible with online credit-card and security features of the other browsers, but it's much easier to shop when your browser responds to your imagination, instead of your keystrokes.

WebStarr, Inc. is a privately held corporation based in Maine. Listed on the NASDUCK exchange, WebStarr has been a leader in the development of high-speed, high-spirited web products. WebStarr products are used by more than 83% of web surfers. With sales of more than $32,000,000 per month, WebStarr is the fastest growing company in Maine.

For further information on our products, visit our web site at http://www.webstarr.com.

Figure 2-2: The original press release.

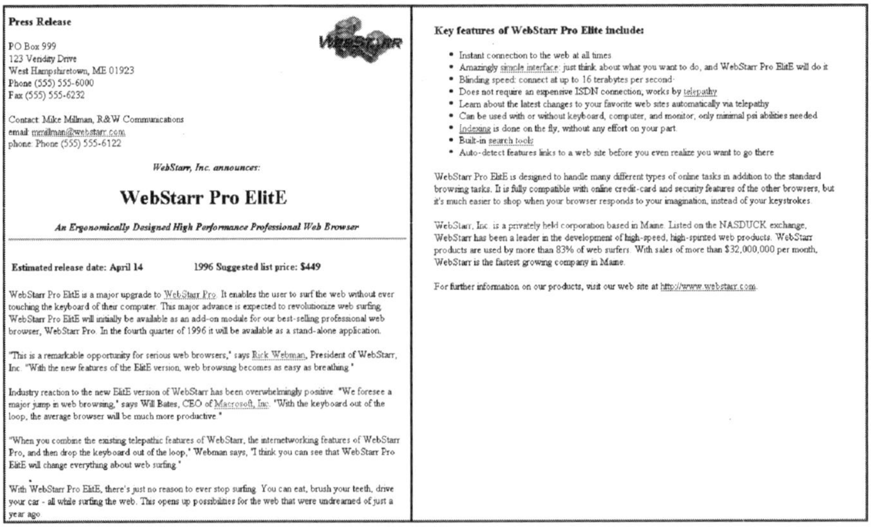

Press Release

PO Box 999
123 Veridity Drive
West Hampshiretown, ME 01923
Phone (555) 555-6000
Fax (555) 555-6232

Contact: Mike Millman, R&W Communications
email: mmillman@webstarr.com
phone: Phone (555) 555-6122

WebStarr, Inc. announces:

WebStarr Pro ElitE

An Ergonomically Designed High Performance Professional Web Browser

Estimated release date: April 14 **1996 Suggested list price: $449**

WebStarr Pro ElitE is a major upgrade to WebStarr Pro. It enables the user to surf the web without ever touching the keyboard of their computer. This major advance is expected to revolutionize web surfing. WebStarr Pro ElitE will initially be available as an add-on module for our best-selling professional web browser, WebStarr Pro. In the fourth quarter of 1996 it will be available as a stand-alone application.

"This is a remarkable opportunity for serious web browsers," says Rick Webman, President of WebStarr, Inc. "With the new features of the ElitE version, web browsing becomes as easy as breathing."

Industry reaction to the new ElitE version of WebStarr has been overwhelmingly positive. "We foresee a major jump in web browsing," says Will Bates, CEO of Macrosoft, Inc. "With the keyboard out of the loop, the average browser will be much more productive."

"When you combine the existing telepathic features of WebStarr, the internetworking features of WebStarr Pro, and then drop the keyboard out of the loop," Webman says, "I think you can see that WebStarr Pro ElitE will change everything about web surfing."

With WebStarr Pro ElitE, there's just no reason to ever stop surfing. You can eat, brush your teeth, drive your car - all while surfing the web. This opens up possibilities for the web that were undreamed of just a year ago.

Key features of WebStarr Pro Elite include:

- Instant connection to the web at all times
- Amazingly simple interface: just think about what you want to do, and WebStarr Pro ElitE will do it
- Blinding speed: connect at up to 16 terabytes per second
- Does not require an expensive ISDN connection; works by telepathy
- Learn about the latest changes to your favorite web sites automatically via telepathy
- Can be used with or without keyboard, computer, and monitor; only minimal psi abilities needed
- Indexing is done on the fly, without any effort on your part
- Built-in search tools
- Auto-detect features links to a web site before you even realize you want to go there

WebStarr Pro ElitE is designed to handle many different types of online tasks in addition to the standard browsing tasks. It is fully compatible with online credit-card and security features of the other browsers, but it's much easier to shop when your browser responds to your imagination, instead of your keystrokes.

WebStarr, Inc. is a privately held corporation based in Maine. Listed on the NASDUCK exchange, WebStarr has been a leader in the development of high-speed, high-spirited web products. WebStarr products are used by more than 83% of web surfers. With sales of more than $32,000,000 per month, WebStarr is the fastest growing company in Maine.

For further information on our products, visit our web site at http://www.webstarr.com.

Figure 2-3: The press release converted into a Web page.

I have set up the situation for this press release as realistically as possible. The key points to note about the conversion are as follows:

➡ The image was black and white for the press release, because it was to be faxed and there was no need for a color image. Color is highly desirable for the Web page, so I have included a color version of the image, rather than black and white.

➡ A press release is a common document produced at WebStarr. It's a good idea to automate the conversion of standard documents. For the automation to be meaningful, your standard documents must use a standard **template** that contains standard styles, and you have to use those styles in your documents. You learn some automation tricks later in this chapter. You can apply these tricks to frequently used document types at your own company or home business.

➡ HTML doesn't support every type of **layout** used in the press release, so we will make some changes to the layout. This is a common occurrence when converting existing documents to the Web. If you will be converting documents for a large company, you may need to work with another department to get approval for the changes. You might even have to develop a standard layout for Web pages, or work with a standard layout created by the art or marketing department. On the other hand, folks who don't understand the requirements of the Web might argue about the need for layout changes. You'll find information in this chapter that you can use to convince non-Web-aware people of the need for the changes.

➡ Putting a document on the Web means that you can add **hyperlinks** to other documents. I have made liberal use of this feature in the tutorial.

Starting the conversion

To begin the tutorial, open the Word document you copied from the CD-ROM earlier. The file to open is

```
\My Documents\My Web Pages\Pressrel.doc
```

Figure 2-4 shows the file opened in Word.

You will not see the black and white image from Figure 2-2 unless you view the document in Page Layout mode (VIEW⇨PAGE LAYOUT). The image is located in the page header. Headers and footers are only visible in Page Layout mode. The toolbar at the bottom of the Word window is the drawing toolbar, which you use to change the position and appearance of imported graphics.

Figure 2-4: The press release open in Word for Windows.

Save button

File Pressrel.doc   Save in drop-down box

Filename

Save as type drop-down box

Figure 2-5: Saving a file as HTML.

Converting the document into an HTML Web page is very easy: Just save it as an HTML document. Begin by choosing FILE⇨SAVE AS. This action opens the Save As dialog box, shown in Figure 2-5. In this dialog box, do the following:

➡ If the current directory shown in the Save In drop-down box is not \My Documents\My Web Pages, change to that directory now.

➡ If the filename is not Pressrel.doc, click the file Pressrel.doc.

➡ Click the small down arrow at the right of the Save As Type drop-down box to display the possible choices for saving files. Use the arrow keys or the scroll bar in the drop-down box to highlight the choice HTML Document (*.htm). Click this choice to select it (see Figure 2-5). You will see the File Name appear as Pressrel.htm.

➡ Click the Save button to save the document as an HTML file.

While Word saves the document as an HTML file, it attempts to convert your existing styles to styles that are legal for Web documents. As a result, the document appears very different after it has been saved. Do not be alarmed; this is normal. Figure 2-6 shows what your document should look like after it is saved as HTML.

The key changes are as follows:

➡ If the filename is not Pressrel.doc, click the file Pressrel.doc.

➡ Some text styles have been changed. For example, the return address was originally right-justified, and now it is left-justified.

➡ Many paragraphs that had styles are now converted to the Normal,P style. These paragraphs retain some special formatting (bold, italic).

➡ Some paragraphs were converted to specific Web-legal styles, such as Heading 1,H1.

⇒ The style with a bottom border, used for the text An Ergonomically Designed High Performance Professional Web Browser, now has a horizontal rule beneath it. There are no Web-legal styles with bottom borders. The **horizontal rule** is the closest approximation, and this is what Internet Assistant uses when it converts the file to HTML.

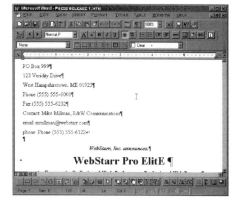

Figure 2-6: The converted document.

In general, Internet Assistant attempts to intelligently convert Word formatting and styles to Web-legal styles. However, there are quite a few Word features that just will not translate to the Web. These features include:

⇒ Annotations

⇒ Borders and shading

⇒ Captions

⇒ Drawing layer elements

⇒ Embedded objects (video clips, equations, clip art, and so on)

⇒ Fields (only the field result is converted)

⇒ Footnotes and endnotes

⇒ Frames (however, top and bottom frame borders are converted to horizontal rules)

⇒ Headers and footers

⇒ Indented paragraphs

⇒ Index entries

⇒ Page breaks/section breaks

⇒ Revision marks

⇒ Tabs in any style not converted to PRE (preformatted) or DL (Definition list)

⇒ Table of Contents entries

If you encounter these Word features in a document that you plan to convert to the Web, take some time *before* you convert to decide how you want to handle them. For example, if you have a document with footnotes, you either need to drop the footnotes completely or find a way to add them to the body of the document.

You can tell Internet Assistant how to convert specific, commonly used styles. The section "Automating Style Conversions," later in this chapter, includes all the gory details.

Although Word and Internet Assistant have tried to convert the press release document to Web-legal styles, some of the decisions aren't very visually appealing. The next step in the conversion process is to examine the result of the automatic conversion and decide how to improve it.

Before we do that, let's look at the kinds of styles that are legal on the Web. After we see what the Web styles look like, we can return to the tutorial and apply several of those styles to the converted document.

Web-legal styles

A limited number of styles are used on the Web. They fall into several broad categories:

➡ Headings: Styles that are good for section headings or document titles

➡ Lists: Great for lists, of course

➡ Miscellaneous: Everything else

I have created several documents, located on the CD-ROM, that illustrate these various styles. If you used the automatic setup earlier in the chapter, those files were copied to your hard disk. If you used the manual setup, and you don't already have the book's CD-ROM loaded, load it now so that it will be handy when you need it.

Headings

Headings are headings; they vary only in size. Use your browser to open the Web page /My Documents/My Web Pages/headings.htm (on the CD-ROM, it is \tutorial\chap02\headings.htm).

You can also open the file by double-clicking it.

This opens the file in your browser. Figure 2-7 shows what you should see: examples of the six levels of HTML headings, plus a line of normal text for comparison.

At the left of each line, you can see the **HTML code** (also called *HTML command* or *HTML tag*) for the heading. If you look at the style names in an Internet Assistant file, you see that each one includes the HTML code for the style. For example, the style name for a top-level heading is Heading 1,H1. If you decide to start learning HTML, the style names can serve as a guide.

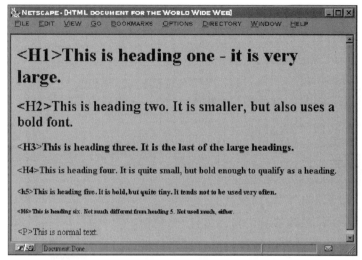

Figure 2-7: Examples of headings in the Netscape browser.

The headings in a Web page are used like the Heading 1, Heading 2, and so on, styles that you see in a typical Word outline. Typically, you use H1 for a page title, H2 for major subdivisions of a page, and H3 for minor subdivisions. H4, H5, and H6 are special-purpose headings, and you don't use them as often as the other three. For example, you might use one of these smaller headings when you use smaller than normal text fonts, or simply to emphasize a line of text.

Lists

There are several different kinds of Web-legal styles for creating lists. The list types are the following:

- **Ordered lists**, also called numbered lists
- **Unordered lists**, also called bulleted lists
- **Definition lists**
- **Compact definition lists**
- **Menus**
- **Directories**
- **Combination lists**

Use your browser to open the Web page /My Documents/My Web Pages/ lists.htm (on the CD-ROM, it is \tutorial\chap02\lists.htm). The figures in this section show what you should see — examples of different kinds of lists. You will find at least one example of each kind of list described here.

Ordered lists

An ordered list is simply a list that has numbers to the left of each list entry. The top example in Figure 2-8 shows an example of an ordered (or *numbered*) list.

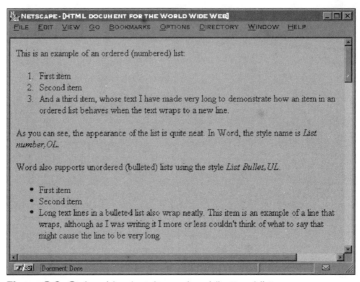

Figure 2-8: Ordered (top) and unordered (bottom) lists.

To create an ordered list, type the list as normal (default) text. Then select the paragraphs you want to include in the list, and click the down arrow at the right of the Styles drop-down box in the Formatting toolbar (that's the drop-down box next to the Internet Assistant icon; see Figure 2-9). Click the style List Number,OL.

Style drop-down box

Down arrow

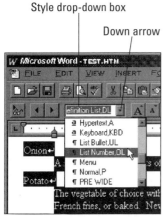

Figure 2-9: Selecting a style.

TIP When you are adding text to which you plan to apply Web styles, leave at least one extra line below the point where you are adding the text. Otherwise, when you press Enter to create a new paragraph, the style you just created will be repeated in the new line.

Unordered lists

An unordered list is simply a list that has bullets to the left of each list entry. The bottom example in Figure 2-8 shows an example of an unordered (or *bulleted*) list.

To create an unordered list, type the list as normal (default) text. Then select the paragraphs you want to include in the list, and click the down arrow at the right of the Styles drop-down box in the formatting toolbar. Click the style List Bullet,UL.

Definition lists

A definition list consists of pairs of terms and definitions. The top portion of Figure 2-10 shows an example of a standard definition list. Note that each term appears on a single line, and the definition is an indented block of text.

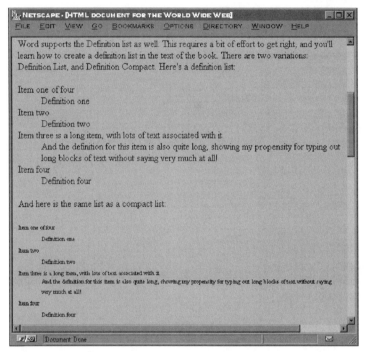

Figure 2-10: Definition lists: standard (top) and compact (bottom).

To create a definition list, follow these steps:

1. Type the first term.

2. While holding down the Shift key, press the Enter key. This key combination adds a soft carriage return. If you have Paragraph Marks turned on (TOOLS⇨OPTIONS⇨VIEW TAB, select Paragraph Marks, and click OK or click the Paragraph symbol in the toolbar), you see the soft carriage return indication shown in Figure 2-11. I recommend leaving Paragraph Marks on at all times while creating, editing, or converting Web-related documents.

Soft carriage return
(Shift + Enter)

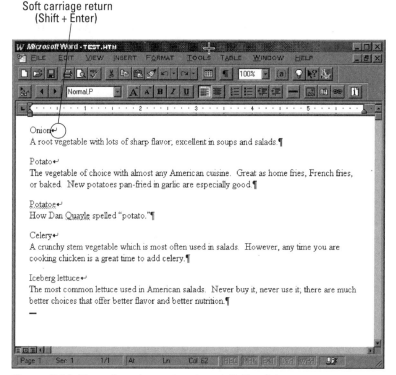

Figure 2-11: The soft carriage return in a definition list.

3. Type the definition of the first term. Press the Enter key when you are finished.

4. Repeat Steps 1 – 3 for each term and definition. Figure 2-11 shows an example.

5. Select all the terms and definitions, and apply the style Definition List,DL (see Figure 2-12). Figure 2-13 shows the appearance of the definition list in Netscape.

You don't have to restrict your use of the definition list to definitions. After all, it is simply a way of organizing information on a Web page. For example, you can use the definition list to add a small catalog of parts to a Web page. The term becomes the part name or number, and the definition can include a description and price.

You can also arrange definitions and terms without using the definition list at all. Figure 2-14 shows an example of an ordered list arranged to work like a definition list. I made the terms bold to emphasize them.

The idea I'm trying to get across is that HTML offers only a small number of ways to arrange your lists. Some of these ways, such as the definition list, were created for a specific kind of situation. Now, with the Web being used for a much wider variety of information, the name "definition list" is too limiting. Feel free to adapt the standard forms of HTML for your own purposes and to use whichever method best suits your needs on any given page.

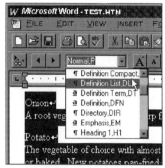

Figure 2-12: Creating a definition list in Word.

Compact definition lists

Internet Assistant also offers you the option of using a *compact definition list.* The bottom half of Figure 2-10 shows an example of a compact list. A compact list is simply a definition list with less space between lines and smaller text. You use a compact list when you want your list to take up less space on the Web page. This is mostly used with very long definition lists. You create a compact definition list the same way you create a standard one. When it comes time to apply a style to the selected text, however, use Definition Compact,DL instead of Definition List,DL.

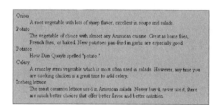

Figure 2-13: The definition list in Netscape.

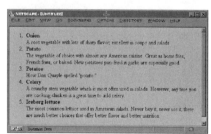

Figure 2-14: Using an ordered list instead of a definition list.

Menu

Many HTML styles have their origins in the dark history of the Web. These styles were created to meet a specific need, but that need may have changed with changing use of the Web. The Menu style is one example of a style whose utility has changed over time.

The first thing to notice about the Menu style is that it looks exactly like the List Bullet,UL style (see Figure 2-15). Originally, the Menu style was used for menus, which were nothing more sophisticated than a list of hyperlinks. The main reason to use the Menu style today is to remind yourself that your list is supposed to act like a menu. You could just as easily create an unordered list and apply hyperlinks to that. Using the Menu style confers no special powers on your list of hyperlinks.

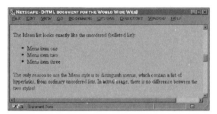

Figure 2-15: *The Menu style looks just like the Unordered List style.*

Figure 2-16: *The Directory style often isn't supported by browsers.*

The list in Figure 2-15, however, won't act like a menu unless you make each of the items in the list a hyperlink. This is easy to do with Word and Internet Assistant: Just select the text, click the Add Hyperlink button, and type in the hyperlink. You add some hyperlinks later in this chapter.

Directory

While we are on the subject of styles that haven't stayed useful, the Directory style is a more extreme example than Menu. As you can see in Figure 2-16, the Directory style is supposed to show a multiple-column list similar to the DOS directory command. Most browsers, however, don't support the Directory style correctly, as you can also see in Figure 2-16.

Should you use the Directory style at all? Probably not. Because most browsers show it just like an unordered list, you should probably stick to the unordered list. The exception is a Web page that you know will be browsed by browsers that support the Directory style.

Combinations

HTML supports nesting of lists to create combination lists. This means that you can create, for example, an ordered list that includes one or more unordered lists. Figure 2-17 shows an example. In most browsers, different bullet characters are used for different levels of indentation in combination lists. It can be tricky to create some types of combination lists in Word, but if you load an existing HTML with a combination list, Word usually accepts it just fine. If you find that you cannot create exactly the kind of combination you want with Word, you should try to find an alternative way to organize the list.

 The indents you find in some of these lists are almost the only support for indented paragraphs that you will find on Web pages. Until a more advanced version of HTML is released, your ability to created indented paragraphs is limited to lists. This is particularly important when you are converting existing documents to Web pages. If those documents contain indents (especially hanging indents), the formatting will be very different after you save the document as a Web page. You'll usually need to reformat manually, and you won't be able to recreate the look of the original document without some tricky work using tables. Also see the style Blockquote, discussed elsewhere in this chapter, which offers one option for indenting paragraphs that has nothing to do with lists.

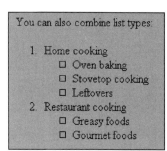

Figure 2-17: An example of a combination of list types.

To create a nested (indented) list, follow these steps:

1. Type the entries into your list.

2. Apply the desired style (List Bullet,UL or List Number,OL) to each entry, one at a time if necessary.

3. Select a group of entries you want to nest within the larger list, and then select FORMAT⇨INCREASE INDENT.

To undo the nesting for an entry, select the entry and then choose FORMAT⇨ DECREASE INDENT.

When you use Increase Indent on an item in a numbered list, you do not see the nested numbering scheme until you save the file as HTML, close it, and then open it again. You can also select FILE⇨PREVIEW IN BROWSER to see the results in your browser after you save to disk.

Miscellaneous

Use your browser to open the Web page /My Documents/My Web Pages/ misc.htm (on the CD-ROM, it is \tutorial\chap02\misc.htm). Figure 2-18 shows what you should see: examples of various miscellaneous Web-legal styles.

Basic character styles

The first part of the file misc.htm shows character-based styles (see Figure 2-18). Web pages can include most of the basic type styles, such as bold, italic, and so on. This is a short list, and it reflects the limitations of HTML as it currently exists. For example, you can't specify a specific font unless you know for certain that it will be installed on the computer of the folks who will view your page!

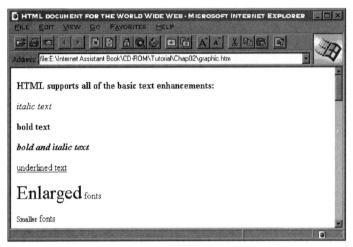

Figure 2-18: The character-based styles supported in Web pages.

Increase font size

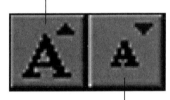

Decrease font size

Figure 2-19: These buttons increase (left) and decrease (right) the size of fonts.

Figure 2-20: You see this warning if you try to make a font too large.

Two styles shown in Figure 2-18 are worth a closer look: enlarged and reduced fonts. When you are editing an HTML document, Internet Assistant adds two buttons to the Formatting toolbar that enable you to increase or decrease the size of a font. Figure 2-19 shows these buttons. Clicking the left button increases size, and clicking the right button decreases size.

HTML supports only a limited range of font sizes. If you try to make the font size of selected text too large or small, you see a warning telling you that you cannot change the size any further (see Figure 2-20).

You can use changes in font size anywhere on a Web page. For example, you can select the first letter of a paragraph, italicize it, and make it larger. This creates a large initial capital letter (see Figure 2-21).

Miscellaneous formatting styles

There are four styles in `misc.htm` that illustrate block-oriented styles. These are Address, Blockquote, PRE, and PRE WIDE. Figure 2-22 shows examples of all four.

The Address style was originally used for addresses on a Web page. In most browsers, however, Address simply shows up as italicized text. Like the Menu style, Address is a style whose name may not match how you want to use it. If you prefer, you can simply use Italic or Bold Italic for addresses or anything else on your Web page. You do not have to use the Address style for addresses!

The Blockquote style was created for setting off text quoted from another source. Because the Web was originally created to facilitate the exchange of university-related information, this made sense. Today, you can use the Blockquote style any time you want an indented paragraph. You can't control the degree of indent, but you get an indent.

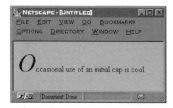

Figure 2-21: Using font size to create a large initial cap.

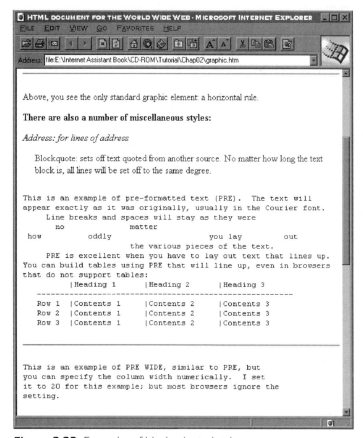

Figure 2-22: Examples of block-oriented styles.

You use the PRE and PRE WIDE styles when you absolutely must have a specific layout in a block of text. As you can see in Figure 2-22, you have complete control over PRE text because it uses a monospaced (usually Courier) typeface. That is, every character, punctuation mark, and space uses the same amount of space on the page. If you want to create tables that can be viewed by someone who does not have a table-enabled browser, PRE text is your only hope.

PRE WIDE simply enables you to specify the width of the text when it is displayed in a browser. As you can see at the bottom of Figure 2-22, not all browsers support this function.

Exotic character styles

There are a number of character-based styles that you can use on your Web pages, and they are shown in Figure 2-23. Like many HTML styles, some of these styles have their origins back in the early days of HTML, and they reflect the way that HTML was used, as well as the purposes of HTML, in those early days. Now that you know what these styles look like, you can decide whether any of them are appropriate to your needs. As I've said before, you are not required to use them as they were designed. Feel free to use them as design elements, not rigid definitions.

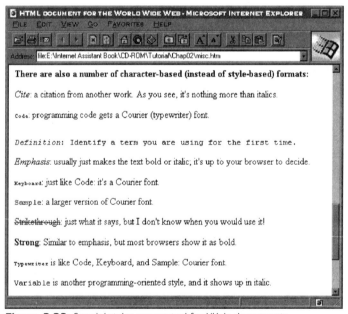

Figure 2-23: Special styles supported for Web documents.

You can find more detailed information about these character styles in the complete list of Web-legal styles included later in this chapter.

The marquee

Microsoft has introduced a new feature in Version 2.0 of its browser, Internet Explorer: the **marquee**. This feature takes its name from scrolling theater marquees. In a nutshell, a marquee enables you to scroll text across the page while the rest of the text is stationary.

If you use a marquee in your Web page, keep in mind that most users (that is, anyone using a browser other than Internet Explorer) will see the marquee as stationary text. If other browsers eventually support the marquee, of course, you can ignore this note!

Figure 2-24 shows a sequence of three images that illustrates the action of a marquee. You can select the color of the marquee background when you create the marquee.

Figure 2-24: A marquee is text that moves across the page.

To create a marquee, first place the cursor where you want the marquee to appear, and then select INSERT⇨MARQUEE. Figure 2-25 shows the dialog box you use to specify the properties of the marquee. Enter the text for the marquee in the top line of the dialog box. Click OK when you are finished.

You can also specify the properties of the marquee as indicated in Table 2-1.

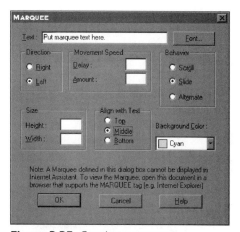

Figure 2-25: Creating a marquee.

Table 2-1	Establishing Marquee Properties	
Property	**HTML Equivalent**	**Description**
Text	\<marquee> Text \</marquee>	Enter the text that will scroll across the page.
Direction	\<marquee direction=...>	Direction the marquee text scrolls in. The default direction is to the right.
Delay	\<marquee scrolldelay=...>	Number of milliseconds to pause between each successive draw of the marquee text. The smaller this number, the faster the marquee text moves.

(continued)

Table 2-1	Establishing Marquee Properties	
Property	**HTML Equivalent**	**Description**
Amount	<marquee scrollamount=...>	Number of pixels the marquee text is to move each time. The smaller this number, the smoother the marquee text moves.
Scroll	<marquee behavior=scroll>	Default setting. Text starts outside the marquee, scrolls horizontally across it, and then scrolls out of the marquee (see Figure 2-24).
Slide	<marquee behavior=slide>	The text originates outside the marquee, scrolls horizontally across it, and then stops at the opposite margin and does not move.
Alternate	<marquee behavior=alternate>	The text originates inside the marquee, scrolls horizontally across it, bounces off the opposite margin, scrolls back across the marquee, bounces off the other margin, and so on.
Height	<marquee height=...>	Number of pixels high for the marquee.
Width	<marquee width=...>	Number of pixels wide for the marquee.
Align with	<marquee align=...>	Relative placement of text next to the marquee. Top, for example, aligns the top of the text and the top of the marquee.
Background Color	<marquee bgcolor=#rrggbb>	Background color of the marquee. (*#rrggbb* is the hexadecimal color-code equivalent to the color you choose.)

Tutorial 2: Begin Again

When we last were working on the tutorial, we had just saved the press release as an HTML file. The layout of the page, however, was a mess as a result of the conversion process. It's time to take what we've learned about styles and apply it to the Web page version of the press release. Figure 2-26 shows the current state of affairs: the two pages of the press release in Word for Windows.

If you closed the file, you should select the file type as HTML Document (*.htm) in the File⇨Open dialog box. The default setting opens only Word documents (*.doc). Choosing HTML Document displays all HTML files in the current folder; double-click the file you want to open or click to select it and then click the Open button.

The converted document isn't a total disaster, which is good news. During a conversion, Word tries to keep as much formatting as it can. The following rules summarize what happens during the conversion:

⟹ Text that has attributes (bold, italic, underline) have those attributes preserved.

⟹ Centered paragraphs are retained as centered.

⟹ Right-justified text becomes left-justified.

⟹ Tabs are converted to a single-space character.

⟹ Font sizes are retained, within the limits of the smallest and largest fonts allowed in a Web page.

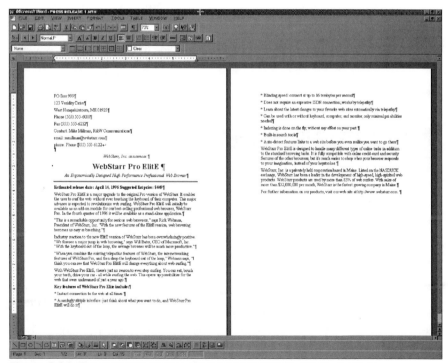

Figure 2-26: The complete version of the converted press release, in Word.

➥ Styles with a top or bottom border usually result in a horizontal rule being added.

➥ Custom spacing between paragraphs is lost; all paragraphs have the same amount of fixed space between them: one line.

➥ Most fonts are converted to the default font.

➥ Word features not supported on the Web are simply dropped.

If the original document was very simple, the automatic conversion options listed here may result in a pleasing Web page. However, it takes graphics and careful layout to have a really good Web page. Unless you are converting a huge number of documents, you probably will want to spend some time enhancing the result of the automatic conversion.

Adding a graphic

The first enhancement that this press release needs is a graphic. In the original document, the image at the top left of the page was actually located in the header. As you learned earlier, headers and footers are simply dropped during the conversion. Additionally, the image was black and white.

To add a color image, position the cursor at the beginning of the document and press the Enter key. This adds a new line to the top of the converted document (see figure 2-27).

Add the blank
line here

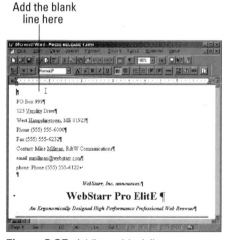

Figure 2-27: Adding a blank line.

TIP It's a good idea to keep **Paragraph Marks** turned on so that you can see exactly where blank lines are. You have better control of the page layout right from the start if you can see tabs, too. Why? Because tabs are not supported in Web pages. They are converted to spaces, and you frequently need to provide cleanup during conversion.

Position the cursor in the new line, and then click the Picture tool in the Formatting toolbar. This action opens the Picture dialog box (see Figure 2-28), which we used extensively in Chapter 1. Click the Browse button, locate the file Webstar3.gif on your hard disk (you copied it to \My Documents\My Web Pages\images earlier). It is a small version of the WebStarr, Inc. logo.

Click the Options tab of the Picture dialog box to display the available options (see Figure 2-29). Type the picture height (78 pixels) and width (140 pixels) in the spaces provided. Then set the alignment of the picture to Right in the Alignment drop-down box. This choice forces the image to the right of the Web page when you view the page in a browser.

Although working in Word gives you a great deal of "what you see is what you get" performance, there are some Web features you will only be able to see in your browser. This is one example.

Now click the OK button to add the picture to the page. Figure 2-30 shows the result. If you see the text Image not loaded instead of the picture, it's the same problem we faced in Chapter 1. You should close and reopen the file to see the picture.

The first thing you notice is that the picture isn't on the right, where we want it. The correct position won't show up until you view the Web page in your browser. To demonstrate this positioning, save your work and choose FILE⇨PREVIEW IN BROWSER or click the Browser button on the Standard toolbar to display the page in your browser. Figure 2-31 shows what the page looks like in a browser. Note that the picture is right where we expected it to be. Note also that the picture has a white background, but the page background is gray. We'll fix that shortly.

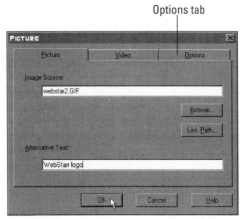

Figure 2-28: Adding a picture.

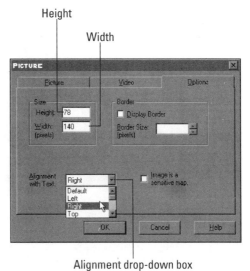

Figure 2-29: Setting picture options.

Figure 2-30: The image has been added.

Adjusting paragraph spacing

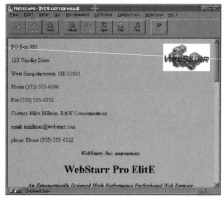

Figure 2-31: The picture shows up on the right in a browser.

In addition to the background issue, there is another problem: The space between lines in the address and contact information is much too wide.

When you see the paragraph mark (that backwards P thing at the end of a paragraph in Figure 2-30) at the end of any paragraph, Word adds white space after that paragraph. The HTML code that does this is the <P> command. There is another HTML command,
 (break), which causes a line break but does not add any space between lines. To tell Word you want a break, use the soft carriage return: Hold down the Shift key and press Enter. I made judicious use of soft carriage returns to close up space in the address and contact text blocks (see Figure 2-32) while still keeping some space between the blocks. The result is much more logical and pleasing than what we started with after the conversion. Figure 2-33 shows what the result looks like in a browser.

Setting background color

To clean up the problem with the white background of the picture versus the gray background of the Web page, we will change the background color of the Web page to white. Select FORMAT➪CHOOSE BACKGROUND AND LINKS to display the dialog box shown in Figure 2-34. Use the Background Color drop-down box shown in that figure to change the Background Color to white. Click OK to save the background color.

Notice that you could also choose a background image. You'll learn how to work with **background images** (and many other goodies) in Chapter 4.

When you specify a page background color, you see a portion of the HTML code for the BODY of your document. It appears just to the left of the image, as the first text in your document. It will be blue, which means one very important thing: *Don't touch!* Blue text, especially blue text in angle brackets, is HTML code, and you should be careful not to delete it.

Soft carriage return

Figure 2-32: Adding soft carriage returns to close up extra space between lines.

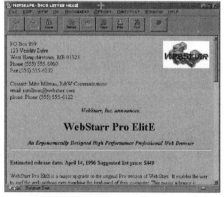

Figure 2-33: The view in a browser.

Word and Internet Assistant work together to convert your Word documents to HTML codes. Because Word can't show the actual appearance of some HTML codes (such as background color), it sometimes uses blue text to indicate the existence of HTML codes. This text is actually a Word **field**; Internet Assistant makes extensive use of fields to do its work. Avoid accidentally changing or deleting such text — the results could be unpredictable. In extreme cases, removing an HTML code could render your entire document useless. If you accidentally delete HTML codes, Undo may not work as you expect. It is much safer to use File➪Revert to go back to the last correct version you saved.

Background Color
drop-down box

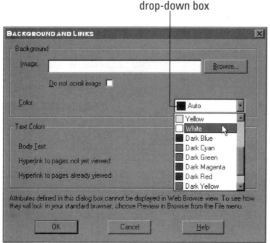

Figure 2-34: Changing the page background color.

Figure 2-35 shows the result of the change in background color when you view the page in your browser. Remember: Always save your work before you try to view it in a browser. The browser loads the file from disk — if you don't save it first, you won't see the changes.

Figure 2-35: The background now appears white in a browser; compare to Figure 2-33.

Making layout changes

Looking at this document in a browser, it's not immediately obvious that it is a press release. A newspaper reporter or marketing manager might know this is a press release, but anyone else might not. Let's add a new paragraph just under the WebStarr logo that spells out the nature of the document. Figure 2-36 shows what I have in mind: a paragraph that says, simply, `Press Release`. As indicated in the figure, select the paragraph and then give it a style: Heading 3,H3. This style makes the text bold and adds some white space above and below to set it off. Figure 2-37 shows what this looks like in Internet Explorer. Headings, like most HTML styles, aren't just for headings; you can use them anytime you want to emphasize a line of text.

At this point, the top portion of the Web press release looks good, and we can move on to the main body of the Web page. The centered text below the address and contact text blocks was converted successfully for us; we'll focus on the problem areas of the release.

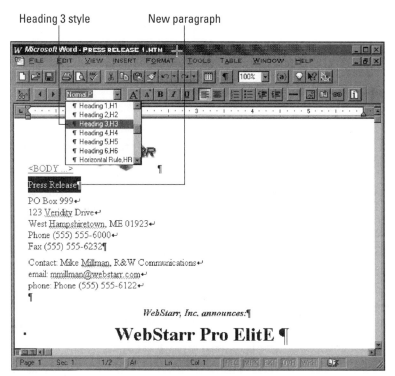

Figure 2-36: Adding a new paragraph of text.

Figure 2-37: The view in Internet Explorer.

The first problem is the line of text immediately below the horizontal rule (see Figure 2-38). In the original, this text was split, with half hugging the left margin and half hugging the right margin. We can't right justify text on a Web page, so let's use a table to move these two phrases apart. Replace the space between the two originally separate portions of the line with a Tab.

TIP The Tab goes between Estimated release date: April 14, 1996 and Suggested list price: $449. Internet Assistant won't save this tab; we're just using it to tell Word where to break the text to create a table.

Text too crowded

Figure 2-38: The (originally tab-separated) text below the horizontal rule looks crowded.

Select all of the text in the line, and choose TABLE⇨INSERT to convert the text to a table (see Figure 2-39).

By default, Word does not save the width of tables or columns when it saves tables to a Web page. This means that, when you view a table in a browser, the column width will be just wide enough to hold the text. You can change this, and force Word to save table width, by choosing TABLE⇨CELL WIDTH AND SPACING. This selection displays the dialog box shown in Figure 2-40. You can

Text now in a table

Figure 2-39: Text converted to a table.

specify exact column widths with this dialog box, but there is a simpler way to get the same result. Simply check the checkbox at the top of the dialog box, WYSIWYG Column Widths, and click OK.

WYSIWYG (pronounced "**wizz**-ee-wig") is short for "What you see is what you get." In this case, it means that the column widths you see in Word are the column widths you get in your browser.

After you have set this **checkbox** to On, you can simply drag to revise column widths. When you save your Web page, the column widths are saved, too. Figure 2-41 shows the result of using WYSIWYG column widths. This isn't quite as nice as right justification, but it's a lot better than what the automatic conversion created.

Click here to preserve column widths

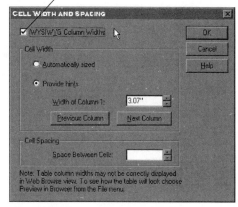

Figure 2-40: Setting column widths.

Later on, you learn about adding HTML commands to your Web pages; this is called HTML **markup**. You can use the ALIGN=RIGHT command to force right justification, but only in a table. See Chapter 7 for details on HTML markup.

Note separation

Figure 2-41: WYSIWYG column widths in the browser.

Adding a list

Most of the text in the press release converted just fine — after all, a paragraph of text is just a paragraph of text. The next item in the press release that needs attention is a list of key features for the new product. Figure 2-42 shows what this area looks like. The paragraphs all start with an asterisk and a space. In the original, there was a tab between the asterisk and text, but the tabs were deleted during conversion. Fortunately, we can use a Web-legal list style for the key features section.

Tabs converted
to single space

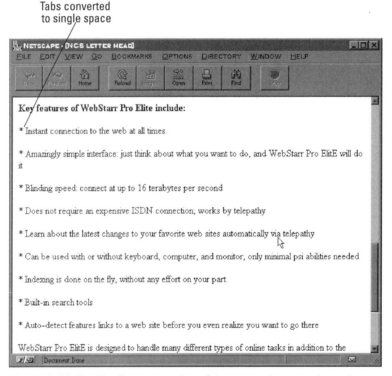

Figure 2-42: The Key Features section of the press release needs work.

First, however, let's apply a heading style to the Key features line itself. This heading will set it off from the surrounding text and increase the font size. Select the line, and then use the Style drop-down box in the Formatting toolbar to apply the style Heading 3,H3.

After the conversion, the items in the key features list have the style Normal,P. To convert these items to a bulleted list, drag to select all the paragraphs in the list, and then apply the style List Bullet,UL (see Figure 2-43). Figure 2-44 shows the result in a browser. To clean up, remove the asterisks and spaces at the left of each line in the list.

At this point, we have solved all the conversion problems found in the press release. Except for highly formatted documents, or documents that use Word features not supported in HTML documents, this is a pretty typical conversion. Most Web documents are quite short and can be converted with just a handful of manual adjustments. Longer Web documents are usually composed of straight text, and straight text converts easily in *most* situations.

Figure 2-43: Converting normal text to a bulleted list.

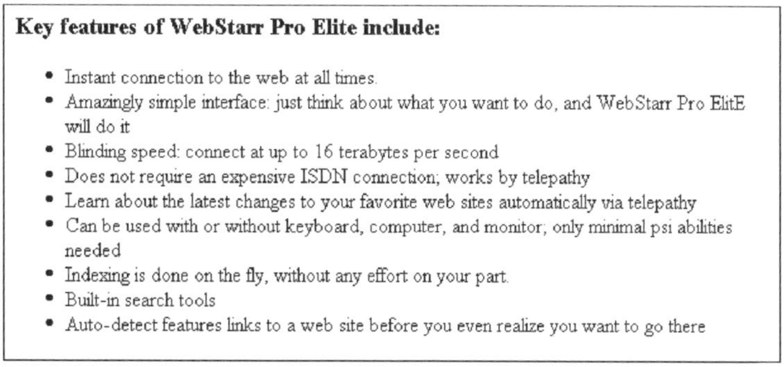

Key features of WebStarr Pro Elite include:

- Instant connection to the web at all times.
- Amazingly simple interface: just think about what you want to do, and WebStarr Pro EliteE will do it
- Blinding speed: connect at up to 16 terabytes per second
- Does not require an expensive ISDN connection; works by telepathy
- Learn about the latest changes to your favorite web sites automatically via telepathy
- Can be used with or without keyboard, computer, and monitor; only minimal psi abilities needed
- Indexing is done on the fly, without any effort on your part.
- Built-in search tools
- Auto-detect features links to a web site before you even realize you want to go there

Figure 2-44: A bulleted list in Internet Explorer.

Adding Web features

What we have done so far is to attend to the layout issues for this press release. We are creating a Web page, however, and we can now add Web-specific features to the press release. These features can make it much more effective than a standard press release. For example, look again at the contact information at the top of the Web press release. One of the contact items is an e-mail address for someone in the public relations department. In Chapter 1, we used a hyperlink to allow browsers to automatically open a mail program. We can do that here, too. Follow these steps:

1. Select the text that is the e-mail address.
2. Click the Add Hyperlink button on the Formatting toolbar.

Display text — Type mailto: text here

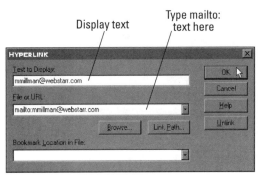

Figure 2-45: Adding a mailto: address in a hyperlink.

3. In the Add Hyperlink dialog box (see Figure 2-45), enter the following in the File or URL text box:

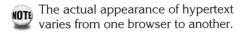

```
mailto:mmillman@Webstarr.com
```

4. Click OK to add the hyperlink; the hypertext shows up colored and underlined.

NOTE The actual appearance of hypertext varies from one browser to another.

There is mention of a Web site at the end of the press release:

```
http://www.Webstarr.com
```

So far, you've been using hyperlinks for **mailto** addresses. It's time to add the most common kind of hyperlink: a link to Web sites. It's quite easy. Instead of typing in **mailto:<address>**, you type in the complete URL of the Web site. Figure 2-46 shows how to fill in the Add Hyperlink dialog box. Figure 2-47 shows the result in Word: underlined text.

Type hyperlink here

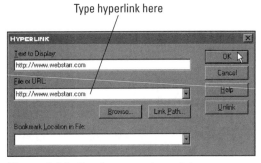

Figure 2-46: Creating a true hyperlink.

TIP Although you can use hyperlinks for a variety of Web tasks, all hyperlinks look the same: underlined text. To find out what is inside a hyperlink, you have to look. Most browsers show the contents of a hyperlink on the status line of the browser when you pass the cursor over the hyperlink. Next time you are on a Web page, check this out.

Another way to enhance this page for the Web is to add hyperlinks to any text that is related to other Web pages. These links can be to pages on the WebStarr server or on other servers. As long as you have a relevant URL to link to, you have all you need for a valid hyperlink.

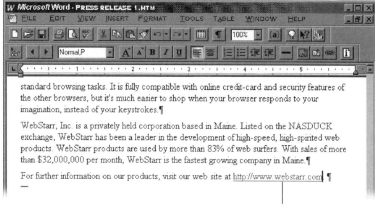

standard browsing tasks. It is fully compatible with online credit-card and security features of the other browsers, but it's much easier to shop when your browser responds to your imagination, instead of your keystrokes.¶

WebStarr, Inc. is a privately held corporation based in Maine. Listed on the NASDUCK exchange, WebStarr has been a leader in the development of high-speed, high-spirited web products. WebStarr products are used by more than 83% of web surfers. With sales of more than $32,000,000 per month, WebStarr is the fastest growing company in Maine.¶

For further information on our products, visit our web site at http://www.webstarr.com ¶

Hyperlink (underlined)

Figure 2-47: The hyperlink in Word.

For example, the first sentence of the press release states:

```
WebStarr Pro ElitE is a major upgrade to the original Pro version
of WebStarr.
```

The reference to the Pro version of WebStarr is a good opportunity for a hyperlink. It's quite likely that WebStarr, Inc. has a Web page for this product. Assuming that the HTML file for WebStarr Pro is on the same **Web server** and in the same directory as this press release, you follow these steps to add a hyperlink:

1. Select the text `original Pro version of WebStarr` and change it to **WebStarr Pro**. This is a much clearer wording for a hyperlink.

2. Click the Add Hyperlink button.

3. Enter **Webpro.htm** as the URL and then click OK.

Presto! You've got a hyperlink to an existing document. Now someone who reads the press release can easily read information about WebStarr Pro. This lets the reader put the information found in the press release into context. A company like WebStarr, Inc. would probably have a large number of such links to add to this press release. Figure 2-48 shows a portion of the press release with the hyperlinks added. For example, the hyperlinks include

Text	Hyperlink	Description
Rick Webman	`ceo.htm`	Links to a file about the CEO of the company and a picture of him
Macrosoft, Inc.	`http://www.macrosoft.com/sw.htm`	Links to the home page of another company
simple interface	`iface.htm`	Links to a file that shows screen captures of the new product
telepathy	`telepath.htm`	Links to a Web page illustrating the "mind reading" capabilities of WebStarr

Hyperlinks

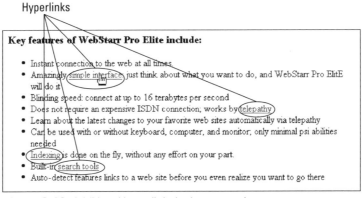

Figure 2-48: Additional hyperlinks in the press release.

Any company should work this hard to link its Web pages. Why? It's all about information: The more information you can convey to someone who is interested, the better the Web page is working. It's important to have content — but the content is useless if someone can't find it.

This completes the tutorial for this chapter. Next, you learn how to automate some parts of the conversion process by customizing the Windows 95 Registry.

Automating Conversion

The press release that you converted during the tutorial required a modest amount of manual changes after the automatic conversion that occurred when you saved the file as HTML. In some cases, you may be faced with many similar files, each one of which requires manual intervention. If, for example, your company were a large one with many press releases or product specifications or any other information that needed to be converted to the Web, it could take a lot of time and effort to convert Word documents to Web pages.

Fortunately, there is a way to cut down on the amount of work involved. It involves diving into the innards of Windows 95: the Registry. The *Registry* stores settings for many, many aspects of Windows 95 and your programs. I'm going to show you the steps you take to modify the Registry, but let's be clear at the outset: *Changes to the Registry should only be made by someone who knows his or her way around Windows 95.* When you change the Registry, you are making changes to the very heart of your Windows 95 system. Making the wrong change could cause unpredictable problems.

Before you make any changes to the Registry, it's a good idea to save the current version of the Registry so that you can go back and restore it if you make a mistake. You'll learn how to do this shortly. Remember that the Registry is a key part of Windows 95, and if you mess it up, you could have a serious problem to deal with. If you have *any* doubt about your ability to handle modifications to the Registry, find someone who knows his or her way around and let that person make the changes for you.

Now that I have you suitably nervous about this, we can start.

Word styles and Internet Assistant

When you create a new HTML document, Internet Assistant loads a specific template that includes only those styles that are legal for Web pages. If you click FORMAT⇨STYLES in any HTML document, you see exactly the same styles. Most of these styles include a text name, a comma, and, when applicable, the HTML code for that style. Table 2-2 shows a complete list of the styles you find in an HTML document in Word. In the table, *Type* refers to character-based ("a" for alpha) or paragraph-based ("P" for paragraph).

Many of these styles were created early in the development of HTML to serve the needs of the academic community. As a result, some of the styles look identical — only the names are different. Unless your organization has requirements about which styles to use, and when, feel free to use the style name that is most convenient for you.

Table 2-2		Legal Web Styles
Type	**Style Name**	**Description**
P	Address	Originally used for address, but all it does it make the text italic.

(continued)

Table 2-2	Legal Web Styles	
Type	**Style Name**	**Description**
P	Blockquote	Used to indent a paragraph; originally referred to a block of text quoted from another source.
a	CODE	Originally used for programming code. Uses a small typewriter font.
a	CITE	Used for citations in academic pages.
a	Default paragraph font	This is the font used by default for all text.
P	Definition Compact,DL	Applies a small font to definition lists.
P	Definition List,DL	Creates a definition list.
a	Definition Term,DT	Created internally when you make a definition list; do not apply it yourself!
a	Definition,DFN	Created internally when you make a definition list; do not apply it yourself!
P	Directory,DIR	A seldom-used HTML list style; many browsers do not support it correctly.
a	Emphasis,EM	Used for text you want to emphasize. Many browsers show this as italic. Strong is used more often.
P	Heading 1,H1	Highest level heading, largest heading font.
P	Heading 2,H2	Second-level heading.
P	Heading 3,H3	Third-level heading.
P	Heading 4,H4	Fourth-level heading.
P	Heading 5,H5	Fifth-level heading.
P	Heading 6,H6	Sixth-level heading, smallest heading font.
P	Horizontal Rule,HR	Used internally when you click the Horizontal Rule tool on the Formatting toolbar.
a	Hypertext,A	Used internally when you create a hyperlink.

Type	Style Name	Description
a	Keyboard,KBD	Another typewriter font style.
P	List Bullet,UL	Creates a bulleted list.
P	List Number,OL	Creates a numbered list.
P	Menu	Another one of those HTML styles that has become less frequently used, this was intended for folks who created menus using hyperlinks.
P	Normal,P	Standard text.
P	PRE WIDE	Preformatted text with a specified width.
P	Preformatted,PRE	Preformatted text; uses a monospaced font.
P	RestartList	Internal use only. Applies to combination lists.
a	Sample,SAMP	Another typewriter font.
a	Strikethrough,STRIKE	Shows text with a horizontal line through it.
a	Strong,STRONG	Usually shown as bold text.
a	Typewriter,TT	Yet another (but more aptly named) typewriter font.
a	Variable,VAR	Originally used for variables in computer program listings.
P	z-Bottom of Form	Internal style for HTML forms; do not use.
a	z-HTML Tag	Internal style for HTML tags you insert.
P	z-Top of Form	Internal style for HTML forms; do not use.

 All styles that start with "z-" are privately used by Word, and you shouldn't apply them to text in your HTML documents. Several other styles are also used internally by Word, and they are noted above. In general, don't use the internal styles for your own work — you could mess up the file and have to start over.

As HTML evolves, and as Microsoft releases new versions of Internet Assistant, there's a distinct possibility that additional styles will be added to this list. To find out which styles your version of Internet Assistant includes, choose FORMAT⇨STYLE to display the current styles.

You also choose FORMAT⇨STYLE to see what styles are used in your own documents. Figure 2-49 shows the Format dialog box with the styles for the press release used in this chapter's tutorial. The available styles are shown in the window, at the left.

The List drop-down box at the lower left enables you to display either styles currently in use or all styles. To see all styles, you choose (as you would expect!) All Styles. When you are examining the styles in a group of documents you plan to convert, you want to see all the styles for that type of document.

Style list

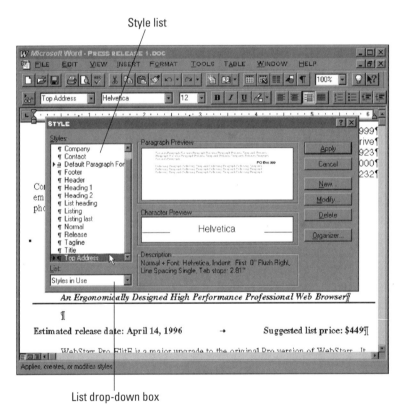

List drop-down box

Figure 2-49: Displaying the styles in a document.

After you know what styles are in your document, what you need is a way to tell Word "Hey, when you find the style MyStyle, convert it to the Web style Heading 3,H3." Ideally, you could prepare a map that tells Word and Internet Assistant how to convert every style in your document. Using the Windows 95 Registry, that's exactly what you can do.

Working in the Registry

There isn't a button or icon you can click to edit the Registry; you have to use the Windows 95 Run command. Click the Start button at the lower left of your desktop to display the Start menu (see Figure 2-50). Click Run to display the Run dialog box (see Figure 2-51).

There is a program in your Windows 95 directory that enables you to edit the Registry. It's called regedit.exe. As shown in Figure 2-51, type **regedit** into the Open drop-down box, and then click OK to run this program. When the regedit program starts, you see something like what you see in Figure 2-52. The width and height of the window may differ, but the entries you see on the left will be similar.

The Registry Editor is divided into left and right halves. The Registry is similar to INI files, which were common in Windows 3.*x* and earlier versions. In effect, the Registry replaces **INI files**. INI files were difficult to work with: You had to find the one you wanted first, out of dozens or sometimes more than a hundred separate files. The Registry is organized hierarchically — it looks a lot like the old File Manager. The left half of the window contains the hierarchy, and the right side is where you select, add, and change values.

The entries for Word and Internet Assistant are buried pretty deep in the hierarchy, so bear with me while we dig down to find them.

Run menu selection

Figure 2-50: The Windows 95 Start menu.

Type program to run here

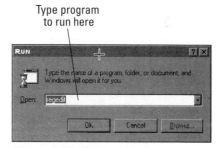

Figure 2-51: The Run dialog box.

Making changes to the Registry is serious business. If you are unsure of yourself, ask someone who knows the Registry to work with you, or to make the changes for you. Remember, you don't have to make these changes to use Internet Assistant — you can always make the changes manually. Changing the Registry is only advisable if you will be converting documents that all use the same styles. If different documents use different styles, you gain nothing by making these changes to the Registry.

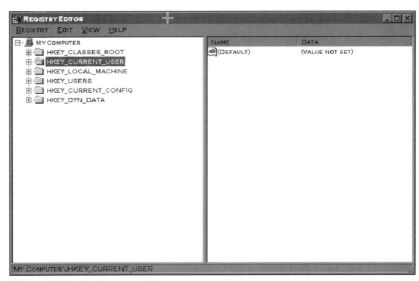

Figure 2-52: *The Registry Editor program.*

Navigating in the Registry

Begin by clicking the folder icon of HKEY_CURRENT_USER. The folder changes to an open appearance (see Figure 2-53), and the value for any entries in the folder appear in the right window (also shown in Figure 2-53). There are no values for HKEY_CURRENT_USER.

Click here to open the hierarchy

Figure 2-53: *Working in the Registry Editor.*

Now click the small plus sign to the left of the folder icon for HKEY_CURRENT_USER. This displays the entries below HKEY_CURRENT_USER in the hierarchy. Figure 2-54 shows the result.

Click here to open next level

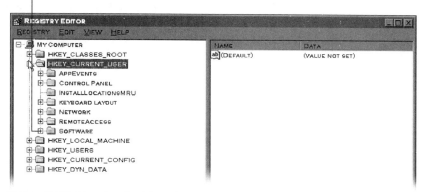

Figure 2-54: Opening the hierarchy.

We have to work down to a deeper level in the hierarchy. Continue by clicking the plus sign to the left of the Software folder. Figure 2-55 shows the result. Notice that the arrangement of the Registry is quite logical — under Software, you find the specific Windows 95 software that is installed on your computer.

The programs you see listed on your computer probably will be different from those shown in Figure 2-55, unless, of course, you have exactly the same software installed that I do! Don't worry about differences. That's one reason for the existence of the Registry: It enables you to customize your copy of Windows 95.

Under Software, you see a listing for Microsoft. Click the plus sign for this entry, which displays Registry entries for whatever Microsoft software you have installed (see Figure 2-56). Find the entry for Word; you should see entries for Word 7.0 and Internet Assistant (see Figure 2-57).

Click here to open next level

Figure 2-55: Opening another level in the hierarchy.

Click here to open next level

Figure 2-56: The Microsoft entries in the Registry.

Click here to open next level

Figure 2-57: Locating entries for Word 7 and Internet Assistant.

We are close to where we want to be now. Click the plus sign for Internet Assistant to display the Registry entries shown in Figure 2-58.

There are three entries for Internet Assistant:

➠ **History.** Contains entries for a history of Web sites visited when using Internet Assistant as a Web browser.

➠ **StyleMap.** This is what we are looking for. It contains a list of styles, and how they should be converted when you convert existing documents to HTML files.

➠ **URLList.** A list of URLs used by Internet Assistant.

Registry entries

Double-click the **StyleMap** entry. This displays two columns of information in the right-hand side of the Registry Editor window (see Figure 2-59). The values in the left column are Word default styles, and the values in the right column are HTML (that is, Web-legal) styles. When you save an existing Word document as an HTML file, Internet Assistant converts the Word styles in the left column into the Web-legal styles in the second column.

Do not remove any of the existing style mappings. Internet Assistant expects to find these entries, and you could cause unpredictable errors if you delete any of the default entries under StyleMap.

By adding your own styles to the left column and adding Web-legal styles for them in the right column, you can have Internet Assistant convert your standard styles — not just Word's.

Before you make any changes to the Registry, however, it's a very good idea to make a backup copy of this portion of the Registry. To do this, click REGISTRY⇨EXPORT REGISTRY FILE to open the dialog box shown in Figure 2-60.

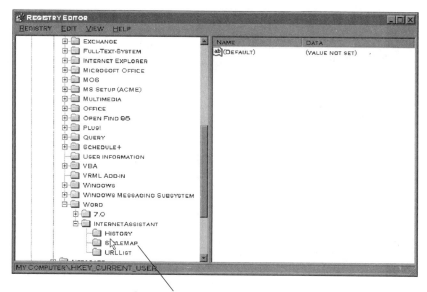

Click here to display values

Figure 2-58: Registry entries for Internet Assistant.

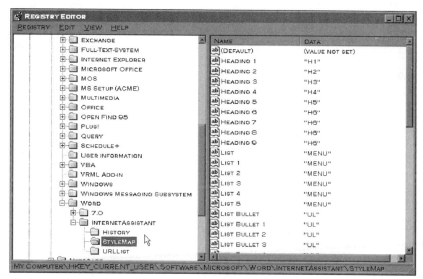

Figure 2-59: Viewing style-mapping information.

File name

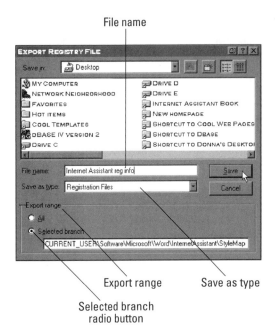

Export range   Save as type

Selected branch
radio button

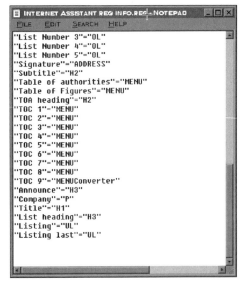

Figure 2-61: This is what the contents of a Registry export file look like.

You could save the entire Registry (and it's not a bad idea to do this periodically), but for now I suggest that you save only the branch of the Registry hierarchy that you are changing. Do the following:

1. Under File Name, type **Internet Assistant reg info.** This isn't a required filename, but it accurately describes the contents of the file.

2. Make sure that the Save As Type is Registration Files.

3. Under Export Range, make sure that Selected Branch is selected, and that the path is

```
HKEY_CURRENT_USERS\Software\
Microsoft\Word\
InternetAssistant\
StyleMap
```

You can save the file anywhere that you can find it later. You can either create a directory specifically to hold Registry files, or you can save it to your desktop. The file is a text file, and you can examine it with any text editor, such as Notepad. Figure 2-61 shows the contents of a Registry file.

NOTE The contents look a lot like an INI file, don't they? This is no accident. The Registry is somewhat like an INI file on steroids.

TIP After you have saved a portion of the Registry in this manner, you can click REGISTRY⇨IMPORT REGISTRY FILE to restore a previous state of the Registry. This is very useful if you make a mistake and can't figure out what you did wrong. It allows you to put things back the way they were before you started. I recommend that you always use the safety net of exporting a Registry file whenever you make changes to the Registry.

Adding entries to the Registry

After you have exported the StyleMap branch of the Registry, it's time to add the styles for your own document to the Registry and to supply appropriate Web-legal styles for conversion. To add a new style to the style map, choose EDIT⇨NEW⇨STRING VALUE (see Figure 2-62). This doesn't display a dialog box (as you might expect). It simply adds the new entry with a default name of "New Value #1" in the left column (see Figure 2-63) and a blank value in the right column.

The default name looks just like a file that is being renamed — the text is highlighted, and you should now type in the name of the entry. This name will be a valid style from whatever document you will be converting. In this example, the entry is one of the styles from the press release: Announce (see Figure 2-64). When you have finished typing the name, press Enter to complete the editing. The box around the new entry disappears.

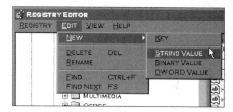

Figure 2-62: Adding a new name to the Registry.

Type name of new value here

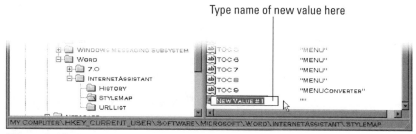

Figure 2-63: Adding a new name.

Typed name replaces original name

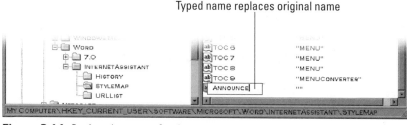

Figure 2-64: Setting the name for the new entry.

Type a valid HTML style name here

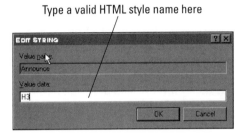

Figure 2-65: Modifying an entry's value.

The entry now has a name, but it doesn't have a value (the Web-legal style that Announce will be converted to). Click the Announce entry to select it if it is not already selected. To enter the value, choose EDIT⇨MODIFY. This time, you see a dialog box, as shown in Figure 2-65.

If you look at the styles assigned to paragraphs in the press release, you will note that the Announce style is used by the line above the product name, WebStarr Pro ElitE. The best Web-legal style to use here is a third-level heading — we'll get a large-but-not-too-large font and bold text.

However, do not enter the Word style (Heading 3,H3); use the HTML command instead — H3. Figure 2-65 shows the proper entry. Click OK when you are finished to save this new entry to the Registry. Figure 2-66 shows what the Registry looks like when all the styles in the press release have been added to the Registry. The five additional styles were added in the same way that the Announce style was added.

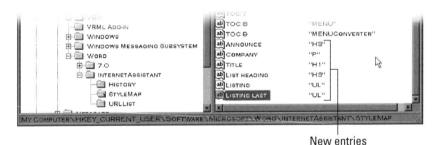

New entries

Figure 2-66: Six styles from the press release have been added to the Registry.

The HTML styles used in the right column were all taken from the style names in the HTML document. Each Web-legal style has the HTML code for that style included in the style name, following the comma. For example, the HTML code for a bulleted list is UL, and you can find it in the style name, List Bullet,UL.

There is no need to save your changes to the Registry; each new style mapping was saved to the Registry as soon as you entered it.

Remember: You should only add Registry entries for styles that appear over and over in your documents. The purpose of these Registry entries for Internet Assistant is to make it easier to convert documents that use your standard styles.

Figure 2-42 showed how the list from the press release originally converted — it didn't take any advantage of HTML's list styles. In Figure 2-67, you can see how the addition of the press release styles to the Registry simplified the conversion process. The list in Figure 2-67 (and the heading above it) now looks just like it did when we did the manual conversion — but this time, the conversion was automatic. Internet Assistant found the styles in the Registry and did the conversions for me. That didn't remove the asterisks, however, so there is still some cleanup to do. However, I can relax because I know that every time I convert a press release that uses the standard press release styles, I will have less work to do.

Using macros

The asterisks could easily be taken care of with a **macro**. The macro goes to each occurrence of the list styles, looks for an asterisk/space combination at the start of the line, and deletes it. Listing 2-1 shows an example of such a macro. The combination of the Registry and macros gives you a lot of power for converting documents to the Web. You can usually create a macro by recording it first, and then modify it for use in a wide range of situations.

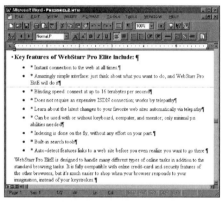

Figure 2-67: The results of automatic conversion after adding the styles from the press release to the Registry.

Before using any macro, you may need to customize it for your particular application. The Word help files contain extensive information about creating and using macros, and many excellent books cover this topic. Be forewarned that macro programming is a complex area. If you aren't already familiar with Word macros, you will probably have to invest a significant amount of time to learn the details.

Listing 2-1: A Word macro to remove asterisks.

```
Sub MAIN
REM Initialize with name of the list style.
SearchStyleName$ = "List Bullet,UL"
REM Is the style of the current paragraph List Bullet?
```

(continued)

Listing 2-1 *(continued)*:

```
        If StyleName$() = SearchStyleName$ Then
          REM Current paragraph uses a list style.
          StartOfLine
          CharRight 2, 1
          EditCopy
          REM See if the selection contains "* ".
          If Selection$() = "* " Then
           REM Delete the selection.
           EditClear
          End If
        End If
        REM Look for first occurrence of slugline style.
        EditFindStyle .Style = SearchStyleName$
        EditFind .Find = "", .Direction = 0, .MatchCase = 0,
        .WholeWord = 0, .PatternMatch = 0, .SoundsLike = 0,
        .Format = 1, .Wrap = 0, .FindAllWordForms = 0
        REM Repeat search until no match is found.
        While EditFindFound()
          StartOfLine
          CharRight 2, 1
          EditCopy
          REM See if the selection contains "* ".
          If Selection$() = "* " Then
           REM Delete the selection.
           EditClear
          End If
          REM Move to next line so we don't repeat the find.
          Result=LineDown()
          If Result = 0 Then
           REM No more lines; stop the macro.
           Stop
          Else
           REM Search again.
           EditFindStyle .Style = SearchStyleName$
           EditFind .Find = "", .Direction = 0, .MatchCase = 0,
        .WholeWord = 0, .PatternMatch = 0, .SoundsLike = 0,
        .Format = 1, .Wrap = 0, .FindAllWordForms = 0
          End If
        Wend
        End Sub
```

Instant Internet: Creating Cool Web Pages from Scratch

In This Chapter

Creating a custom Web page

Viewing the HTML code created by Internet Assistant

Working with **bookmarks**

Working with outlines

Using **table headers**

Customizing the appearance of tables

Using **directory structure** to organize your Web pages

In the first chapter, you experienced true instant Internet by plugging new text and images into a template. Chapter 2 also provided instant thrills: converting what you already have. Now comes what you might imagine to be the really difficult task: creating a Web page from scratch.

I have news for you: It's not a whole lot different than what we've done in the first two chapters. Don't expect a big, fat chapter full of challenges. Creating a Web page from scratch isn't a tough job. In fact, if you follow a few simple steps before you start creating the Web page, it can be downright easy. Because creating a brand-new Web page isn't the difficult part of the process, this chapter also covers a few goodies to expand your Web-page capabilities.

Setting Up the Tutorial

This chapter shows you, step by step, how to create your own custom Web page. Before starting the tutorial, you set up the tutorial by copying files used in the tutorial from the CD-ROM to your hard disk. You may choose to run automatic setup or to set up the files manually.

Automatic setup

If you haven't already installed the software for automatic setup of the tutorials, turn to Appendix A and do so now. Otherwise, if you choose not to use automatic setup, see the next section, "Manual setup," which tells you how to copy the necessary files for this tutorial manually. If you didn't use automatic setup earlier, you can find complete instructions for starting, running, and using the automatic setup program in Chapter 1.

To run automatic setup, click the Start button, then Programs, and then click the Autopage icon, shown here.

Click here for Chapter 3

Figure 3-1: Automatic setup for Chapter 3 tutorial.

This is the Chapter 3 tutorial, so click the Chapter 3 Files radio button to display the files for this chapter (see Figure 3-1).

To copy the files for the tutorial to your hard disk, click the Copy to Hard Disk button. The files are copied to the My Web Pages subfolder of the My Documents folder. If you installed Microsoft Office to your C drive, the following is usually the folder:

    C:\My Documents\My Web Pages

NOTE This is the same folder you have been using for all of the tutorials. From time to time, you may notice that one or more additional subfolders is created in the My Web Pages folder; this is normal, and all is explained during the tutorial.

After you have copied the necessary files, skip ahead to the start of the tutorial. If you choose not to use the automatic setup, read the next section to find out how to copy the necessary files manually.

Manual setup

Before you start the tutorial, open the folder called My Web Pages on your hard disk. If you already completed the tutorial in Chapter 1, you created it as a subfolder of the My Documents folder (usually C:\My Documents).

The tutorial in this chapter uses six image files from the CD-ROM. They are located in the folder \tutorial\chap03. Before you continue, copy the following image files from the \tutorial\chap03 folder on the CD-ROM to the My Web Pages\images folder you created earlier on your hard disk (see Chapter 1 for complete details):

```
plogo.gif
wstarr.gif
pro.gif
server.gif
allbtns2.gif
Webstar4.gif
```

You are now ready to begin the tutorial.

Tutorial 3A: Creating a Web Page from Scratch

At the start of this chapter, I made the following claim:

> If you follow a few simple steps before you start creating the Web page, it can be downright easy.

It's not my habit to make outlandish claims just to get your attention. I meant what I said, and now I'm going to prove that to you.

The first step is the most critical: If you don't follow the first step, the others will be much, much more difficult. Just follow along, and everything should go well.

Step 1: Start with a plan for the page

As a matter of fact, if you make an honest effort to come up with a plan for your page, you are already more than halfway finished with your work. Writers and artists know this simple fact of the creative life: If you know what you plan to do, doing it is much, much easier.

The plan doesn't have to be complicated, fancy, or overly detailed. A plan for a Web page is much like a plan for a house: It needs to show the broad picture. You can fill in the details after you have the broader pieces in place.

How do you develop a plan, you ask? There are several good ways to start. I suggest you use the following methods, in the order shown:

1. Look at other pages on the Net. Find one that appeals to you and has a layout that looks appropriate for the content you want to put on the page. This is a lot like working from a template, and it can be the easiest way to create a page from scratch. If you can't find a page that suits you, move to the next step.

2. Write down the major content areas you plan to put on the page, and then organize them logically. It takes a little time to decide what the major areas are (I suggest no more than three areas), but after you know what they are, they should almost organize themselves. If they *don't* organize themselves, you probably don't have the right areas defined yet. If they refuse to organize themselves despite your best efforts, cut your losses and move to the next step.

3. You can sometimes sketch a layout and then fit the material to the layout. If you haven't been able to organize the material in the preceding step, it's likely that the material may not have a single best organizing principle. In such cases, you can impose the organization by arbitrarily creating a layout. Trust your intuition in such cases: You may surprise yourself with just how effective an arbitrary layout may be.

This third step is often a good point to look at the templates included with this book. Even if the template isn't perfect, a little fiddling usually gives you what you want. Don't expect to find a perfect layout for every Web page. Sometimes, forcing the material into a layout that is at least close reveals good ideas that lead to a great Web page.

Figure 3-2 shows an example of a sketch for a layout. Other than knowing I had three major points to cover, it's an arbitrary layout. The layout allows me to have three major topics and three minor topics. I have also included the general layout of a logo for the page, and I added a **tagline** (a short, catchy phrase or sentence) below the logo to describe the page.

Figure 3-3 shows the result of creating a page from this layout. Note that I made some changes during development of the page. This is typical. You can't anticipate everything.

Don't try to include every level of detail on your layouts. You are bound to face some surprises as you create the Web page, and you need room to make changes. Focus on the large-scale organization of the page.

Step 2: Choosing a strategy

There are several different ways to create a Web page based on the layout sketched in Figure 3-2. For example, the upper portion of the page could easily be laid out as a table, with headlines and text in the left columns, and pictures in the right column.

Another option is to use some picture options to flow the text around the images. That's the method we use in the tutorial to create the page. The bottom portion could be created as a single Definition List, or we could create headlines and use the Blockquote style to indent the text under each headline.

Because you learned how to create a Definition List in Chapter 2, we'll use the head-line/Blockquote technique here.

When you create your own Web pages from scratch, you make similar decisions. When in doubt, you can simply try several different approaches and decide which one works best.

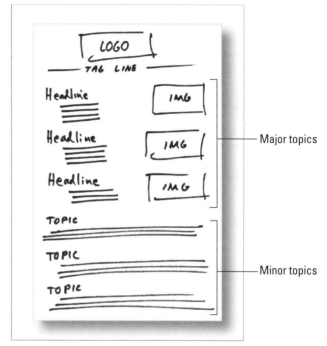

Figure 3-2: A sketch of a layout for a Web page.

Figure 3-3: A Web page created from the layout in Figure 3-2.

In some cases, you may find that you have too much material to fit on one Web page. In these cases, you need to create additional pages and add **hypertext links** to your main page so that readers can access the additional pages. In fact, that's the strategy we use for this tutorial.

The nature of the tutorial

As with other tutorials, this one is based on the fictitious company WebStarr, Inc. This Web page is part of the company's Web site. If you refer to the page we created in Chapter 1, you see a button near the top of the page labeled "Products." In this tutorial, we create the Web page that appears when you click the Products button.

Here's the memo that came from the Vice President of Marketing, who has overall responsibility for the Web site:

```
Dear X,

I met with Bob Webman to discuss the contents of our Products Web
page, and we have determined the information that needs to be on
the page.

The primary focus areas will be our three main products:
WebStarr, WebStarr Pro, and WebStarr Server Edition. There's
obviously too much information for one page, so we want you to
provide lots of hyperlinks. Some of the hyperlinks will be new
pages; some links will be to pages you have already created.

We also want to provide information about the new product show-
case that the Sales team has created; it includes fancy interac-
tive examples of our key products. We also want links to Web
sites where the Server Edition is used.

Sincerely,



Ethel Webster, VP Marketing
```

The memo loosely defines the nature and content of the Web page, but leaves a lot of room for flexibility of interpretation. Look again at the sample layout in Figure 3-3, and note how it defines a Web page that is attractive, organized, and able to meet the requirements of the memo:

➡ There are three main focus areas on the page.

➡ We need a minor area to provide the link to the product showcase.

➡ We may need another minor area to provide the link to customer sites.

In addition, we also are assuming that, based on a meeting last week with the Director of Company Morale, there is a strong desire to provide opportunities for client feedback on company Web pages. We'll add a third minor topic for feedback.

Step 3: Creating the Web page

Creating a Web page from scratch is an interactive process. By starting with a layout, you have set the broad strategy for the page. As you actually add text, images, or other elements to the page, you may find you need to make changes. These changes may involve rearranging the sequence of major focus areas, using lists instead of straight text, reducing the size of images, and so forth. We cover a few of these possibilities during the course of this tutorial.

To begin creating the page, I started in an **image program** (Fractal Design Painter). I created a **logo** for the page that combines the company logo and Products button from the page you created in Chapter 1. If you have copied the files for this tutorial to your hard disk, the file is ready for loading into your Word for Windows page. To begin, follow these steps:

1. Choose FILE⇨NEW to create a new file. Choose the basic HTML template as the template for this new document. The file is called `HTML.DOT` and is located in the General folder of the New dialog box.

2. Save the new file as `\My Documents\My Web Pages\products.htm`. Remember from Chapter 1 that you should always save a file before adding images to it, so that Internet Assistant can put correct relative path names into your HTML file.

3. Click the Add Picture tool on the Formatting toolbar, and then click the Browse button in the Picture dialog box to display the images available in the folder `\My Documents\My Web Pages\images`. Select the image `plogo.gif` and click OK (see Figure 3-4).

4. Note that the *Image Source* text box contains a relative path. This indicates that the image is found in the subfolder `images`. Enter the following in the Alternative Text text box:

    WebStarr, Inc. Products

5. Click OK to add the image. In most cases, you do not see the image; you see the alternate text instead. To view the image, save your work, close the file, and then re-open it. The result is shown in Figure 3-5.

Image preview

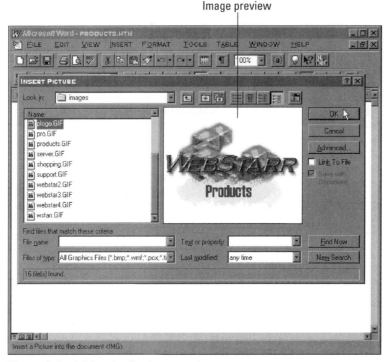

Figure 3-4: Adding the first image to the page.

Figure 3-5: The first image added to the page.

6. Next, center the paragraph by positioning the cursor in the paragraph and clicking the Center Text icon in the Formatting toolbar. This is the same Center Text icon you normally see when working in Word.

7. Now press Enter and add the **tagline** beneath the image, as follows:

> **WebStarr: what the pros use to surf the net in style.**

Make the tagline text italic (select it and click the I button on the Formatting toolbar) and center this paragraph, too. Figure 3-6 shows the result.

TIP Make it a habit to always have at least one additional blank paragraph below your current working position in the file. This allows you to move quickly to the next task. Word makes the formatting of a new paragraph identical to the formatting of the current paragraph. Thus, if you center a paragraph and then press Enter to create a new paragraph, the new paragraph is centered, too. Keeping an extra paragraph with the Normal style at the bottom of your document avoids your having to frequently reformat. If you do need to repeat a style, you can place the cursor at the end of the paragraph and press Enter. If you do not need that style again, go to the Normal paragraph and press Enter.

Taglines aren't perfect for every Web page, but they can be very useful. A good tagline describes the contents of your page quickly and lets the readers know right away whether this page will give them what they want or need.

Add Horizontal Rule icon

Figure 3-6: Adding a tagline beneath the image.

The logo and tagline serves as a page header; add a horizontal rule beneath the tagline by positioning the cursor at the beginning of the line after the tagline and selecting INSERT⇨HORIZONTAL RULE. Figure 3-7 shows the result.

You can also add a horizontal rule by clicking the Add Horizontal Rule icon on the Formatting toolbar (see Figure 3-6). This is one of the tools that Internet Assistant adds to the Word toolbars.

The layout that I sketched for this page includes three images, each of which uses Right alignment to force it to the right edge of the page. We will insert each image just prior to the text that is to appear to the left of it on the Web page. To insert the picture and set the correct options, do the following:

Figure 3-7: A horizontal rules separates the header from the rest of the page.

1. Position your cursor at the beginning of the line immediately below the horizontal rule.

2. Click the Add Picture icon on the Formatting toolbar.

3. Use the Browse button in the Picture dialog box to locate the correct image file: `\My Documents\My Web Pages\images\wstarr.gif` (see Figure 3-8). Click OK to load the image.

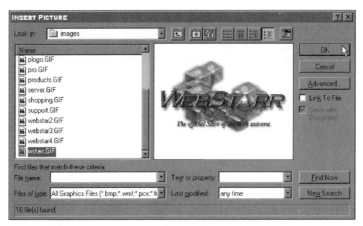

Figure 3-8: Loading the image for the first major topic.

4. Click the Options tab and set Alignment with Text to Right (see Figure 3-9). Add the dimensions of the image (160 high, 265 wide) at the top left in the dialog box so that your browser sets up the page properly even before the image has completed loading. Click OK to close the dialog box and load the image. If the image is not immediately visible, then save, close, and reopen the document. If the paragraph with the image is centered, click the Align Left button on the Formatting toolbar to remove centering.

5. Add a headline to the right of the image, without any intervening space: **WebStarr: Free and Powerful.** Give it a Heading 1, H1 style, and make the first word (**WebStarr**) italic. Change the text to italic *after* you apply the style.

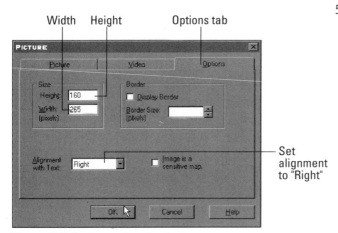

Figure 3-9: Setting options for the image.

The result is shown in Figure 3-10. Even though we set the picture to align itself to the right of the text, Word does not show this alignment. This is a limitation of using Word for creating Web pages — not every feature of the Web is a feature of Word. When you view the page in your browser, the picture will be correctly aligned.

Now add a block of text below the headline that tells visitors how to get a free copy of WebStarr (so they can find out whether the second half of the headline is actually true!):

WebStarr is available just for the **downloading.** Try downloading from the following sites. If you have difficulty downloading from one site, try another. The current version of WebStarr is 3.02.01.

If it is not using the Normal,P style, apply that style. Add a list of five make-believe Web sites below this text block, and apply the style List Bullet,UL to turn it into a list (see Figure 3-11), as follows:

> Download from Misula State University
>
> Download from Crocket Pickle Foundation
>
> Download from Surreal Tapestries, Inc.
>
> Download from Marginal Presentations Co.
>
> Download from Maine Events, Inc.

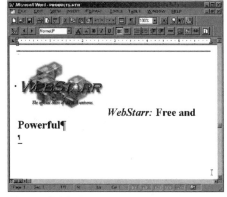

Figure 3-10: The image and headline in Word.

Figure 3-11: Adding text and a list of Web sites.

Save your work. Figure 3-12 shows what the page looks like in a **browser.** The exact appearance varies from one browser to another. Note that the images have a white background, whereas the browser is using a gray background. We'll change the page background to white later.

TIP You can leave the page background color until last. Having the page a different color allows you to see exactly how your browser is treating the spacing around your images.

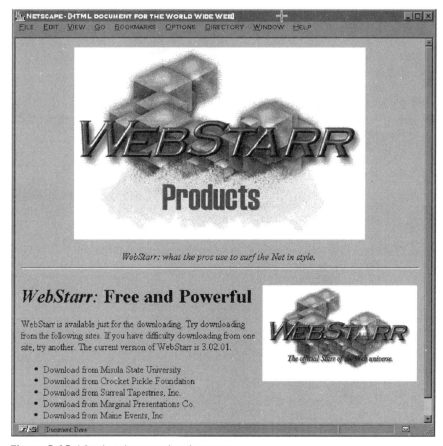

Figure 3-12: Viewing the page in a browser.

Adding hyperlinks

Following the text block for this topic, we have a list of Web sites that visitors can use to download a free copy of WebStarr. It does no good at all to merely list them; we need to add hyperlinks to these Web sites so that the visitor can get immediate gratification. Isn't that what the Web is *really* about? Yes, the author has his tongue firmly in his cheek.

To add hyperlinks, follow these steps:

1. Select the text.

2. Click the Add Hyperlink button on the Formatting toolbar.

3. Type the URL of the Web site in the File or URL text box of the Hyperlink dialog box. (See Figure 3-13 for an example.)

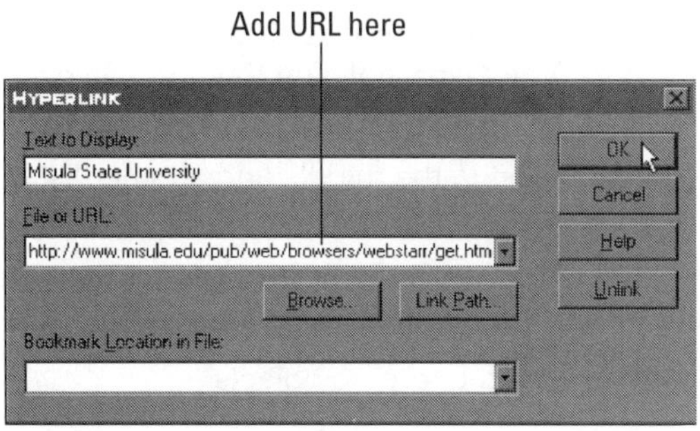

Add URL here

Figure 3-13: Adding a URL.

Here are the make-believe hyperlinks if you care to add them:

Web Site	Make-Believe URL
Misula State University	http://www.misula.edu/pub/Web/browsers/Webstarr/get.htm
Crocket Pickle Foundation	http://www.crocketpickle.com/files/Webst
Surreal Tapestries, Inc.	http://www.unearthly.com/public/files/ws
Marginal Presentations Co.	http://www.ontheedge.com/index.htm
Maine Events, Inc.	http://www.mainevents.net/

All the make-believe URLs are patterned after URLs you can find on the Net. For example, the "pub," "public," and "files" subdirectories are commonly found on servers. They usually contain **shareware** or other software that was provided by someone other than the owner of the Web site. The "edu" in the domain name of Misula State University indicates it is an educational site, "com" indicates commercial sites, and "net" stands for network sites.

This completes the tasks for the first major topic area. Now we'll add two more major topics. To add a topic for WebStarr Pro, the professional version of the WebStarr browser, follow these steps:

1. Position your cursor at the beginning of the line immediately below the last item in the list of download sites.

2. Click the Add Picture icon on the Formatting toolbar.

3. Use the Browse button in the Picture dialog box to locate the correct image file: \My Documents\My Web Pages\images\pro.gif. Click OK to load the image.

4. Click the Options tab, and set Alignment with Text to Right. Add the dimensions of the image (160 high, 265 wide) at top left. Click OK. If the image is not immediately visible, then save, close, and reopen the document.

5. Add a headline to the right of the image, without any intervening space: **WebStarr Pro: You Get What You Pay For.** Give it a Heading 1,H1 style, and make the first two words (**WebStarr Pro**) italic.

6. Add a text block, with a list in the middle and another list at the end (apply the style List Bullet,UL to the list items):

> For personal use, you can't find a better browser than WebStarr. But you want the best in features, such as:
>
> > support for embedded Espresso objects
> >
> > concurrent Latte
> >
> > a little Cream & Sugar
>
> There is no other product that gives you everything you need: WebStarr Pro. With WebStarr Pro, you can go anywhere on the Web and know that your browser supports any and every feature you encounter.
>
> > Currently supported third-party objects
> >
> > A list of vendors developing objects for WebStarr Pro
> >
> > Guidelines for WebStarr Pro developers
> >
> > Submit ideas for the next version of WebStarr Pro
> >
> > Download our current beta release, WebStarr Pro version 3.5B

The first list contains information about WebStarr Pro features, and the second list is intended as a list of hyperlinks to various related subjects.

As a general rule, you can best organize information within a topic as follows: Add hyperlinks that are directly related to a topic within the text of the topic itself; add related hyperlinks after the topic text.

There are some appropriate spots for hyperlinks in the preceding text. If you want some practice in adding hyperlinks, here they are:

Hyperlink Text	URL
Espresso	`espresso.htm`
Latte	`latte.htm`
Cream & Sugar	`cs.htm`
third-party objects	`http://www.misula.edu/pub/Web/browsers/Webstarr/thirdpty.htm`

vendors	vendors.htm
Guidelines	guidelin.htm
next version	newvers.htm
Download	ftp://Webstarr.com/ftp/beta/wsp35.zip

One URL in this batch has a different look (the last one). Instead of starting with "http," it starts with "ftp." Web pages commonly use **HyperText Transfer Protocol (http)** for moving data across the Internet. Before there were Web pages, however, there was still a need to move files across Internet links. FTP (File Transfer Protocol) filled that need. FTP is awkward compared to http, but it got the job done for many years. You still run into it; for example, you can use ftp on a Web page when all you need to do is download a file, rather than view it online. In the preceding ftp example, WebStarr has made a beta version of its software available at an ftp site, not an http (Web) site, but just about every Web browser also lets you contact and work with an ftp site. When you visit an ftp site, you usually see nothing more interesting than a list of files (see Figure 3-14).

Your **Webmaster** or system administrator can tell you whether you have an ftp server, and how to use it for file downloading.

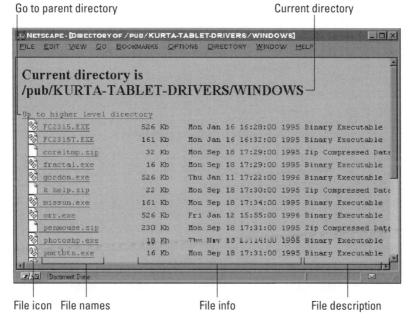

Figure 3-14: An ftp site doesn't have the visual appeal of an http (Web) site.

This completes the work for the second major topic area. Now we'll add the third major topic. To add a topic for WebStarr Server Edition, follow these steps:

1. Position your cursor at the beginning of the line immediately below the last item in the list of items related to WebStarr Pro.

2. Click the Add Picture icon on the Formatting toolbar.

3. Use the Browse button in the Picture dialog box to locate the correct image file: `\My Documents\My Web Pages\images\server.gif`. Click OK to load the image.

4. Click the Options tab, and set Alignment with Text to Right. Add the dimensions of the image (160 high, 265 wide) at top left. Click OK. If the image is not immediately visible, then save, close, and reopen the document.

5. Add a headline to the right of the image, without any intervening space: **WebStarr Server: Best Back End in the Business**. Give it a Heading 1,H1 style, and make the first two words (**WebStarr Server**) italic.

6. Add a text block, with a list in the middle and another list at the end (apply the style List Bullet,UL to the list items):

   Someday, perhaps everyone will have personal servers sitting on the Web. For now, if you want the best server for your site, there is only one choice: WebStarr Server Edition. You'll get a full suite of server tools:

   Development tools

   Espresso support

   Latte support

   Visual Cream & Sugar development

   Included with Server Edition, you'll get complete support for indexing, database links, CGI, and more back-end goodies than any other server provides.

   Features supported in WebStarr Server Edition

   Development Tools included in WebStarr Server Edition

   Information about our forthcoming third-party architecture

As with the text associated with the second major topic, the first list contains directly related information, and the second list is more loosely associated with the topic.

As always, there are appropriate spots for hyperlinks in the text. There are a few twists in the hyperlinks that are worth a closer look. Consult the following list if you want further practice with hyperlinks:

Hyperlink Text	URL
tools	`tools.htm`
Espresso	`espress.htm`
Latte	`latte.htm`
Visual Cream & Sugar	`cs.htm#visual`
Features	`wserver.htm#features`
Development Tools	`wserver.htm#tools`
third-party architecture	`wserver.htm#architecture3`

The last four items in the list include something new in the way of URLs: There's a pound sign (#) sitting in the middle of the text. The pound sign indicates a link to a *bookmark* in an HTML file. Before we finish up the tutorial, let's take a short side trip into the world of bookmarks. Save your work first!

What is a bookmark?

A bookmark is a reference point on a Web page. It has a name, and you can go to the bookmark by referring to its name.

How do I create a bookmark?

To create a bookmark, position the cursor at the location on the page where you want the bookmark. For example, click to place the cursor to the left of the image for the first major topic (that's the file `wstarr.gif`).

If you have trouble placing the cursor to the left of the image by clicking, click *on* the image, and then use the left-arrow key to move to the left of the image.

Click the Add Bookmark tool on the Formatting toolbar (see Figure 3-15) to display the dialog box shown in Figure 3-16. Type the name of the bookmark — in this case, **Webstarr**.

Add Bookmark tool

Figure 3-15: The Add Bookmark tool.

TIP The bookmark names in any one file must be unique. You cannot use the same bookmark name twice in one HTML file.

To add the bookmark, click the Add button at upper right of the Bookmark dialog box (see Figure 3-16).

Bookmark name

Add bookmark

Figure 3-16: Naming a bookmark.

Bookmark location (hidden from view)

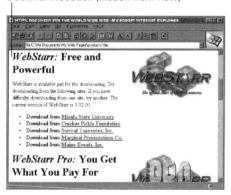

Figure 3-17: When you go to a bookmark with a hyperlink, the bookmark is at the top of the page.

Sort by name   Sort by location in file

Figure 3-18: Multiple bookmarks sorted by name.

How do I manage bookmarks?

You can have any number of bookmarks in an HTML file, but, as a practical matter, you won't need a large number of bookmarks in the average Web page. When you add a hyperlink to tell a browser to go to a book-mark, the browser positions the Web page so that the referenced bookmark is at the top of the browser window. For example, if you used a hypothetical hyperlink to go to the Webstarr bookmark from the preceding section, you would see something like Figure 3-17.

Word and Internet Assistant work together to allow you to conveniently manage book-marks. For example, Figure 3-18 shows a situation with multiple bookmarks in an HTML file. They are listed alphabetically, by name. Note that, at the bottom of the dialog box, there are two methods for sorting: by name and by location. Location refers to the location in the HTML file. Figure 3-19 shows what you see when you list bookmarks by location — the first bookmark in the file is shown first, the second next, and so on. This lets you view bookmarks in the order in which they occur.

Which method of sorting you use depends on what you are trying to do. If you want to jump to a particular place in the file, sort by location. If you are trying to recall the name of a bookmark, sort them by name.

For example, you may want to add a hyperlink that jumps to the top of your Web page. If you added a bookmark at the top, you can sort by location to quickly find the right bookmark, even if you don't recall the name of it.

Figure 3-19: Bookmarks sorted by location in the file.

How do I link to a bookmark?

Let's take another look at the process of creating a hyperlink to see how easy it is to create a link to a bookmark. After selecting the appropriate text, click the Add Hyperlink tool. This displays the dialog box shown in Figure 3-20. See that drop-down list at the bottom of the dialog box, conveniently labeled "Bookmark Location in File"? That's where you can find a list of bookmarks in the current document. Just click to select the one you want.

If you use the Browse button in the Hyperlink dialog box to access a different file, you do not see bookmarks for that outside file. The bookmarks at the bottom of the Hyperlink dialog box refer only to the current file. This means that you need to know what bookmarks are available in the outside file. Look for this to change in a future version of Internet Assistant; the capability to look up bookmarks in outside files is too important to be neglected!

Bookmark drop-down list

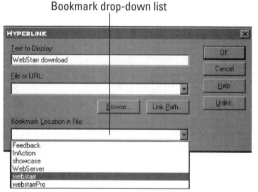

Figure 3-20: Adding a bookmark link.

If you *do* link to a bookmark in another file, the correct way to specify the bookmark is as follows:

```
FileName.htm#BookmarkName
```

Do not use spaces anywhere in the reference. There are several examples of external bookmark references in the hyperlinks for the third major topic in the tutorial; let's look at them in detail.

Bookmarks

The first bookmark reference in the list of hyperlinks mentioned so far in this chapter is to `cs.htm#visual`. You may have noticed that we added a hyperlink earlier to the file `cs.htm`, using the text Cream & Sugar to indicate the link. Cream & Sugar is an **add-on product** for WebStarr's browsers, and there is a page — `cs.htm` — that tells the visitor about this product. We'll assume that there is a bookmark on that page that leads to a special section of the page that describes *Visual* Cream & Sugar. The hyperlink `cs.htm#visual` takes the visitor directly to that part of the page.

 You can also create a link to a bookmark by putting the URL in the File or URL text box, and typing the bookmark name in the Bookmark text box. In my experience, this can lead to confusion with any bookmarks in the current file. That's why I recommend that you specify the bookmark by using the # symbol. If you highlight a hyperlink that contains a bookmark reference to an external file, and click the Add Hyperlink button, you'll see that Word properly separates the URL and the bookmark (see Figure 3-21).

File/URL   Bookmark

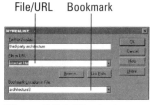

Figure 3-21: Word separates the URL and the bookmark in the Hyperlink dialog box.

The other hyperlinks with bookmarks work exactly the same way. All of them jump to the `wserver.htm` Web page, but to different positions on that Web page.

To make the current Web page, `products.htm`, callable via bookmark-based hyperlinks from other Web pages, we can add bookmarks to appropriate locations in the file. You have already added a bookmark at the left of the image for the first topic. Now add two more bookmarks: a bookmark named *WebStarrPro* just left of the image for the second topic, and a bookmark named *WebServer* just left of the image for the third topic. Save your work.

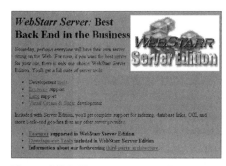

Figure 3-22: The appearance of major topic three in a browser.

You may have noticed that the bookmark references use various mixtures of case. You can use upper- or lowercase in a bookmark, and you can use upper- or lowercase to refer to bookmarks — most browsers do not care about case when searching for a bookmark.

Figure 3-22 shows the results of our work so far in a browser. Notice that there is absolutely no indication of the presence of the three bookmarks. They are invisible when you are browsing a Web page. The only way to access a bookmark is with a hyperlink.

All three major topics are now complete, and we can move on to the minor topics.

Minor Topics

Let's add the text for two of the minor topics, and then format it. Add the following text below the third major topic:

Visit our fun-filled product showcase.

We have created a special Web page that features screen shots and interactive examples of our key products. Don't leave without visiting this exciting, cutting-edge example of WebStarr power!

WebStarr Server Edition in action.

Many leading companies have already put our WebStarr Server Edition to work on their Web sites. Visit them and see what WebStarr Server Edition can do for *you!*

Format the text by following these steps:

1. Apply the style Heading 3,H3 to the two headlines (first and third paragraphs).

2. Apply the style Blockquote to the two larger paragraphs (second and fourth). This indents the two paragraphs to create a more interesting layout.

3. Add a hyperlink to each of the headlines. For the first headline, select the text `product showcase` and add a hyperlink to `showcase.htm`. For the second headline, select the text `in action` and add a hyperlink to `inaction.htm`.

Figure 3-23 shows what the result looks like in a browser.

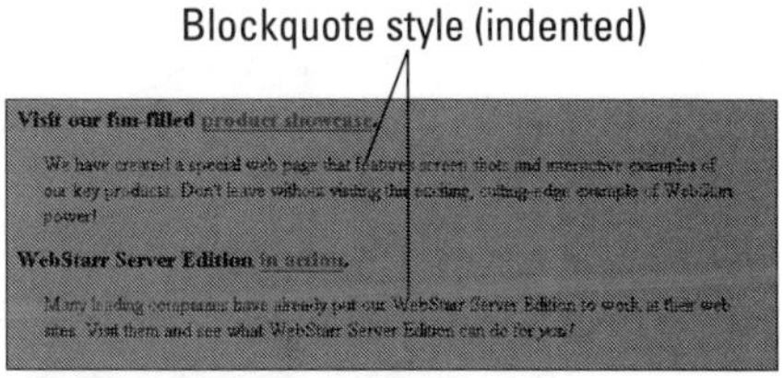

The third minor topic concerns feedback. Add the following text:

Feedback!

Blockquote style (indented)

Figure 3-23: Two minor topics using the Blockquote style.

We'd like to know what you think of us. Tell us about your reactions to our Web pages. Speak your mind on our product features. If you have something to say, we want to hear it at Feedback Central!

Format the text by following these steps:

1. Apply the style Heading 3,H3 to the headline.

2. Apply the style Blockquote to the second paragraph.

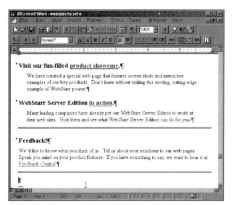

Figure 3-24: The last minor topic is complete.

3. Select the text Feedback Central and add a hyperlink, with the following in the File or URL text box: feedback.htm.

   We could have used something like mailto:feedback@Webstarr.com, but I have something more sophisticated in mind. Later, in Chapter 6, we build a survey form to use for feedback. This form asks visitors certain questions, and provides a place for free-form feedback, too.

4. Add a horizontal rule above and below the feedback topic to clearly distinguish it from the other two minor topics. Figure 3-24 shows the result.

The End of the Page

The content of the page is complete, but there is still a bit of work to do. It would be convenient to have a quick way to visit the other key pages at the WebStarr Web site. This is the Products page, and it serves as a gateway to quite a few other pages. We need a method for jumping quickly to the Support page, or the FAQs page, and so on. I have prepared a graphic that is a miniature version of the buttons from the top of the home page for WebStarr, Inc. (see Chapter 1).

Position the cursor below the last horizontal rule and click the Add Picture tool. Use the Browse button to locate the file \My Documents\My Web Pages\ images\allbtns2.gif (see Figure 3-25). Click OK to load the image, click the Options tab and add the height (20) and width (300) of the image, and then click OK to load it. Use the Center tool to center the paragraph containing the image. As always, save, close, and reopen the file if the image doesn't load.

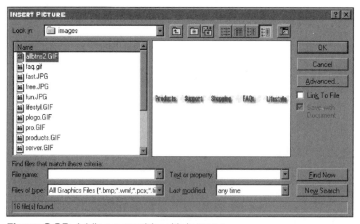

Figure 3-25: Adding a graphic with buttons.

Create a new paragraph below the button image, and add a small version of the logo (\My Documents\My Web Pages\images\Webstar4.gif). Center the image. Add the following two lines of text below this image to indicate who created the page. Apply the Normal,P style if the text does not already use that style:

Web site designed and maintained by WebStarr Page Art, Inc.

Copyright 1995 by WebStarr Page Art, Inc.

It's common in the Web page business to add information about yourself or your company at the bottom of key pages at a Web site. This lets the world know who created the page.

Are you getting tired of adding hyperlinks, bits of text here and there, and repeating the steps needed to load images? Welcome to the real world of creating Web pages. It's not difficult, but the details are many and they don't vary a whole lot. I had to make a choice about whether to include every step necessary to create each Web page, or just include the exciting stuff. Everything about Web pages isn't exciting. Sometimes, success is in the details, so I've elected to cover each and every detail in each and every Web page that is included in the tutorials. That way, you won't have to worry that you missed something important. It's all here.

Center both lines of text. Select both lines, and click the Decrease Font Size button three times to reduce the font size. Figure 3-26 shows the result in a browser.

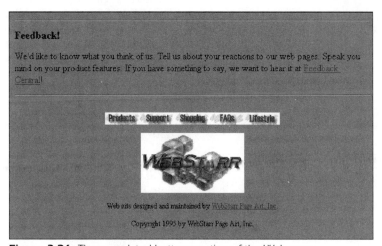

Figure 3-26: The completed bottom portion of the Web page.

All that remains is to set the background color of the Web page. Choose FOR-MAT⇨BACKGROUND AND LINKS to display the dialog box shown in Figure 3-27. Because all the images use a white background, the page should, too. Select white in the Color drop-down box, and then click OK to save. Save the file, and then view it in your favorite browser (see Figure 3-28).

Figure 3-27: Setting the background to white.

Figure 3-28: The page background appears white in a browser.

The page is complete, but there is more information to cover. Let's take a look at Word's ability to create good-looking tables for the Web.

Tutorial 3B: Fancy Tables

One of the most powerful features of HTML is its capability to use tables to organize the layout of text and graphics on a Web page. You saw one example of a table in Chapter 1, where we used a table to line up graphics on the left side of the page and text on the right. Another, simpler example of a table was used in Chapter 2 to separate two paragraphs on a line.

There is a lot more to Web tables than what you've seen so far. Unfortunately, some features of Web-legal tables are not supported in Word/Internet Assistant. The most important feature that is missing: nesting one table inside another table. For example, the table structure shown in Figure 3-29 (designed and written for me by my evil twin brother) is legal on the Web.

Word itself does not support nested tables, so there is no way to create or to maintain nested tables on Web pages with Internet Assistant. If you try to load an HTML file with nested tables in it, Word loads the entire outer table, followed by the first nested table,

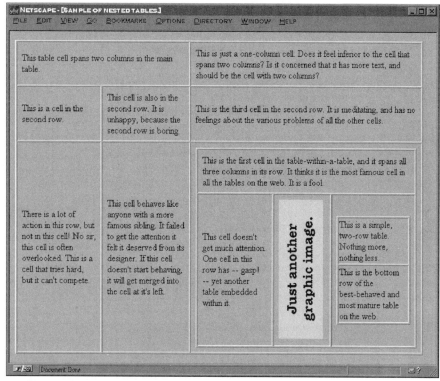

Figure 3-29: Nested tables are legal on a Web page, but you cannot create or maintain them with Internet Assistant.

followed by the next nested table, and so on. All the tables will be combined into one giant table — not what you would expect. If you then save the file, you destroy the nesting and have a real mess on your hands.

Never load an HTML file that contains **nested tables** into Word. If you do load it, never, ever save it: Word will completely mix up the tables, and it will take a great deal of work to re-create the nested tables. This is true even if you never touch the nested tables while the file is loaded into Word.

There are other Web-legal table features that are not supported by Internet Assistant, but the problem isn't as severe. For example, you can specify the distance between the edge of a table cell and the text within that cell by using the CELLPADDING parameter of HTML. Word does not currently support this parameter, but if you add the parameter manually, word tolerates it. You learn about manually adding HTML commands in Chapter 7.

Let's create a table from scratch using Word and Internet Assistant. In the HTML file you created earlier in this chapter, products.htm, you added a hyperlink to a Web page with the URL tools.htm. That Web page contains a list of development tools for the WebStarr Server Edition software.

Create a new HTML file (select FILE⇨NEW, and then choose the HTML.DOT template), and save it as tools.htm in the \My Documents\My Web Pages directory. Saving the file now avoids any problems and error messages later.

For this example, we'll create a table four columns wide and four rows long. To do this, click the Create Table icon in the Standard toolbar, and drag to indicate a 4 × 4 table (see Figure 3-30). This isn't any special feature of Internet Assistant; this is the normal way to create a new, blank table in Word. When you are finished, you see a blank table, as shown in Figure 3-31.

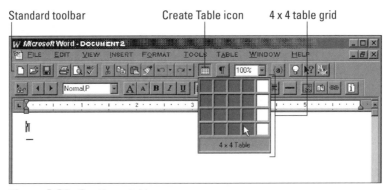

Figure 3-30: Creating a table.

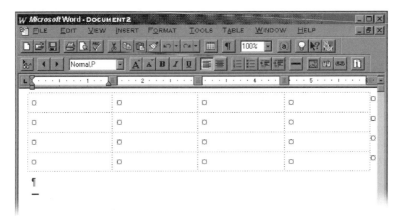

Figure 3-31: An empty table.

Table headers

HTML enables you to specify that cells in a table are headers rather than just table data. Browsers usually show headers as bold, centered text.

You do not have to specify an entire row or column as a header. HTML being what it is, you can make any cell a header. As a practical matter, a useful header consists of an entire row or column, and usually is the first row or column of the table.

To create a header row, select the top row of cells in the table, then choose TABLE⇨CELL TYPE to display the dialog box shown in Figure 3-32. There are just two types of cells: table header and table data. The default, of course, is Table Data. To make the selected row of cells header cells, just click the radio button marked Table Header, and then click the OK button.

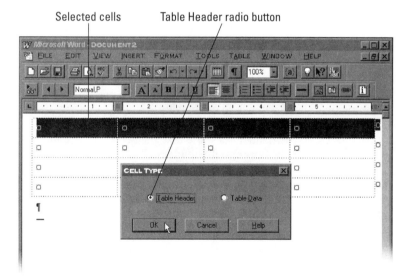

Figure 3-32: Setting cell type.

The appearance of the selected row changes, as shown in Figure 3-33. Each cell contains an underlined, blue asterisk. This is actually a Word field. Internet Assistant uses the field to mark the cells as header cells. When Word saves the file, Internet Assistant adds — to each cell — the HTML codes for table header to the file.

Do not delete these fields; they contain important information needed by Internet Assistant.

Header cells

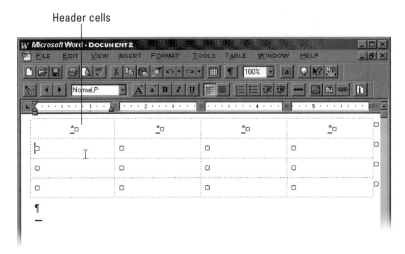

Figure 3-33: *The top row is now made up of header cells.*

For this example, the cells in the first column also need to be header cells. Select the column and then select TABLE⇨CELL TYPE to change them to Table Header cells, just as you did for the first row of cells. Note that the default radio button is now Table Header, because that was the previous selection. You see the same underlined asterisk in each cell.

If you add text to the header cells, the text will be bold and centered. Add the text shown here to the appropriate header cells:

Save your work now. If you view the result in your browser, you see that the text appears organized like a table, but without borders and without any kind of title. We'll add those details shortly.

	Description	Products	Costs/Benefits
CGI Scripting			
Document Management			
Indexing/Search Tools			

Table cells

Adding text to an HTML table is as easy as adding text to a normal Word table: You just type it in. If you want, you can apply styles to the text. For example, you can make words italic or bold. You can also apply Web-legal styles. For example, you can put a list inside a table cell. Type the following information in the first row of cells:

CGI Scripting	When you create forms for your Web site, you'll need flexible, efficient CGI scripts to process the data. And, just as you need to manage sites with many Web pages, script management tools will save time and money.	ScriptMagic ScriptText ScriptMan ScriptTool CGI Manager BatchLint	For a large Web site, custom scripting costs can be your largest software expenditure. With WebStarr scripting tools, you can cut costs with better script management and reusable tools.

Type the following information in the second row of cells:

Document Management	Large numbers of documents — especially when you automate conversion of existing documents — can eat up resources if you don't have good management tools.	DocuMagic VersaManager Chapter & Verse Text Magic FormatMagic	By automating document conversions, you can save up to 95% of the cost of manual conversion. Need we say more?

Type the following information in the third row of cells:

Indexing/ Search tools	Large Web sites accumulate a tremendous amount of information. So much, in fact, that finding the right	Indexer IndexMagic Search & Rescue	A large site without indexing can be worthless — if you can't find information, why visit the Web site?

(continued)

(continued)

	piece of data can be real trouble. Indexing makes it easy to find key information.	Find It Fast	Indexing and search tools help you retain the value of your data.

Notice that the third column contains lists. Select the entire list in the first row of the second column (begins with ScriptMagic), and apply the List Bullet,UL style (see Figure 3-34). Do the same for the other two lists. Figure 3-35 shows what the lists look like in a browser.

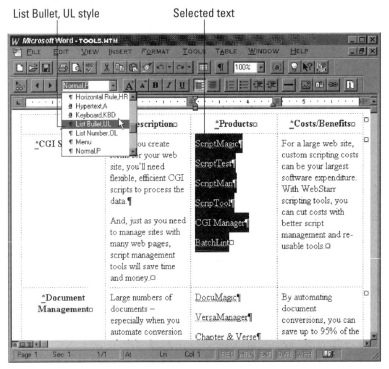

Figure 3-34: *Creating a list inside a table cell.*

The table elements are all there, but the layout is crowded and not easy to interpret. The text for each cell is centered vertically in the cell, and it's not easy to figure out which text lines up with what. In short, the table is confusing. It needs modifications.

Table enhancements

There are six steps you can take to make this table look better:

- Use WYSIWYG to set exact widths for the table columns

- Add borders to the table cells

- Add color to emphasize headers (works only with Internet Explorer, however)

- Add space between table cells

- Add a table caption

- Align all cell text with the top of the cells

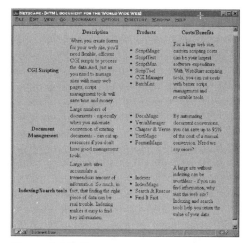

Figure 3-35: The table looks like this in a browser.

Let's see how we can use these techniques to improve the appearance of the table.

Step 1: Use WYSIWYG to set exact widths for the table columns

To set exact widths for the table columns, choose TABLE⇨CELL WIDTH AND SPACING. Click the WYSIWYG Column Widths checkbox at the top of the dialog box if it is not already checked (see Figure 3-36). You could use the Width of Column control to adjust the width of the current column, but it's much, much easier to simply click OK and then adjust column widths manually. Simply place the mouse over the vertical border between two columns and then drag left or right to adjust the column width.

Click here before setting column widths   Width of Column control

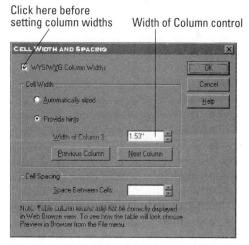

Figure 3-36: Setting table column widths.

Column too narrow

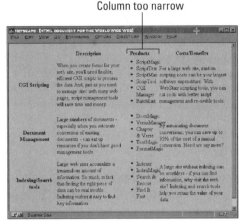

Figure 3-37: Fix layout problems by changing column widths.

No border   Border grid

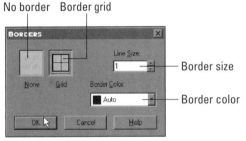

Border size

Border color

Figure 3-38: Adding a border to a table.

To check column widths, save your work and preview the HTML file in your browser. Figure 3-37 shows the kind of problem you might encounter: The third column is too narrow, and the list text isn't displaying properly.

> **CAUTION** When using lists in a table, remember that all lists are indented. This means that you will have extra space to the left of the list. The extra space may make the list too wide for its column. Always check the appearance of a table that uses lists in your browser.

Step 2: Add borders to the table cells

Adding a border is simple: Click TABLE➪ BORDERS to display the dialog box shown in Figure 3-38. Click the Grid icon to add a border. You can also set the width of the border, but the simple truth is that, in most browsers, table widths other than the default, 1, just don't look very good. I recommend that you accept the default value for border width. Click OK to close the dialog box and add the border.

Step 3: Add color to emphasize headers

Some browsers support color in individual table cells, and some don't. At the time this book is being written, only the Microsoft Internet Explorer supports color this way. With most browsers, you can set the color for the page, but not for anything else. With the rapid growth of HTML, it's reasonably likely that other browsers will support color in table cells; the only question is whether they will support it the same way Internet Explorer and Internet Assistant do. You can determine which browsers support color in cells by simply setting the color of some table cells and then viewing the HTML file in your browser.

To set the color of one or more cells, select the cells (drag across the cells you want to select) and select TABLE➪BACKGROUND COLOR to choose the color, and to determine whether the color applies to the entire table or to just the selected cells. For example, to give the first row of cells a light blue background, click to select the row, then choose TABLE⇨BACKGROUND COLOR to display the dialog box shown in Figure 3-39.

Set the color to Cyan by using the Background Color drop-down list. Click the Selected Cells **radio button** to make sure that the color applies only to the cells you selected. Click OK to save the changes. Figure 3-40 shows the appearance of the table in Word. You also see the color if you view the file in the Internet Explorer browser.

Step 4: Add space between table cells

The text of most cells is currently crowded up against text in other cells. This makes the table look awkward and makes it more difficult to interpret. To adjust the spacing between cells, click to place the cursor within the table, and click TABLE⇨CELL WIDTH AND SPACING to display the dialog box shown in Figure 3-41. At the bottom of the dialog box, in the section marked Cell Spacing, set the Space Between Cells to 0.2 inch. Click OK to save the change. You won't see any difference in Word; cell spacing shows up when you view the file in a browser (see Figure 3-42).

 If you adjusted column widths manually, you may see a column width in the box to the right of Width of Column. You don't need to do anything with this number.

Apply to all cells in table
Background color | Apply to selected cells

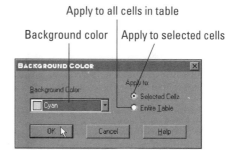

Figure 3-39: Setting the color for a range of cells.

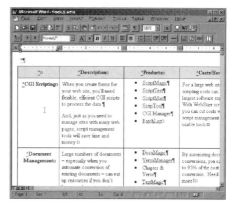

Figure 3-40: Table cells with color.

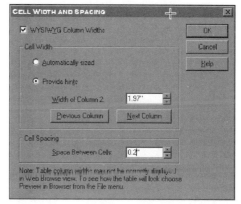

Figure 3-41: Setting cell spacing.

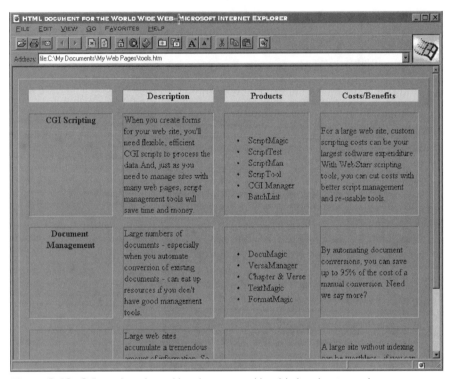

Figure 3-42: Cell spacing viewed in a browser, with table borders turned on.

By adding space, we've taken away the need for borders in the table. In general, if you can make a table read clearly without borders, you should do so. In many cases, borders cause as many problems with layout as they solve. At times, however, a border is just what you need, and now you now how to create one. To remove the borders, select TABLE⇨ BORDERS to open the Borders dialog box and then select None to remove the borders.

Table alignment   Text alignment

Step 5: Align all cell text with the top of the cells

To align the text within cells, select the cells in the usual manner, then choose TABLE⇨ALIGN to display the Align dialog box (see Figure 3-43). For this example, select the leftmost column of cells.

The Align dialog box is divided into two major areas. The top area controls the alignment of the table as a whole; you can align tables to the left margin or center them on the page. In this case, click the Left radio button under Entire Table.

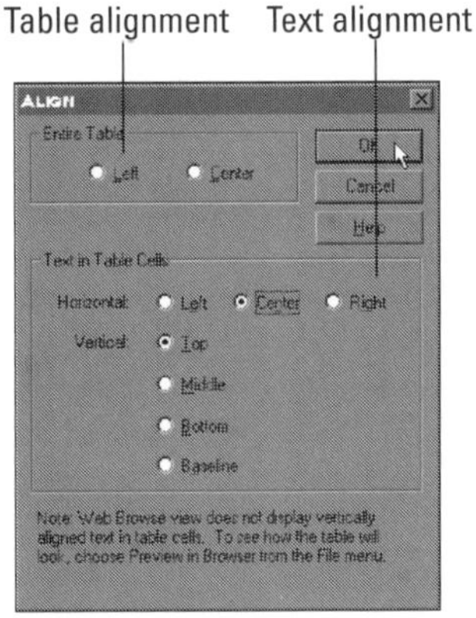

Figure 3-43: Setting cell text alignment.

Word does not display vertical alignment correctly in all cases. Verify vertical alignment by using a Web browser.

As for the cell text, these are header cells, so set the Horizontal alignment to Center. Click the Top radio button for Vertical text alignment, and then click OK to save the changes. Next, select the nine cells that contain text (that is, all the non-header cells), and set the Vertical alignment to Top. Save your work and check it in your Web browser. The text of all cells should now start at the top of the cell.

Step 6: Add a table caption

To add a table caption, click to place the cursor in the table and click TABLE⇨CAPTION. This choice brings up the Caption dialog box, shown in Figure 3-44. Type the caption **WebStarr Server Edition Development Tools**, and make sure the Above Selected Table radio button is selected. Click OK to save the caption.

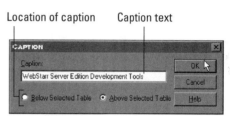

Figure 3-44: Adding a table caption.

The caption appears as a single cell above the existing table, spanning the entire width of the table (see Figure 3-45).

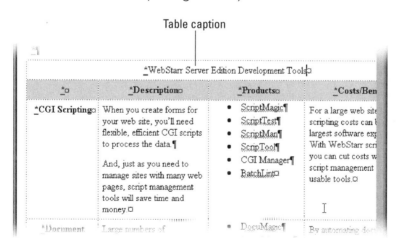

Figure 3-45: The initial appearance of a table caption in Word.

The caption looks pretty wimpy in normal text. Place the cursor in the caption cell, and apply the style Heading 2,H2. You may also want to apply a large type style to the top row of header cells. Select each cell and apply the style Heading3,H3. Finally, if you want, apply a light color to the page background (select FORMAT⇨BACKGROUND AND LINKS).

Figure 3-46 shows the results of the changes. Notice the following:

➡ The table has a caption.

➡ Cell text is aligned with the top of the cells.

➡ Cell spacing is wide enough to allow the table to be read clearly.

Save your work; this page is complete. You can now test the hyperlink to the `tools.htm` file from the `products.htm` page. Open the Products page in your browser, and click the hyperlink. The table you just completed should appear. If not, check the hyperlink to make sure that it points to the file `tools.htm`, and that the `tools.htm` file is in the same directory as the `products.htm` file.

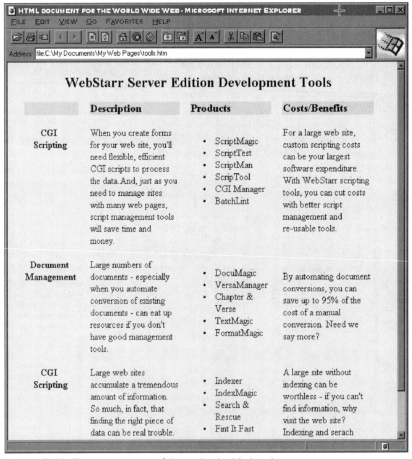

Figure 3-46: The appearance of the revised table in a browser.

Mastering the Internet: Images and Image Maps

In This Chapter

Customize the appearance of images in your Web pages

Work with colors and backgrounds

Create interlaced images

Create transparent images with Snap/32, a shareware tool

Create Image Maps with MapThis!, a freeware tool

Use clip art effectively

Use image-editing software to create or modify images for maximum impact

Master the art of the button

The Internet has been around far longer than most people realize. When most of us think about the Internet, we're really thinking about the World Wide Web (WWW). The Web transformed the Internet by making it possible to include graphics. Pictures converted the Internet from a static network of files to an interactive network of Web pages.

Images are what make the Web so useful and interesting. By learning how to create, edit, and work with images on Web pages, you gain an enormous amount of power that you can apply at your Web site.

Setting Up the Tutorial

In the first three chapters, you created complete Web pages during the tutorials. In this chapter, we jump around — some of the tutorials build on what you created in earlier chapters, and some start from scratch. You can view this chapter as a collection of mini-tutorials.

Automatic setup

If you haven't already installed the software for automatic setup of the tutorials, turn to Appendix A and do so now. Otherwise, if you choose not to use automatic setup, see the next section, "Manual setup," which tells you how to copy the necessary files for this tutorial manually. If you didn't use automatic setup earlier, you can find complete instructions for starting, running, and using the automatic setup program in Chapter 1.

To run automatic setup, click the Start button, then Programs, and then click the Autopage icon, which is shown here.

This is the Chapter 4 tutorial, so click the Chapter 4 Files radio button to display the files for this chapter (see Figure 4-1).

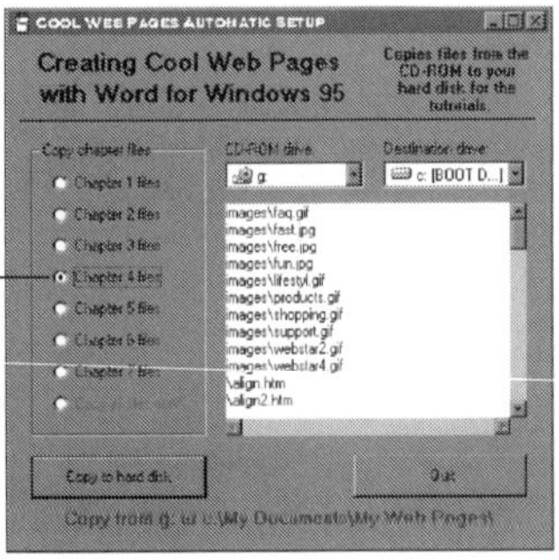

To copy the files for the tutorial to your hard disk, click the Copy to Hard Disk button. The files are copied to the My Web Pages subfolder of the My Documents folder. If you installed Microsoft Office to your C drive, the following is usually the folder:

`C:\My Documents\My Web Pages`

NOTE This is the same folder you have been using for all the tutorials. From time to time, you may notice that one or more additional subfolders is created in the My Web Pages folder; this is normal, and all is explained during the tutorial.

Click here for Chapter 4

Figure 4-1: Automatic setup for Chapter 4 tutorial.

After you have copied the necessary files, skip ahead to the start of the Tutorial. If you choose not to use the automatic setup, read the next section to find out how to copy the necessary files manually.

Manual setup

Before you start the tutorial, open the folder My Web Pages on your hard disk. If you already completed the tutorial in Chapter 1, you created it as a subfolder of the My Documents folder (usually C:\My Documents).

The tutorial in this chapter uses images and other kinds of files from the CD-ROM. They are located in the folder \tutorial\chap04. Copy the following HTML (Web page) files

align.htm	align2.htm	bkg.htm
blur01.htm	both01.htm	clouds.htm
clouds2.htm	hyperimg.htm	ilace.htm
line01.htm	line02.htm	mess01.htm
mess01.htm	mess02.htm	pastel.htm
pattern2.htm	pattern3.htm	test.htm
transp.htm	zebra1.htm	zebra2.htm

from the \tutorial\chap04 folder on the CD-ROM to the \My Documents\My Web Pages\ folder you created earlier on your hard disk (see Chapter 1 for complete details).

Copy the following image files

absbot.gif	absmid.gif	baseline.gif
clipart.gif	clouds.jpg	clouds2.jpg
default.gif	ilace.gif	imagemp3.gif
lace.gif	lace2.gif	left.gif
line01.gif	line02.gif	middle.gif
pattern3.jpg	pattern4.jpg	right.gif
texttop.gif	top.gif	wallst.gif
webserve.gif	whale.gif	wire.jpg
wircblur.jpg	wirelite.jpg	wirelite.jpg
wirex.jpg	wow_cash.gif	wow_cash2.gif
zebra1.pcx		

from the \tutorial\chap04 folder on the CD-ROM to the \My Documents\My Web Pages\images folder. If the My Web Pages\images folder doesn't already exist, create it now.

Copy the map-related files

`allbtns2.gif`	`allbtns2.map`
`imagemp3.gif`	`imagemp3.map`

from the `\tutorial\chap04` folder on the CD-ROM to the `My Web Pages\maps` folder. If the `My Web Pages\maps` folder doesn't already exist, create it now.

You are now ready to begin the tutorial.

Tutorial 4A: Background Images

When it comes to using graphics to spice up a Web page, backgrounds are often the easiest to start with. There are a surprising number of different ways you can work with backgrounds. You can

➡ Add a background color

➡ Use a picture for a background

➡ Use repeating textures as background

➡ Use a single row or column of pixels to create a background

➡ Create a nonscrolling background, called a *watermark*

➡ Integrate foreground and background elements to create striking designs

Figure 4-2: Don't let your background colors clash with the text! Here, the text is only slightly darker than the background.

It is also possible to go too far with your backgrounds. The worst problem is the background that makes it difficult to read the page's text, or that conflicts with the images used on the page. Figure 4-2 shows an example of a background color that makes it difficult to read the text. In the original, the background is bright yellow and the text is bright blue. The image is actually more readable in black and white here. You may be asking yourself, "Who would use that color combination?" The truth is that such mistakes are made on the Web every day — as anyone who has browsed the Web can see for themselves. Another common Web page mistake is the busy background. The background texture in Figure 4-3 shows how easy it is to make a mess of the very same Web page.

Now that you know how to do it *wrong*, let's find out how to do it *right*.

Background (and other) colors

Internet Assistant makes it very easy to work with background colors. We've used background colors in all the sample pages so far — including Chapter 1, where the background color was included as part of the template.

To set a background color with Internet Assistant, choose FORMAT⇨BACK-GROUND AND LINKS to display the dialog box shown in Figure 4-4.

To set the background color, click the Color drop-down box in the top portion of the dialog box, and then select the color you want to use.

This dialog box also enables you to set the colors for three kinds of text found in HTML files:

Body Text
This sets the color of all normal text on your Web pages.

Figure 4-3: Background textures that fight with the text for attention can also spoil the appearance of your pages.

Hyperlink to Pages Not Yet Viewed
This sets the color of all hyperlinks that you have not yet clicked. The visitor's browser keeps track of sites visited and not visited for this to work.

Hyperlink to Pages Already Viewed
This sets the color of all hyperlinks that you have already clicked. The visitor's browser also tracks visited sites for this.

The background and text color options limit you to a fixed number of colors. HTML supports many more. To use a color other than the ones that Internet Assistant provides, however, you must use HTML markup (Chapter 7). To add a custom page background color:

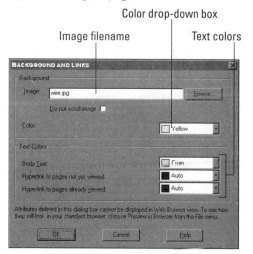

Figure 4-4: Setting the background color.

1. Set the body color of your document by selecting FORMAT⇨BACK-GROUND AND LINKS. Use any color as the background color except Auto. For this example, I used white.

2. Choose VIEW⇨HTML SOURCE to display the HTML codes for your Web page. You should see something like Figure 4-5. (Ignore that little floating palette for now; I'll get back to it shortly.) Find the line that contains the <BODY> codes. For example, it looks like the following if you chose white for a background color:

```
<BODY
BGCOLOR="#ffffff">
```

3. The funny-looking part of the BODY code — "#ffffff" — is what specifies the background color. The bad news: This is a hexadecimal code that specifies the red, green, and blue values that make up a color. The good news: You can use shareware utilities such as ColorHEX (http://firehorse.com/colorhex) to figure out the hex values for your favorite color. After you get the correct hex value, simply edit the BODY code while you are viewing the HTML source. For example, to use a background color that is a creamy off-white, change the BODY code to the following:

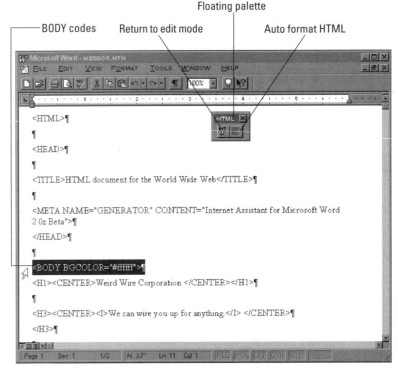

Figure 4-5: Viewing the HTML source codes for your web page.

```
<BODY
BGCOLOR="#ffffdf">
```

This reduces the amount of blue in the background from #ff (hex for 256) to #df (hex for 223). Now click the pencil icon in the floating toolbar (I said we'd get back to it; see Figure 4-5) to return to Word. You see the dialog box shown in Figure 4-6.

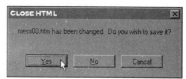

Figure 4-6: *Saving changes made in View HTML Source mode.*

4. Click OK to save the changes you made. When you view the page in your browser, you see a nice, off-white background color.

In addition to the shareware program ColorHEX, you can find many Web pages to assist you in creating a HEX string for your background color specification. Some examples are the following:

➥ http://www.dsphere.net/rgb2hex.html

➥ http://www.missouri.edu/~c588349/colormaker.html

➥ http://durandal.res.cmu.edu/~john/colorcalc.html

➥ http://www.stardot.com/~lukeseem/hexed.html

➥ http://www.imagitek.com/bcs.html

➥ http://www.users.interport.net/~giant/COLOR/hype_color.html

The other button in the floating toolbar autoformats your HTML document. This can be handy if you know a little HTML, because it makes HTML code easier to work with. Figure 4-7 shows what formatted HTML looks like. You can't see the colors in the black-and-white image, but I've noted in the image which portions of HTML code get which colors. HTML tags, for example, are in red, and values you enter (such as that **"ffffff"** for the BODY color) are in light blue. Because different kinds of HTML commands appear in different colors, it's easier to interpret what you see.

It is easier to diagnose HTML problems if you can see the various kinds of HTML codes in different colors. You learn much more about HTML codes and how to work with them in the section "View HTML Source mode," in Chapter 7.

Background pictures

You use the same method to add a picture to your page background: Select FORMAT➪BACKGROUND AND LINKS. Look again at Figure 4-4. Notice that the first text box at the top of the dialog box is sitting there, waiting for the name of an image file. You can click the Browse button to look for images on your hard disk.

Red for HTML tags   Floating toolbar

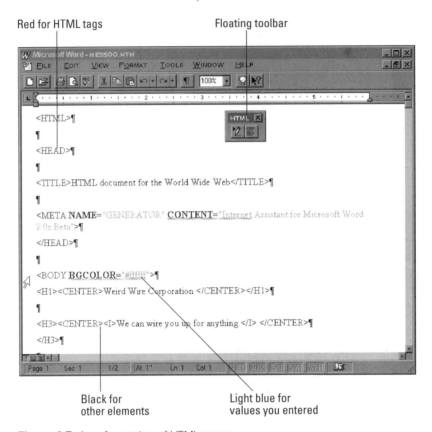

Black for
other elements

Light blue for
values you entered

Figure 4-7: Auto-formatting of HTML source.

When you set up the tutorials for this chapter, you copied an HTML file to \My Documents\My Web Pages folder. Open the file mess01.htm in Word (choose FILE⇨OPEN); you see the same page shown earlier in Figure 4-3. Let's use a different background picture to correct the problems presented in this Web page — a background that is far too busy.

The image of a bundle of wire, used for the background, competes with the foreground text and images so that the eye has a difficult time deciding what is what. One quick solution is to simply remove the background image. A better solution is to retain the wire image in some fashion — this is, after all, a Web page for a company that makes wire products!

For a Web page designer, two possible solutions come to mind:

➡ Change the wire image so that it acts like a background.

➡ Use a wire image as a logo, and use a plain, colored background.

There are several tricks you can use to convert an image like the wire bundle into a suitable background. To use these tricks, however, you need an *image-editing program*. One excellent image editor is Adobe Photoshop, and there are several shareware paint programs that also have the power to work magic on a background, such as Paint Shop Pro. If you have a paint program that supports filters, you can use the filters to change the character of the background image so that it does, in fact, visually appear to be in the background.

A *blur filter* applied to the wire bundle image, shown in Figure 4-8, is moderately effective in transforming the image into a true background image. Blurring is commonly used in photographic backgrounds for exactly this reason. Blurring also creates a slight 3D effect, which can add pizzazz to an otherwise ordinary Web page. Blurring by itself isn't the solution, however. The image is still too dark to be truly effective as a background, even with the light text.

Figure 4-8: Blurring improves the image for use as a background.

Lightening the image, shown in Figure 4-9, is somewhat effective. I also changed the text from light to dark. Unfortunately, even though the background is lighter, the crisp details intrude on the readability of the text.

Figure 4-9: Lightening the image also improves the background.

The most effective result comes from applying both filters, as shown in Figure 4-10. The combination of blurring (to send the image truly into the background) and lightening (to reduce visual competition with the text) gets the job done effectively.

Figure 4-10: A combination of lightening and blurring does the best job.

The methods at your disposal for changing potential background images into real background images varies with the image-editing software you use. For example, with Photoshop, I was able to add a creative twist to the wire bundle background (see Figure 4-11). I applied a filter to crystallize the image, then I brightened the image and reduced contrast. I added a slight 3D texture with the Lighting filter, and then added a blur to move the result

Figure 4-11: Creative use of filters can create imaginative backgrounds.

Figure 4-12: A texture with obvious repeating boundaries.

Figure 4-13: A texture without obvious boundaries.

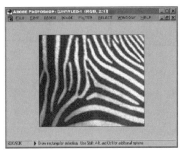

Figure 4-14: This is the image to be converted into a repeating pattern.

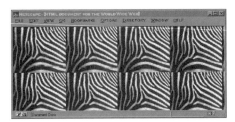

Figure 4-15: Edges of the tiles do not match.

firmly into the background. Your imagination is the only limitation with the more powerful image-editing programs.

Repeating textures

Most browsers repeat (or *tile*) the background image if the background image is smaller than the window size. Because large files take longer to download, you usually will want to use fairly small image files for your textures. In most cases, you can improve the appearance of the texture if the boundaries between tiles are not visible. Figure 4-12 shows a repeating texture with obvious boundaries between tiles, and Figure 4-13 shows the same texture changed to remove the boundary problem. In this section, you learn how to smooth the boundaries between tiles by using Adobe Photoshop.

The wire bundle texture used earlier is not a repeating texture. This wasn't a critical problem, though, because the images blended together reasonably well. However, a keen eye can pick out the boundary. In many cases, though, you want to avoid showing the boundary between tiles of the background image. There are two techniques you can use to create seamless tiles:

➡ Copy from one edge of the tile to another, and then blend.

➡ Use software specifically designed to create tiles.

Copy and blend

Let's see how you can create a tile by using the copy-and-blend technique in Adobe Photoshop. This basic technique also works in other image-editing programs that offer similar tools.

 Photoshop is not included on the CD-ROM that comes with the book. If you do not have Photoshop already installed, you cannot do this part of the tutorial.

Figure 4-14 shows the starting image for this exercise: a swatch of zebra hide, extracted from a photo of a zebra in the Digital Stock clip art collection. If we tile this image (see Figure 4-15), the borders between the tiles are completely obvious — the edges of the image simply do not line up.

To create a tile in Photoshop, we edit the image so that the edges match —
top to bottom, left to right. Follow these steps if you own a copy of Photoshop
(they assume a basic working knowledge of Photoshop):

1. Load the image `zebra1.pcx` into Photoshop. The image was copied
    to your `\My Documents\My Web Pages` folder when you set up for
    this tutorial. Choose SELECT⇔ALL to select the entire image. Then use
    the rectangular selection tool while pressing the Ctrl key to remove
    the center portion of the image from the selection. This leaves only
    the border of the image selected (the area between the two dotted
    lines in Figure 4-16).

The image itself
determines how
much of the center
portion of the image
you should remove
from the selection. If
the details in the
image are small,
you only need a
narrow border area
for blending. If the
image has large
details, you need a
wider border area for
blending. If you are
unsure, experiment
with different border
widths to see what
works best.

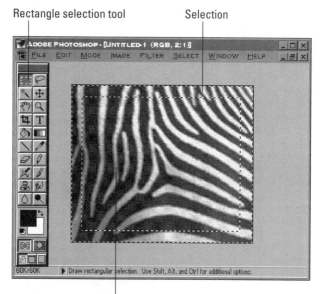

Figure 4-16: Only the edge of the image is selected.

2. We now can modify this
    selection, but you need to
    use this exact same selec-
    tion again. Save the selec-
    tion by choosing
    SELECT⇔SAVE SELECTION.
    This action displays the
    dialog box shown in Figure
    4-17; click OK to save it.

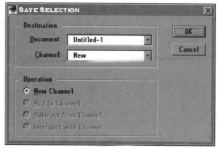

Figure 4-17: Saving a selection for later use.

3. Using the Lasso tool while you hold down the Alt and Ctrl keys, remove all but the top edge of the selection, as shown in Figure 4-18. Notice that I made the left and right edges of the selection beveled, so that no part of the left or right borders are included as part of the selection. Copy the result to the Clipboard (Ctrl+C), and then paste it into the image (Ctrl+V). Figure 4-19 shows the result.

Lasso tool   Selection

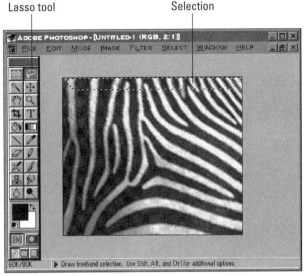

Figure 4-18: Modifying the selection.

Selection

Figure 4-19: Copying the edge of the image and pasting it.

TIP Holding down the Alt key enables you to click points along a path with the Lasso tool. Without the Alt key, the Lasso tool draws a selection. Holding down the Ctrl key enables you to remove portions of a selection; holding down the Shift key enables you to add to a selection. See the Photoshop documentation for complete details on use of the Lasso tool.

4. The selection you just pasted will become the bottom border of the image. First, however, flip the selection vertically by choosing IMAGE⇨FLIP⇨ VERTICAL, and then drag the selection to the bottom edge of the overall image (see Figure 4-20).

5. Load the selection you saved earlier, by choosing SELECT⇨ LOAD SELECTION. This choice displays the dialog box shown in Figure 4-21. Because you have only one saved selection, click OK to load it. (The entire image border is once again selected.)

Selection

Figure 4-20: The selection has been flipped and moved into position.

6. Use the Lasso tool while holding down the Alt and Ctrl keys to remove all but the left edge of the selection, creating a smaller selection, as shown in Figure 4-22. Figure 4-22 shows clearly why we used a beveled selection; this new selection matches the edge of the first selection perfectly, and there is no overlap.

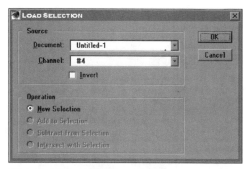

Figure 4-21: Loading a selection.

Figure 4-22: Select just the left edge of the border.

7. Copy the selection to the Clip-board, and then paste it into the image. Choose IMAGE⇨FLIP⇨ HORIZONTAL to flip the selection from left to right, and then move it to the right edge of the image, as shown in Figure 4-23.

8. So far, everything we have done is merely preparation. The top and bottom edges now match, and the right and left edges now match, but those edges don't match the middle portion of the image at all! It's time to use a little magic, in the form of the Photoshop Blend tool. The Blend tool enables you to drag color from one part of an image into an adjoining part. Click SELECT⇨NONE to paint anywhere in the image. (Photoshop only lets you paint in the current selection if a selection exists.) Now use the Blend tool to modify the edges of the former selections to remove the harsh, linear boundary between the middle of the image and the edges.

Figure 4-23: The right edge of the image now matches the left edge.

Figures 4-24 through 4-26 show three steps in this process. Your work need not look identical to these examples. In fact, feel free to experiment with the Blend tool to create any degree of blending that suits your eye. To save the file as a GIF file, choose FILE⇨EXPORT⇨GIF 89A. Save the image interlaced (click the Interlaced checkbox), without transparency (click OK when you see the Transparency dialog box), with the filename `zebra1.gif`.

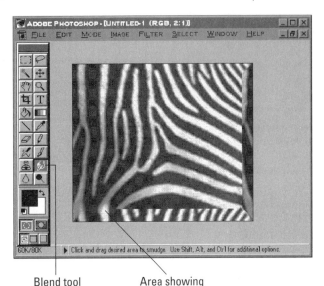

To see what the image looks like tiled, create a new HTML document, and use the file you created, `zebra1.gif`, as a background. You can also view the files `zebra1.htm` and `zebra2.htm` (found in the `\My Documents\My Web Pages` folder) in your browser. Figure 4-27 shows the result when you tile the image. You can still tell that the pattern repeats, but the harsh edges between tiles are completely missing. This version, in fact, gives the appearance of an undulating 3D surface. If you want a more smoothly blended tile, with less apparent repetition, simply use a wider border when you begin the process.

Blend tool   Area showing blending

Figure 4-24: First stage in blending at lower left.

Figure 4-25: The entire bottom edge is blended.

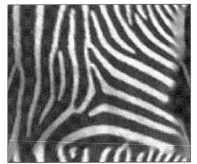

Figure 4-26: The left and right edges are blended now.

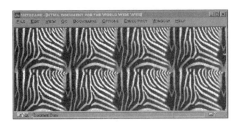

Figure 4-27: Tiling the zebra-skin image.

You can create repeating background textures from almost any image by using this technique, and many image-editing programs give you the tools you need to create tiles. This tutorial was specific to Photoshop, but you should be able to duplicate the process (with minor modifications) with any competent image editor.

Software for creating tiles: Painter

One of the most powerful image-editing programs available is Fractal Design Painter. Version 4.0 includes not only a host of dazzling features, but full support for working with Web images (more about that later).

Painter is not included on the CD-ROM that comes with the book. If you do not have Painter already installed, you cannot do this part of the tutorial.

To create a tile in Painter, we will define an image as a tile, and then use Painter's natural media tools to paint the pattern. Follow these steps:

1. Open a new file in Painter, 256 pixels wide by 256 pixels high (see Figure 4-28). Notice that Painter uses a number of floating palettes to give you access to its features. During this mini-tutorial, you use the Art Materials palette and the Brushes palette.

2. To convert the image into a pattern, click the Pattern menu in the Art Materials palette (see Figure 4-29). Click the DEFINE PATTERN menu selection. You don't see any difference, but the image file is now a pattern file. This means that, when you paint or draw in the image, your brush automatically wraps around the top/bottom and left/right borders.

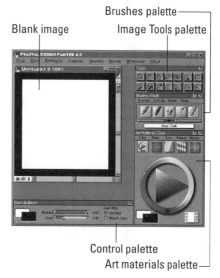

Brushes palette
Blank image   Image Tools palette

Control palette
Art materials palette

Figure 4-28: Opening a file in Painter.

3. Paint a flower by using Painter's tools. I used the Chalk, Pencil, and Pastel brushes to create the flower shown in Figure 4-30. Be careful not to let your work reach the edges of the image.

4. Now let's create a pattern behind the flower to illustrate the clever way that Painter wraps your brush strokes. Figure 4-31 shows some curling, diagonal lines that I drew. Notice that only the background is selected (note the selection boundary in Figure 4-31). This makes it easy to avoid spoiling the flower with the diagonal lines.

   Figure 4-32 shows the completed pattern, with red dots added for fun. I didn't add a dot in every open space. Because Painter is automatically wrapping brushstrokes, the top/bottom and left/right edges meet, and dots should only be placed in the center of each open area. If this doesn't seem clear right now, you'll understand during the next step.

Figure 4-29: Changing the image into a pattern.

Figure 4-30: Painting a flower with Painter's tools.

Diagonal lines　　　　　Selection boundary

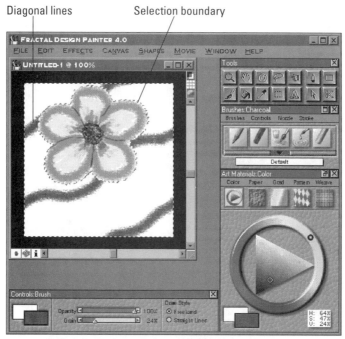

Figure 4-31: Adding lines to the drawing.

Figure 4-32: Adding more design elements.

5. To see how neatly Painter has turned the image into a pattern, click in the Tools palette on the Grabber tool (shaped like an open hand). Hold down the Shift key while you drag in the image window to slide the image aside. Instead of moving outside the window, the image wraps perfectly (see Figure 4-33).

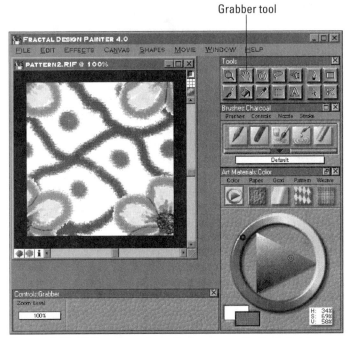

Figure 4-33: Sliding the pattern displays how effectively Painter controls the edges of the pattern.

You can, if you want, use Painter's vast array of painting tools and special effects to modify the pattern. Figure 4-34 shows the pattern modified to appear three-dimensional, and Figure 4-35 shows a sample Web page using a lighter, softer version of the pattern.

In addition to creating your own background textures, you can use clip art collections, many of which contain textures that can work well as a background. Clip art is covered later in this chapter. When using any background, remember to verify that it does, indeed, behave like a background. If the background competes with the text for attention, it's probably in need of some lightening, blurring, or some other technique to tone it down.

Both Painter and Photoshop include a ton of features that go beyond what I've shown here. If you are serious about Web images, you can't find better software than these two products. Each complements the other, giving you an impressive range of features.

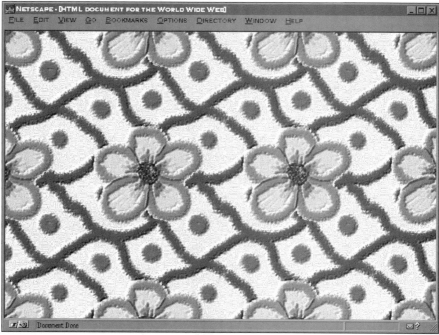

Figure 4-34: A 3-D version of the pattern.

Figure 4-35: A Web page that uses a lighter version of the pattern.

Lines and columns

Because browsers simply repeat (tile) an image used for a background, you can play some tricks with creatively shaped image files. For example, you can create an image that is just one pixel wide or high, and use it as a background. Consider an image just one pixel high, and 1,024 pixels wide. If you apply a graduated fill to the image, you'll get a graduated fill across the Web page. Figure 4-36 shows a one-pixel-high image, and Figure 4-37 shows a page that uses the image as a background.

Figure 4-36: An image file made up of a single row of pixels.

When you put a solid color near the left edge, as shown in Figure 4-38, it's important to make sure that text will not compete with the block of color. I used the Blockquote style to move the "normal" paragraphs away from the left margin, and I used a table with a blank first column to force the bulleted list even farther from the left margin.

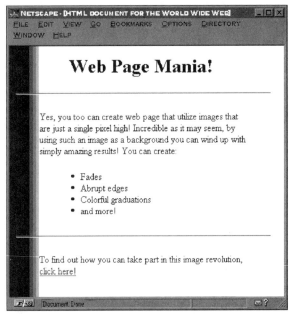

Figure 4-37: A Web page using the image from Figure 4-36 as a background image.

To force the empty left column of the table to actually eat up space, you must click TABLE⇨ CELL WIDTH AND SPAC- ING to turn on WYSIWYG support.

You can also use images made up of a single column to create a Web page. Figure 4-39 shows such an image, and Figure 4-40 shows a Web page using the image as a background.

Blockquote style

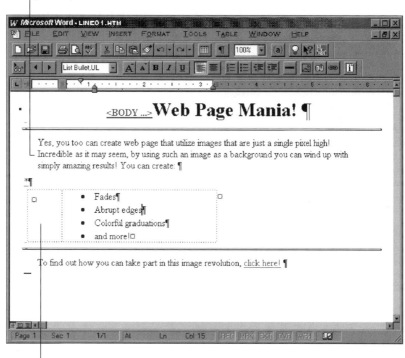

Table with blank
first column

Figure 4-38: Using formatting to control the left margin.

Figure 4-39: An image file made up of a single row of pixels.

It is the small file size of these single-row, single-column images that makes them ideal for a background. You can take the idea a step farther and use just a few pixels of width or height to create more interesting patterns, while still keeping the file size small. Figure 4-41 shows an example of such a background image. When the colored portion of the image is this wide, all the text on the page must be in a table — the Blockquote style simply can't move the text far enough from the left margin. Figure 4-42 shows how I used fixed-width table cells to keep the page under control. Note that the text below the bottom horizontal rule is in a separate table.

Figure 4-40: A Web page using the image from Figure 4-39 as a background image.

Image height

Figure 4-41: Using an image 1,024 pixels wide by 64 pixels high to create a more interesting background pattern.

Blank first column

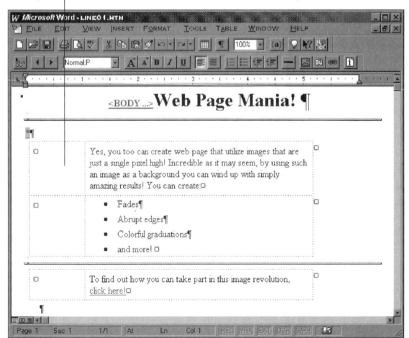

Figure 4-42: Using tables to control text placement.

Watermarks

Internet Assistant supports a slight variation on the background theme: *nonscrolling* backgrounds. This kind of background is also referred to as a **watermark**. As of the date this book is being written, however, only Microsoft's Internet Explorer browser supports nonscrolling backgrounds. This may change; check the documentation or help file for your favorite browser to see whether it supports watermarks.

 Originally, a watermark was an embossed mark applied to paper, usually to show the name or symbol of the manufacturer.

Like a standard background, a watermark is a repeating pattern. The only difference is that the background image does not scroll even when the text on the page does scroll. Figure 4-43 shows a Web watermark that looks like — you guessed it: a real-life watermark. The "W" and the "R" stand out because they have deeper shadows in the original artwork. Some time and effort with Photoshop would be needed to smooth this out.

Watermark

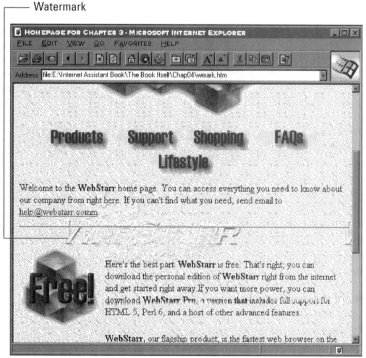

Figure 4-43: An example of a watermark.

Page samples

I have included a number of files on the CD-ROM that illustrate the various situations described in this chapter. Some of those files have already been mentioned. Table 4-1 is a complete list of these files, including the filename and what the file is intended to illustrate. All the files were copied to your hard disk when you set up for the chapter earlier.

Table 4-1	CD-ROM Files for Chapter 4
Insert File	**Contents**
blur01.htm	Uses a blurred background image
both01.htm	Uses a blurred and lightened background image
clouds.htm	Illustrates a pattern without edge correction
clouds2.htm	Illustrates a pattern with edge correction
hyperimg.htm	Uses a small file as a hyperlink to a larger version
ilace.htm	Displays interlacing of a large image
line01.htm	Demonstrates use of a one-pixel-wide image as a background
line02.htm	Demonstrates use of a one-pixel-high image as a background
pastel.htm	Demonstrates use of a custom color for a background
mess01.htm	Illustrates the hazards of a dark, unblurred background image
mess02.htm	Illustrates the hazards of clashing text and background colors
pattern2.htm	Shows an example of a patterned background
pattern3.htm	Same pattern as pattern2.htm, but made much lighter
test.htm	An example of a transparent image
transp.htm	Another example of image transparency
bkg.htm	Illustrates the benefits of a light, blurred background
zebra1.htm	Uncorrected tile of zebra skin
zebra2.htm	Zebra skin tile with edges corrected so that they match properly

Tutorial 4B: Images on the Page

HTML supports a limited number of options for putting images on the page. You've already seen in Chapter 3 how Internet Assistant lets you define where on the page an image should appear. In that example, you used the Options tab of the Picture dialog box to set the Alignment with Text to the value Right. Let's see what else we can do with the Picture dialog box.

Table 4-2 lists settings for Alignment with Text that the Options tab gives you.

Table 4-2	Alignment with Text Options	
Setting	**HTML Code**	**Description**
Default	none	This setting results in no ALIGN parameter in the HTML file. The image is positioned in the default location according to whatever browser is used. This usually is the baseline of the current text line.
Left	ALIGN=LEFT	Creates a left-aligned, floating image. Text flows to the right of the image, wrapping around it.
Right	ALIGN=RIGHT	Creates a right-aligned, floating image. Text flows to the left of the image, wrapping around it.
Top	ALIGN=TOP	The top of the image is aligned with the top of the tallest item in the line. This can be the largest font, or another image.
TextTop	ALIGN=TEXTTOP	The top of the image is aligned with the top of the tallest *text* in the line.
Middle	ALIGN=MIDDLE	The middle of the image is aligned with the baseline of the text in the line.
AbsMiddle	ALIGN=ABSMIDDLE	The middle of the image is aligned with the middle of the text in the line.
Baseline	ALIGN=BASELINE	Same as Bottom. The bottom of the image is aligned with the baseline of the text in the line. The baseline does not include any descenders (that is, the tail of the letter "y").
Bottom	ALIGN=BOTTOM	Same as Baseline. The bottom of the image is aligned with the baseline of the text in the line.
AbsBottom	ALIGN=ABSBOTTOM	The bottom of the image is aligned with the actual bottom of the text in the line. For example, if the text has a "y" in it, the image will be aligned with the bottom of the "y."

Figure 4-44: A Web page with numerous examples of image alignment.

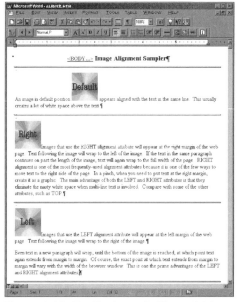

Figure 4-45: The file shown in Figure 4-44 as seen in Word. Note the differences from Figure 4-44.

If you need more precise image locations than these options provide, you probably will have to make creative use of tables to position your images.

Figure 4-44 shows a portion of a Web page that includes images of every type listed in Table 4-2. To create this page yourself, open the file `align.htm` in Word. This file was copied to the `\My Documents\My Web Pages` folder during chapter setup. Figure 4-45 shows what this file looks like in Word. Generally speaking, Word seldom aligns an image the way it appears on a Web page in your favorite browser.

To add the image to this file (yes, they were also copied during setup!), drag to select the bold text entries of the form **Image images\xxxxx.gif**, where `xxxxx.gif` is the filename of the image. Load the named image, which deletes the text you selected and inserts the image.

For example, the second such text is **Image images\right.gif**. Delete the bold text, then click the Add Picture tool on the Formatting toolbar, and use the Browse button to locate the image file in the `\My Documents\My Web Pages\images` folder. Click the Options tab and then set Alignment with Text to Right. Click OK to load the image. Repeat for all images. You might want to spend a little time reading the text that describes each alignment setting. I've included some tips and suggestions you may find helpful when using these attributes.

I encourage you to experiment with the results in several different browsers. You will probably discover that there is a surprising variation in how the browsers interpret these various alignment settings. For example, Navigator 2.0 does not distinguish at all between the BOTTOM and ABSBOTTOM attributes, whereas Internet Explorer properly displays both.

Image Tricks and Tips

Images you see on the Web take time to download. The time spent waiting often seems to exceed the time spent actually viewing and using Web pages. There are some things you can do to reduce the frustration of waiting for images to download. **Interlacing** enables the image to start displaying immediately, for example. You can also display a small version of your images, and allow visitors to view a larger version by using a hyperlink.

You can use **transparency** in your images. In the first three chapters, we used images that had backgrounds the same color as the page color. You can also create transparent images that look great against *any* page color.

Interlacing

If you have spent time on the Internet, you have probably already encountered interlaced images. When an image is not interlaced, it appears very slowly from the top down. When an image is interlaced, a rough-looking version of the image appears quickly, and then the image details are filled in. Figure 4-46 shows several stages in the loading of an interlaced image.

Figure 4-46: An interlaced image starts out rough (left) and fills in details as it loads (center, right).

Interlacing is a feature of the GIF file format. Other file formats, such as bitmaps (BMP files), do not offer this feature. A regular image file stores information in the same order in which you view it: from the top down. When the file is downloaded over the Net, it is displayed by the browser as it is received: from the top down. An interlaced image file stores the information in a different way. The data for the top line of pixels is stored first, then the data for the fifth line of pixels, then the ninth, and so on. This continues to the bottom of the image. Then the data for the third line, then the seventh line, and so forth. Finally, the data for the second, fourth, sixth, eighth, and so on, lines is downloaded to complete the image.

But you don't need to worry about the details. The work of storing files in interlaced form is a job for an image editor or a utility program. In Photoshop, for example, you simply click the Interlace checkbox to indicate that you want the GIF file saved in interlaced format (see Figure 4-47). Fractal Design Painter also offers a checkbox, along with other useful Web-oriented image features (more about that later, in the section on transparency). The shareware program SnapShot/32, included on the CD-ROM, also enables you to interlace GIF images.

If you haven't already installed SnapShot/32, do so now. See Appendix A for information.

Interlace checkbox

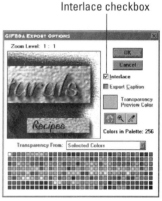

Figure 4-47: Saving a GIF file in Photoshop.

Load the image file `\My Documents\My Web Pages\images\lace.gif` into SnapShot/32 by choosing FILE⇨LOAD. This file was copied to your hard disk as part of the setup for this chapter. To make the image interlaced, choose FILE⇨SAVE AS to display the dialog box shown in Figure 4-48. Type the filename **ilace.gif** as the new name, and verify that you are saving it in the folder `\My Documents\My Web Pages\images`. (If necessary, navigate to the correct folder.) Click the Options button, which displays the dialog box shown in Figure 4-49. Click the Interlaced checkbox, click OK, and then click OK again. The file is saved in interlaced format.

To see the effect of interlacing, you must create an HTML file that uses the interlaced image. Create a new HTML document in Word, then add the image you created as an image (select INSERT⇨PICTURE). Save the file, and then preview it in a browser. You can also load the file `\My Documents\My WebPages\ilace.htm` into a browser. In either case, the interlaced file loads quickly from your hard disk, so you need to watch carefully to see the interlacing effect while the image loads. I deliberately made the image large (much larger than you would for a real Web page!) so that it takes longer to load, and you have a better chance to see the interlacing effect. If you use the ilace.htm example, note that the file contains transparent colors (the blue background shows through the lace).

Filename

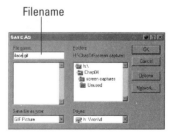

Figure 4-48: Saving a GIF file as interlaced in SnapShot/32.

If you use a different image editor, check the documentation or help file for information about saving GIF files in interlaced form.

Interlaced checkbox

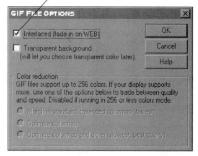

Figure 4-49: Setting the interlaced option in SnapShot/32.

 As this chapter is being written, a new JPG format offering interlaced support is just coming into use. Other file formats may also join the interlacing game. Until a wide spectrum of browsers supports interlacing for other file formats, however, stick with GIF files.

Transparency

Transparency enables you to specify a color that is transparent when a GIF file is loaded onto a Web page. You have probably seen many Web images that use the transparency feature. Figure 4-50 shows an example of transparency. (These images are the same ones shown as samples of clip art in Chapter 1.) The image on the left shows the image without transparency, and the image on the right shows it with transparency.

To create an image that uses transparency, you need a background color that surrounds the main content of the image. The background color does not have to be white; it can be any color.

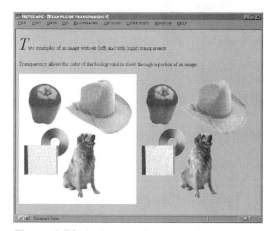

Figure 4-50: An image using transparency.

 Whatever color you use for the background, be careful never to use that color in the body of the image! For example, if you use black for the background, and have black pixels in the image, every black pixel becomes transparent. This can destroy the appearance of your image.

If you create your image by using a true-color image editor (that is, 24-bit color), be especially careful when you convert from 24-bit color to the 8-bit color supported by the GIF file format. Because the image editor picks the colors for the 8-bit image, there is always a chance that the color you chose for the background will wind up somewhere in your image.

Here's how to create image transparency with three different programs:

Photoshop: Photoshop comes with an export filter that supports both transparency and interlacing. To save a file as a GIF file, first convert the image to 8-bit color, then choose FILE⇨EXPORT⇨GIF 89A to display the dialog box shown in Figure 4-51. Select interlacing (you'll want interlacing for almost every GIF file), then click the background of the image to identify the color you want to use as the transparent color. Figure 4-51 shows the transparent color already selected. A heavier black outline around the palette color shows which color is transparent, and the original color (white) has been replaced with a medium gray. With Photoshop, you can define more than one color as the transparent color. When you click OK to save the file, Photoshop changes all the colors you selected to be transparent into a single color (that same medium gray), and marks the color as transparent by adding the heavy black outline. This means that the file will look different the next time you load it into an image editor! Figure 4-52 shows the image from Figure 4-51 in an image editor.

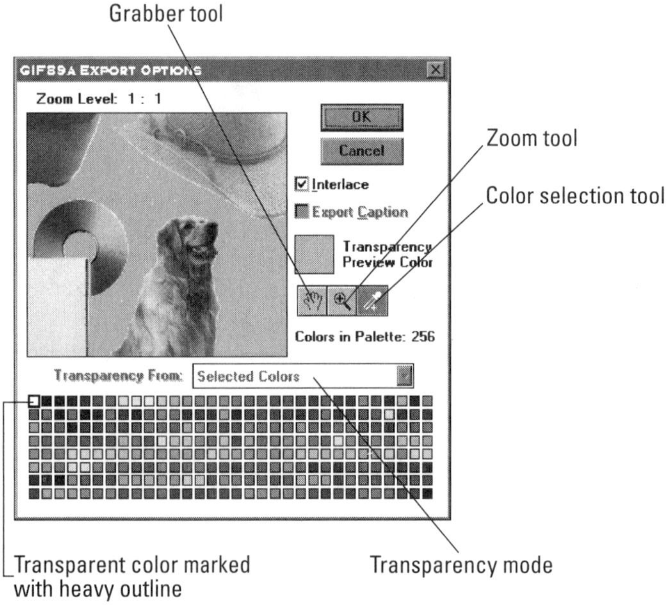

Grabber tool

Zoom tool

Color selection tool

Transparent color marked with heavy outline

Transparency mode

Figure 4-51: The Photoshop dialog box for exporting GIF files.

Figure 4-52: Figure 4-51 after adding transparent colors, viewed in an image editor.

Painter: You have to work a bit harder to get transparency in an image created with Painter. Painter's masking tools are very powerful, and the result can be worth the effort when you are dealing with a complex image. Figure 4-53 shows an image loaded into Painter (yes, that's the image for WebStarr Server Edition, from Chapter 3). I selected EDIT⇨MAGIC WAND, and then I clicked the magic wand in the background area of the image. You can't see it clearly in black and white, but all the white colors in the image are shown as red — they are a Painter mask. When you are working on an image, the mask defines those portions of the image that will be affected. Areas outside the mask cannot be changed. Note that the Value slider in the Magic Want dialog box has been changed to include not just pure white, but also several off-white shades.

TIP To make sure that *all* white areas are part of the mask, I used the Rectangle selection tool to first select the entire image.

Typically, this technique selects more than you want to select. Fortunately, Painter allows you to edit the mask. Click the Path List icon at the top of the Objects palette to display the mask paths (see Figure 4-54). Click to select paths that should not be part of the mask, and delete them by clicking the Clear button in the Objects palette. You can check which paths to delete by visually inspecting the image after each deletion — if you make a mistake, press Ctrl+Z to undo, and move on to the next path.

TIP If you create a mask that covers those areas of the image you *don't* want to make transparent, choose EDIT⇨MASK⇨INVERT MASK now.

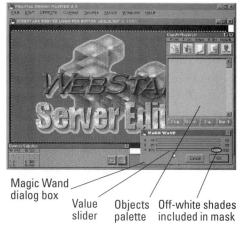

Magic Wand dialog box — Value slider — Objects palette — Off-white shades included in mask

Figure 4-53: *Selecting an image area with the Magic Wand.*

Path list

Selection boundary — Clear button

Figure 4-54: *Deleting extra paths in the mask.*

After the mask is set correctly, choose FILE⇨SAVE AS to open the Save dialog box. Select GIF as the file type, add a filename, and click the Save button to display the dialog box shown in Figure 4-55. This dialog box enables you to set the properties for the GIF file. You can set the number of colors for the file (fewer colors means smaller files, but check the results with the Preview button!), whether to interlace the file, how to convert from 24-bit color (Imaging Method), and transparency options. There are even settings for creating a MAP file (see Tutorial 4C for information). For most GIF files, the settings shown in Figure 4-55 are optimal.

Figure 4-56 shows what the file looks like when you press the Preview Data button. Figure 4-57 shows the file in an actual Web page, viewed with the Netscape browser.

Number of colors
Transparency
checkbox
Dithering

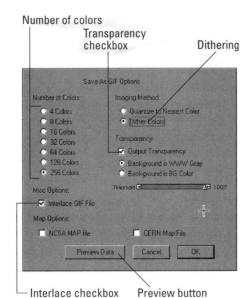

Interlace checkbox   Preview button

Figure 4-55: Setting properties for a GIF file in Painter.

Transparent area

Figure 4-56: The Painter preview of the image transparency.

Figure 4-57: Transparency demonstrated on a Web page.

TIP Note that there is a light fringe around the drop shadow behind the text *Server Edition*. The image originally had a white background, and the Web page uses a gray background. If you plan to use any kind of gradation or drop shadow, always create the image on a background similar to the color you plan for the Web page background.

SnapShot/32: Load the image you saved earlier, `ilace.gif`, into SnapShot/32. Click FILE⇨SAVE AS to open the Save As dialog box, and then confirm that the filename is `ilace.gif`. Click the Options button to display the GIF File Options dialog box. Click to turn on the checkmark for Transparency. Click OK, and then click Save. This action changes the cursor to a crosshair, and the title of the SnapShot/32 window changes to a prompt telling you to click the image to select a transparent color (see Figure 4-58). When you click a color, SnapShot/32 shows you the color and asks you to confirm your choice. After you confirm by clicking OK, the file is saved.

Many other image editors support transparency for GIF images. Check the documentation or help files for information on how to save with transparency when using your favorite image editor.

Crosshair cursor

Figure 4-58: Selecting a transparent color in SnapShot/32.

Sizing

Internet Assistant supports a feature of HTML that enables you to specify the size of an image. Modern browsers use this feature to reserve space for the complete image. If you do not specify the image's size, the browser doesn't reserve space for the image, and the browser has to rearrange the Web page after downloading each image. This results in a very messy page download, from the reader's point of view. Figure 4-59 shows a page after the text has been downloaded, and before the images are downloaded. No size data was included for the images. When size information is included, space is reserved for each image right from the start (see Figure 4-60).

Adding image size data to a picture reference in Word requires an extra step, but it is well worth it when you consider that the result is a page that looks more professional to your visitors. To add size information, click the Options tab whenever you insert a picture. Enter the height and width of the image in the appropriate text boxes.

Image size info
used for layout

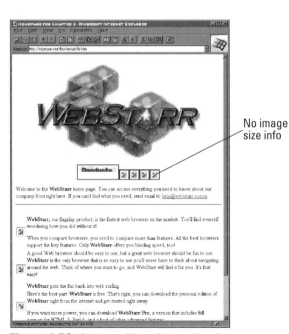

No image
size info

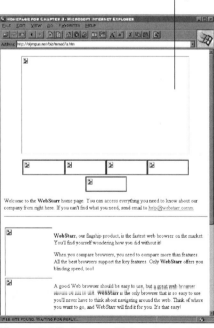

Figure 4-59: A page without image size data.

Figure 4-60: A page with image size data.

Image with hyperlink

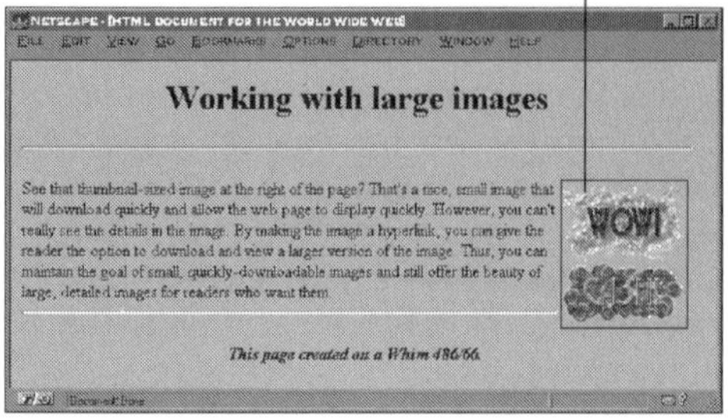

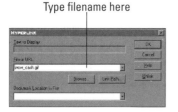

Figure 4-61: *A page with a small version of a picture on it. The border indicates a hyperlink.*

You can also use size information to cause the browser to display images in a size other than actual size. If you do this to display a smaller-than-life-size representation, however, the browser must still download the entire file — you might as well display it life size. If you use this feature to display a larger representation, the pixelation that results may make the image visually unappealing — the image's pixels will appear enlarged, and the edges will be jagged. As a general rule, it is usually not advisable to display an image at other than its actual size.

Hyperlinks

Type filename here

Figure 4-62: *The filename in the File or URL text box points.*

Because it takes time to download image files for a page, you usually will include small images on your Web pages. If the image is important, you can create a hyperlink that downloads a larger version of the image with a click from the user. The hyperlink simply provides a path and filename for the location of the larger image on the Web server.

The buttons you work with in Chapter 1 show how to create a picture-based hyperlink. Those hyperlinks point to other Web pages. You can also point to a file with a hyperlink. When the reader clicks the hyperlink, his or her browser either downloads the file to disk (if the file is an .exe file), or downloads the file and displays it (if the file is an image file). This is completely automatic. All you need to do is specify which file is to be downloaded.

For example, if you have a small version of a picture on a page (see Figure 4-61), you can select the picture in Word, click the Add Hyperlink tool, and supply a filename for a larger version of the picture in the File or URL text box (see Figure 4-62). If the image is in a subfolder, be sure to include the full relative path name!

The picture appears with a border in a browser, indicating that it is a hyperlink. When the reader clicks the picture, most browsers show the larger image on a page by itself (see Figure 4-63).

Figure 4-63: *Hyperlinks to image files result in a page with only the larger image displayed.*

Tutorial 4C: Image Maps

Image maps are images that contain **hot spots**. When you click a hot spot, a hyperlink is executed. You can use any kind of hyperlink — jump to another Web page, display a picture, download a file, and so on. Figure 4-64 shows an example of the kind of image that is perfect for an image map. It contains a group of buttons at the right of the image, and each one can be a hot spot with its own hyperlink.

Buttons

Figure 4-64: An image that is typical of those used for an image map.

Although it is possible to create an image map by hand, it is vastly simpler to create an image map by using software designed for that purpose. I have included the program MapTHIS! on the CD-ROM. MapTHIS! uses the following steps to create an image map:

➥ Load an existing GIF image

➥ Draw hot spots (circles, rectangles, free-form polygons, and so forth)

➥ Attach a hyperlink to each hot spot

➥ Save the results in a `.map` file

Both the map file and the image file are then placed on the server. There are several options (called *conventions*) for MAP files, and you need to contact your Web administrator to find out which convention your Web server uses. See the later section, "The Conventions," for details.

To place an image map in your Web page with Word and Internet Assistant, use the Add Picture tool in the normal manner. Click the tool, browse to find the image, and then click the Options tab. There is a checkbox labeled Image Is a Sensitive Map. Click to set this checkbox to on, and then click OK to save the changes. Clicking the checkbox adds the HTML code `ISMAP` to the image in the HTML file. This tells the browser that the image has an associated map file. To add the name of the map file, select the image you just added and then click the Add Hyperlink tool. Enter the name (and path, if appropriate) of the MAP file in the File or URL text box. Click OK to save the change.

To make management of MAP files easier, I recommend that you place the GIF for the map, and the MAP file itself, in a folder reserved for map files. This folder should be different from that containing other image files. If you used the automatic setup feature of the software supplied with this book, you already have a `map` subfolder of your `\My Documents\My Web Page` folder.

Let's create a typical server-based image map to illustrate how MapTHIS! works, and then we'll use a clever feature of MapTHIS! to create an image map for the Web page you created in Chapter 3.

Server-based image maps

A server-based image map has a MAP file that resides on the Web server. This is the most common form of image map. New versions of some browsers (such as Netscape 2.0), include support for client-based maps, and these are covered in the next section.

Tools

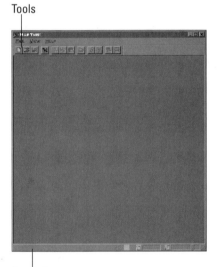

Status bar

Figure 4-65: The opening window of MapTHIS!

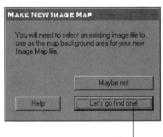

Click here
to continue

Figure 4-66: MapTHIS! is full of cute messages like this.

 If you have not already installed the MapTHIS! software from the CD-ROM, now is the time to do it. See Appendix A for information on installing MapThis!

Begin by double-clicking the MapTHIS! icon. The opening window of the program is shown in Figure 4-65. Click FILE⇨NEW to start a new map file.

You cannot start a new map file by opening a GIF file; you must click FILE⇨NEW.

When you create a new file for the first time, you see the cute dialog box shown in Figure 4-66. MapTHIS! is freeware (there is no shareware fee you have to pay to use it), and, judging from the number of exclamation points in the name, dialog boxes, and help file, the author clearly had fun creating the software. To continue, click the Let's Go Find One! button. Locate the file \My Documents\My Web Pages\maps\imagemp3.gif and load it. This is a relatively large image. Maximize the child window that contains the image, and adjust the size of the MapTHIS! window so that you can see all of the image (see Figure 4-67).

The main tools you use for creating and editing hot spots are shown in Figure 4-67. For this exercise, you create hot spots for each of the five buttons located at the right of the image. To create a rectangular hot spot, click the Rectangle tool, then drag over the outline of the first button, Recipes (see Figure 4-68). Notice that the cursor changes to the shape shown in Figure 4-68 when creating a hot spot. If you have trouble being precise, click the Zoom In tool to correct your work (see Figure 4-69). To change the hot spot, just drag the selection handles (those black squares). Add four more hot spots, one for each button.

To add a hyperlink to each hot spot, double-click the hot spot (click anywhere

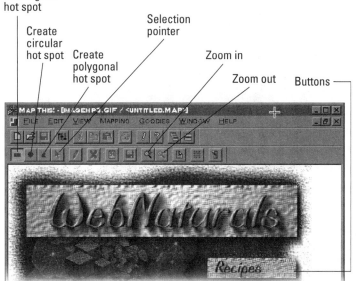

Figure 4-67: Loading an image into MapTHIS!

Figure 4-68: Creating a hot spot.

Selection handle   Selection outline

Figure 4-69: You can zoom in to check the accuracy of your hot spots.

inside the hot spot's boundary) to open the dialog box shown in Figure 4-70. Because this is yet another hypothetical company, the hyperlinks don't actually exist. We have to make them up. Let's assume that there are Web pages with the following names for each button:

Button	URL
Recipes	recipes.htm
Books	books.htm
Natural Chat	chat.htm
Links	http://www.Webstarr.com/hotsites.htm
Resources	resources.htm

Yes, the URL for the Links button jumps to an old favorite: a page on the WebStarr server. If you are wondering why, it's because the Vice President of Marketing at WebNatural used to work as Sales Manager over at WebStarr, and he's still friends with the crew over there. Hey, I said this was all hypothetical!

Add the URL for each button by double-clicking the hot spot for each button, and then typing the URL into the top text box in the URL to Activate When This Area Is Clicked (Required) text box. If you forget to add a URL for every hot spot, MapTHIS! warns you when you try to save the file. A hot spot without a URL causes nothing but trouble if the MAP file finds its way onto your server.

That's all there is to creating hot spots. Before we save the file, click EDIT⇨EDIT MAP INFO to display the dialog box shown in Figure 4-71. Fill in the dialog box exactly as shown in Figure 4-71. The bottom portion of the dialog box establishes the convention that is used for the MAP file; see the next section for information about the conventions.

To save the file to your hard disk, select FILE⇨SAVE AS to save the file in the same directory as the GIF file: `\My Documents\My Web Pages\maps\imagemp3.map`. Note that MAP files have the file extension `.map`. I strongly recommend that you give all MAP files the same filename as the associated GIF file, so that you can easily manage them as a pair (p1.gif, p1.map).

Type the URL here

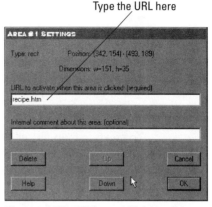

Figure 4-70: Adding a URL hyperlink to a hot spot.

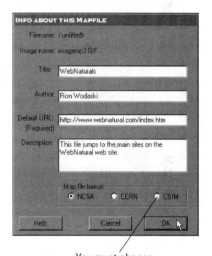

You must choose a convention here

Figure 4-71: Editing map file information.

MapTHIS! contains a number of other useful features. For example, you can create a grid to allow precise alignment of hot spots, and you can view the list of current hot spots — and their URLS — by choosing VIEW⇨AREA LIST. You can also test the map for accuracy, or vary the grid settings.

One common use of MAP files is for groups of buttons. You may recall that we added a row of buttons near the bottom of the `products.htm` Web page, in the tutorial for Chapter 3. MapTHIS! has a feature that makes it very, very easy to work with rows or blocks of same-sized buttons. We'll create a map file for the `allbtns2.gif` image from `products.htm`. Each of the buttons in the image will have a hyperlink to a specific page. These are the same hyperlinks that are used as buttons near the top of the Web page you created in Chapter 1: Products, Support, Shopping, FAQs, and Lifestyle.

To create a map file with MapTHIS!, follow these steps:

1. Close the current MAP file by clicking FILE⇨CLOSE. Then create a new MAP file (choose FILE⇨NEW), using the image file `\My Documents\My Web Pages\maps\allbtns2.gif`. If necessary, adjust the size of the child window to show the whole image (see Figure 4-72).

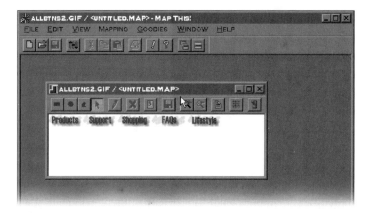

Figure 4-72: *Starting a new MAP file.*

2. Choose GOODIES⇨CREATE GUIDES to display the dialog box shown in Figure 4-73. This dialog box more or less explains itself. Notice that the size of the image is included for easy reference. There are five buttons, and the image is 300 pixels wide, so each button must be 60 pixels wide (one-fifth of 300). Enter **60** in the Width text box. Enter **20** for Height, **5** for Across, and **1** for Down.

   The Create Guides dialog box also enables you to specify a base URL for the hot spots it is creating. You can use this feature to name your Web pages with numerically consecutive names — `Web01.htm`, `Web02.htm`, and so forth. To have MapTHIS! automatically generate the names, you use an old C programmer's trick: **%d** in place of the number that is changing. For example, to implement the sequence I just mentioned, you enter the following into the Base URL text box:

   Web0%d.htm

TIP

In my opinion, the Create Guides dialog box is misnamed. It doesn't just create guides; it creates the actual hot spots. This means that you do not have to use the guides to create hot spots; they are created for you.

3. For this example, we did not use sequentially numbered Web pages, so enter the actual base URL, as follows:

   http://www.Webstarr.com/

4. Click OK, and you have five neatly arranged hot spots, one for each button (see Figure 4-74).

5. Because we did not use numeric sequencing, we need to add the name of each page file to each hot spot. The easiest way to do this is to click VIEW➪AREA LIST to display the list of hot spots (see Figure 4-75). Highlight a hot spot, and click the Edit button to edit the URL in the dialog box shown in Figure 4-76. Repeat this for each hot spot, adding the appropriate URL, as follows:

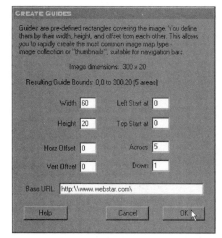

Figure 4-73: Creating guides for hot spots.

Hot spot

Figure 4-74: Five hot spots added.

Selected hot spot

Type URL here

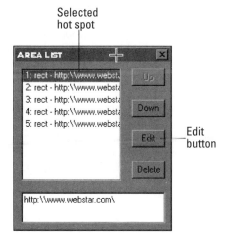

Edit button

Figure 4-75: Displaying hot spot data.

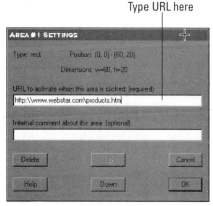

Figure 4-76: Editing hot spot information.

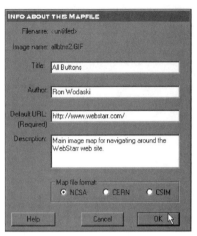

Figure 4-77: Add map information.

http://www.Webstarr.com/products.htm
http://www.Webstarr.com/support.htm
http://www.Webstarr.com/shopping.htm
http://www.Webstarr.com/faqs.htm
http://www.Webstarr.com/lifestyl.htm

6. Add the Map info as shown in Figure 4-77 and save your work to the file `\My Documents\My Web Pages\maps\allbtns2.map`.

The conventions

At the bottom of the Info About This Mapfile dialog box, you see a set of three radio buttons labeled Map File Format. These are the conventions that I have mentioned several times previously. The conventions are nothing more than specific ways of putting the MAP information into a file. The first two, NCSA (National Center for Supercomputing Applications) and CERN (European Laboratory for Particle Physics), are methods for putting the MAP information into a MAP file. The third, CSIM (Client-Side Image Map), puts the information into an HTML file.

There is no advantage to choosing the NCSA or CERN conventions. They are nothing more than different methods for storing MAP information. To determine which convention to use, you simply contact your Web server administrator and ask which one your server supports. It will be one or the other, and that's all there is to it. You don't even need to know what the differences between the two conventions are — MapTHIS!, and most other mapping software, handles it for you. If you are interested in knowing the differences, however, I'll describe them shortly.

After you know which convention to use, you always use that convention on that server, unless, of course, your Web administrator changes server software — and he'll almost certainly let you know. If your image maps ever stop working (this really happened to me!), it could be because the server software was changed, and no one let you know about it. Charge right down to your Web administrator and find out what happened. On second thought, it might be better to send e-mail!

NCSA

I created three different versions of the `allbtns2.map` map file. Here is the NCSA version of the map file created by MapTHIS!:

```
#$MTIMFH
#$-:Image Map file created by Map THIS!
#$-:Map THIS! free image map editor by Todd C. Wilson
#$-:Please do not edit lines starting with "#$"
#$VERSION:1.20
#$TITLE:All Buttons
#$DESCRIPTION:Main image map for navigating around the WebStarr
Web site.
#$AUTHOR:Ron Wodaski
#$DATE:Thu Jan 25 20:38:36 1996
#$PATH:C:\My Documents\My Web Pages\maps\
#$GIF:allbtns2.GIF
#$FORMAT:ncsa
#$EOH
default http://www.Webstar.com/
rect http://www.Webstar.com/products.htm 0,0 60,20
rect http://www.Webstar.com/support.htm 60,0 120,20
rect http://www.Webstar.com/shopping 120,0 180,20
rect http://www.Webstar.com/faq.htm 180,0 240,20
rect http://www.Webstar.com/lifestyl.htm 240,0 300,20
```

The first 13 lines of the MAP file are comments inserted by MapTHIS!. If you deleted them, the MAP file would still work. As you can see, a comment line begins with the characters #$. If you wanted to insert your own comments, you could simply open the MAP file in Notepad, and add your comments — with each comment line starting with these two characters, of course. The remaining six lines come in two varieties: the first line, which specifies the default hyperlink, and the five lines for the five buttons.

The format of the default line is:

```
default <URL>
```

The format for the hot spots is:

```
<type> <URL> <coordinates>
```

where the type is rect, circle, or polygon. The coordinates vary with the type of hot spot — a circle, for example, is defined by the coordinates of its bounding rectangle. Why a rectangle? Because a "circle" can also be shaped like an ellipse.

You could define your own hot spots using this syntax, but MapTHIS! makes it so easy, there's no reason to do so.

CERN

The CERN version of the MAP file created by MapTHIS! looks like this:

```
rect (4096,4096) (4096,4096) mt:#$MTIMFH
rect (4096,4096) (4096,4096) mt:#$-:Image%20Map%20file%20
created%20by%20Map%20THIS!
rect (4096,4096) (4096,4096) mt:#$-
:Map%20THIS!%20free%20image%20map%20editor%20by%20Todd%20
C.%20Wilson
rect (4096,4096) (4096,4096) mt:#$-
:Please%20do%20not%20edit%20lines%20starting%20with%20"#$"
rect (4096,4096) (4096,4096) mt:#$VERSION:1.20
rect (4096,4096) (4096,4096) mt:#$TITLE:All%20Buttons
rect (4096,4096) (4096,4096)
mt:#$DESCRIPTION:Main%20image%20map%20for%20navigating%20
around%20the%20WebStarr%20Web%20site.
rect (4096,4096) (4096,4096) mt:#$AUTHOR:Ron%20Wodaski
rect (4096,4096) (4096,4096)
mt:#$DATE:Thu%20Jan%2025%2020:38:49%201996
rect (4096,4096) (4096,4096)
mt:#$PATH:C:\My%20Documents\My%20Web%20Pages\maps\
rect (4096,4096) (4096,4096) mt:#$GIF:allbtns2.GIF
rect (4096,4096) (4096,4096) mt:#$FORMAT:cern
rect (4096,4096) (4096,4096) mt:#$EOH
default http://www.Webstar.com/
rectangle (0,0) (60,20) http://www.Webstar.com/products.htm
rectangle (60,0) (120,20) http://www.Webstar.com/support.htm
rectangle (120,0) (180,20) http://www.Webstar.com/shopping
rectangle (180,0) (240,20) http://www.Webstar.com/faq.htm
rectangle (240,0) (300,20) http://www.Webstar.com/lifestyl.htm
```

Once again, there are 13 comments, although the syntax for the comments is different. The format for the default line is the same, but the format for the hot spot lines is different. The format for hot spots is:

```
<type> <coordinates> <URL>
```

Note also that the type is spelled out completely, and the coordinates are specified by using parentheses.

As I mentioned earlier, you probably will never have a need to edit a MAP file, but now you know what's inside one. You can even tell the convention used by a MAP file by looking at its contents.

Client- (browser-) based maps

MapTHIS! also enables you to specify CSIM as a file format for the MAP file. Strictly speaking, the CSIM format doesn't use a MAP file at all. It spits out HTML code. The code it spits out, however, is (so far) only recognized by Netscape Navigator 2.0. If you are comfortable requiring that visitors use the Navigator 2.0 browser, or if the situation changes and other browsers support the Navigator syntax for client-based image maps, this section may come in handy.

The best thing about client-based image maps is that they are much easier to test. You can test these maps right on your own computer. Regular image maps make use of scripts or programs on the server, and can only be tested over a live Internet connection.

When you select CSIM as the file type, MapTHIS! requires that you supply a filename that uses the .htm extension. The output from MapTHIS! looks something like this:

```
<BODY>
<MAP NAME="All Buttons">
<!- #$-:Image Map file created by Map THIS! ->
<!- #$-:Map THIS! free image map editor by Todd C. Wilson ->
<!- #$-:Please do not edit lines starting with "#$" ->
<!- #$VERSION:1.20 ->
<!- #$DESCRIPTION:Main image map for navigating around the
WebStarr Web site. ->
<!- #$AUTHOR:Ron Wodaski ->
<!- #$DATE:Thu Jan 25 20:39:24 1996 ->
<!- #$PATH:C:\My Documents\My Web Pages\maps\ ->
<!- #$GIF:allbtns2.GIF ->
<AREA SHAPE=RECT COORDS="0,0,60,20"
HREF=http://www.Webstar.com/products.htm>
<AREA SHAPE=RECT COORDS="60,0,120,20"
HREF=http://www.Webstar.com/support.htm>
<AREA SHAPE=RECT COORDS="120,0,180,20"
HREF=http://www.Webstar.com/shopping>
```

(continued)

```
(continued)
<AREA SHAPE=RECT COORDS="180,0,240,20"
HREF=http://www.Webstar.com/faq.htm>
<AREA SHAPE=RECT COORDS="240,0,300,20" HREF=
http://www.Webstar.com/lifestyl.htm>
<AREA SHAPE=default HREF=http://www.Webstar.com/>
</MAP></BODY>
```

The output uses HTML tags. The outermost tags, <BODY> and </BODY>, represent body text. If you are inserting the output from MapTHIS! into an existing Web page, you should delete the BODY tags before proceeding. (If you don't, your Web page might be mistaken for something out of an Agatha Christie novel!)

After we remove the BODY tags, the first line is:

```
<MAP NAME="All Buttons">
```

This line contains the starting HTML tag for the map definition — MAP — and the name of the map, specified in MapTHIS! (select EDIT⇨EDIT MAP INFO). The end of the map definition is the last line:

```
</MAP>
```

Between these two framing HTML tags, we find a bunch of comment lines (note that HTML comment lines begin with "<!—"and end with "—>".

The default URL is specified as follows:

```
<AREA SHAPE=default HREF=http://www.Webstar.com/>
```

AREA is an HTML tag. SHAPE is a parameter, as is HREF. The typical hot spot is defined like this:

```
<AREA SHAPE=RECT COORDS="0,0,60,20"
HREF=http://www.Webstar.com/products.htm>
```

In this example, the SHAPE is a rectangle, and its coordinates are specified with the HTML parameter COORDS. The HREF (hypertext reference) is the URL to link to when the hot spot is clicked.

As with the other output formats that MapTHIS! supplies, you *could* create this yourself. Fortunately, there should never be a need.

How does a MAP file work?

One thing I haven't covered until now is how the MAP file (or the <MAP> tags in an HTML file) actually provides the hyperlink. Here's what happens:

➡ When you click an image map (also referred to at times as a *sensitive map*), the coordinates where you click are noted.

➡ If the image map is a server-based map file, the coordinates you clicked (together with some other information, such as the name and location of the map file) are sent to a program on the server. This program has just one job: handling image map clicks.

➡ The program on the server reads the map file to learn the coordinates of the hot spots in the map file. It then determines whether the click was on a hot spot. If it was, it jumps to the URL for that hot spot. If the click was not on a hot spot, it jumps to the default URL.

It's really just as simple as that. The hard work is elsewhere — in creating a great image for the map file, in laying out the hot spots, in working with your Web administrator to get the image map working properly. I recommend that you allow yourself extra time to get the bugs worked out of your first image map — you almost certainly will discover one or two idiosyncrasies regarding your server's implementation of image maps.

By far the safest way to implement an image map is with client-based maps. This puts all the work on the visitor's computer. The only disadvantage — and it may be a big one — is that your visitor must be using Netscape 2.0. If more browsers support client-based image maps, they will definitely become the best way to implement image maps.

Clip Art Collections

Implicit in the material covered in this chapter is that you will find some way to create or obtain good-looking images for your Web pages. The reality is that creating images takes time, effort, and (sometimes) talent. Programs like Fractal Design Painter are extraordinarily powerful, but it takes time and effort to learn such complex software. In addition, you may find that you need special hardware to get the most out of image-creation software. For example, you will probably start lusting after a digitizing tablet and pressure-sensitive stylus (see Figure 4-78), which allows you to draw freely into a drawing pro-gram like Painter or Photoshop. Let's face it — the mouse is great for mousing around, but not so great as a drawing tool.

Figure 4-78: *Calcomp drawing tablets are a marvelous tool for creating original art — far better than a mouse.*

You may also find that a scanner is a great asset when creating Web pages. With a scanner, you can scan not only your own photographs, but also materials at hand for textured backgrounds, company logos, client artwork, and even your own hand-drawn sketches. One of the best scanners for serious work is the Hewlett-Packard IVc. I generally recommend against hand-held scanners, because they are difficult to use for serious work — they are unsteady, and they require many attempts to get a clean, accurate scan.

By far the easiest way to get your hands on images is to simply purchase them. Clip art collections are an economical solution. If you want access to a wide variety of clip art collections, I strongly suggest that you contact Publisher's Toolbox, a mail-order company that supplies hardware, software, and images to the desktop and Web publishing trades. You can call 800-390-0461 to request a catalog. You'll learn about clip art collections from many different vendors.

Corel offers tens of thousands of images in a searchable database (see Figure 4-79). Corel images are inexpensive, and quality ranges from low to high. Because images are so affordable, you can build a huge collection with only a small investment.

DiAMAR also offers a huge variety of images, classified by broad subject areas. Image quality is extremely high, but the cost per image is higher than for Corel. Figure 4-80 shows an image of a farmer in silhouette at sunset, with text added in Painter to create a logo for a Web page.

Image information

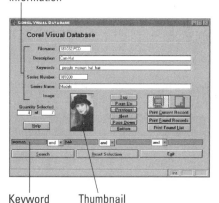

Keyword selection   Thumbnail image

Figure 4-79: *An example of clip art from Corel.*

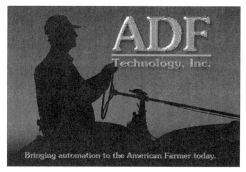

Figure 4-80: *An example of clip art from DiAMAR.*

PhotoDisc offers several classes of images — individual objects, scenics, sunsets, and many more. Figure 4-81 shows an image of a winter highway, with the sky removed and made transparent for use on a Web page.

Figure 4-81: An example of clip art from PhotoDisc.

Digital Stock offers a truly staggering collection of images. All are high quality, but not all are suitable for Web page work. Fortunately, you only pay for images you use, so you can select just those images that work for you. Figure 4-82 shows a beat up old wreck, with the background removed and made transparent.

Figure 4-82: An example of clip art from Digital Stock.

Screen Caffeine Pro offers a unique collection of images that includes buttons and textured backgrounds. Figure 4-83 shows an example of a button collection; there are hundreds of buttons to choose from. Screen Caffeine Pro also includes hundreds of backgrounds that you can use as textures (as-is, or modified in an image editor), such as the one shown in Figure 4-84.

You'll also find Screen Caffeine Pro's catalog full of interesting image tools that enable you to modify stock clip art images to make them uniquely your own.

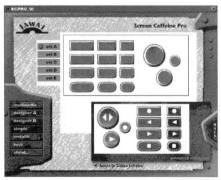

Figure 4-83: An example of button clip art from Screen Caffeine Pro.

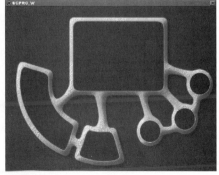

Figure 4-84: An example of texture clip art from Screen Caffeine Pro.

Mastering the Internet: Multimedia

Working with **full-motion video**

Using sounds, including both auto-play and click-play

Finding alternatives for **low-bandwidth** connections

Working with alternative multimedia tools

Multimedia represents a double-edged sword on the Internet. On the one hand, **multimedia** is a powerful tool. The ability to deliver **video clips**, to add background sounds to a page, means that you can go beyond the limits of mere words and still pictures. On the other hand, with most people connecting to the Net with 28.8 Kbps modems, the time it takes to deliver your messages becomes a significant factor. If your multimedia elements take too long to **download**, you risk losing the attention of your visitors.

Today's Internet browsers support a full range of multimedia, including images, sounds, videos, animations, and more. In this chapter, you learn how to create multimedia, how to add it to your Web pages, and how to minimize download times.

Setting Up the Tutorial

In this chapter, we once again jump from one tutorial to the next. Video is video, audio is audio, and each has a different set of tools and requirements. Some of the tutorials build on what you created in earlier chapters, and some start from scratch. Like Chapter 4, this chapter is a collection of mini-tutorials.

Automatic setup

If you haven't already installed the software for automatic setup of the tutorials, turn to Appendix A and do so now. Otherwise, if you choose not to use automatic setup, see the next section, "Manual setup," which tells you how to copy the necessary files for this tutorial manually. If you didn't use automatic setup earlier, you can find complete instructions for starting, running, and using the automatic setup program in Chapter 1.

To run automatic setup, click the Start button, then Programs, and then click the Autopage icon, shown here.

This is the Chapter 5 tutorial, so click the Chapter 5 Files radio button to display the files for this chapter (see Figure 5-1).

Click here for Chapter 5 files

Figure 5-1: Automatic setup for Chapter 5 tutorial.

To copy the files for the tutorial to your hard disk, click on the Copy to Hard Disk button. The files are copied to the My Web Pages subfolder of the My Documents folder. If you installed Microsoft Office to your C drive, the following is usually the folder:

    C:\My Documents\My Web Pages

NOTE This is the same folder you have been using for all the tutorials. From time to time, you may notice that one or more additional subfolders is created in the My Web Pages folder; this is normal, and all is explained during the tutorial.

After you have copied the necessary files, skip ahead to the start of the tutorial. If you choose not to use the automatic setup, read the next section to find out how to copy the necessary files manually.

Manual setup

Before you start the tutorial, open the folder named My Web Pages on your hard disk. If you already completed the tutorial in Chapter 1, you created it as a subfolder of the My Documents folder (usually **C:\ My Documents**).

The tutorial in this chapter uses image and other kinds of files from the CD-ROM. They are located in the folder \tutorial\chap05. Copy the following image files

allbtns2.gif

cat01.gif

cat02.gif

dog01.gif

dog02.gif

ear.gif

vid01.gif

vid02.gif

from the \tutorial\chap05 folder on the CD-ROM to the My Web Pages\images folder you created earlier on your hard disk (see Chapter 1 for complete details).

Copy the following document files

bgsound.htm

shopping.htm

shoplogo.gif

shopping2.htm

from the \tutorial\chap04 folder on the CD-ROM to the My Web Pages\video folder. If the My Web Pages\video folder doesn't already exist, create it now.

Copy the following video files

sample.avi

sample2.avi

tshirt.avi

tshirt2.avi

from the \tutorial\chap04 folder on the CD-ROM to the My Web Pages\video folder. If the My Web Pages\video folder doesn't already exist, create it now.

Copy the following audio files

    doggie.wav

    doggie2.wav

    doggie3.wav

from the \tutorial\chap04 folder on the CD-ROM to the My Web Pages\audio folder. If the My Web Pages\audio folder doesn't already exist, create it now.

You are now ready to begin the tutorial.

Tutorial 5A: Adding Video

When video first arrived on the PC, the biggest problem was the small size of the playback image. Sizes of 160×120 were typical. This is quite small by today's standards. For example, Figure 5-2 shows the size of a 160×120 video clip on a $1,024 \times 768$ desktop. It's difficult to see interesting details at such a small size, but this was the standard when video first arrived. The reason for the small size was limited **bandwidth**: PC hardware could only move the data around so fast. The limit was about 120,000 bytes per second (120K/second).

Today, data rates of more than a megabyte per second are not only possible, but commonly achieved. With faster processors, and cheaper and better video playback hardware, video playback sizes jumped all the way to full-screen. As a result, video is now a part of many applications, from games to online help.

On the Internet, bandwidth takes a giant step backwards. If 120K/second was not quite enough, consider that a 28.8 baud modem is moving 28.8 **Kilobits**, not **kilobytes**, across the phone line each second. This translates into about 3.6K/second! This represents just a small fraction of the bandwidth needed to move video across phone lines at normal sizes and frame rates.

Television comes across at 30 frames per second, full-screen. That's about 27 megabytes (MB) *per second.* When you compare that to the 3.6K/second of the phone line, something has to give — television has a data stream that is more than 400,000 times larger than what your modem can deliver! You simply can't expect high-quality video across a standard phone line.

Video Clip

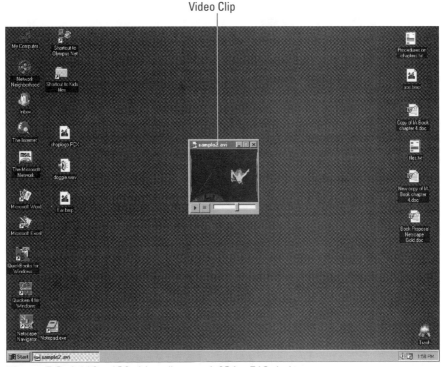

Figure 5-2: A 160 × 120 video clip on a 1,024 × 768 desktop.

Of course, if you and your visitors have ISDN or other kinds of high-speed connections, you enjoy higher data rates. But even an **ISDN** line can deliver only 128K/second, 1/200th of what television delivers — barely enough for postage stamp-sized video clips.

There are several strategies you can use to deal with the realities of limited bandwidth over phone lines:

➡ Use the smallest possible image size.

➡ Reduce the **frame rate**.

➡ Give up the idea of live video entirely, and ask the visitor to download the video clip before viewing it.

In the real world, the third strategy is the one used most frequently. At 3.6K/second, you would be lucky to achieve a frame rate of one frame per second, even with a very small image size. At larger frame sizes, frame rates drop to one frame every 5, 10, or even 15 seconds. This isn't really video.

In this chapter, you learn how to add downloadable video to your Web pages. If you want to explore the possibilities of real-time audio and video, see the sections "Real Audio" and "VDOLive Video," later in the chapter.

Video variations

Internet Assistant makes it almost trivially easy to add video clips to your Web pages, but not all browsers support video clips. As with many other high-end Web features, you should use different browsers to test your Web pages containing video. Internet Explorer supports the video techniques used by Internet Assistant, but other browsers may not. As with just about everything connected with the Web, you should verify handling of video files in several Web browsers to see whether video support has changed since this was written.

To add a video clip with Internet Assistant, click on the Add Picture tool. Instead of adding the name of a picture, click on the Video tab and add the name of a video clip. It's really just that simple. You can even use the Options tab with video clips. We'll add a video to a WebStarr page to see how this works.

Back in Chapter 1, you created a home page for WebStarr, Inc. That page had a row of five buttons on it that provide hyperlinks to other WebStarr pages. In Chapter 3, you created a page for the Products button. In this tutorial, you work with the Shopping page.

You already know how to create a basic page (if not, refer back to the tutorial in Chapter 3), so I've created the basic text and layout for the Shopping page. It was copied to your hard disk during setup. Open the file \My Documents\My Web Pages\shopping.htm in Word now.

Figure 5-3: The shopping.htm HTML page in Word.

Figure 5-3 shows what the file looks like. The logo at the top of the page is just like the logo for the Products page, but it says "Shopping" instead. Like all the other graphics for the fictitious company WebStarr, it was created in Fractal Design Painter.

Position the page so that you can see the text below the Shopping logo (see Figure 5-4).

This page has two major topics. One is for purchasing tickets to events sponsored by WebStarr. The other is for purchasing WebStarr memorabilia, such as T-shirts, mugs, and so on. The page also has the miniature buttons for navigating to key points on the WebStarr site. This is an image map, just as in the example in Chapter 4. Because WebStarr wants its Web site to reflect the very latest advances in technology, the marketing department has created two video clips, and they want you to add them to this page. One clip shows a circus that is sponsored by WebStarr, and the other shows someone modeling a WebStarr sweatshirt.

To add the first video clip, position the cursor at the beginning of the title line for the first topic (tickets). Click on the Add Picture tool to display the Picture dialog box (see Figure 5-5). Click on the Video tab to display the video version of the dialog box (see Figure 5-6).

During setup, you copied the video clip `sample.avi` to the `\My Documents\My WebPages\video` folder. Use the browse button to locate the file and load it.

The Video tab has three settings related specifically to video clips:

Start Play: This determines when the video will start playing. The default setting is FileOpen, which plays the video as soon as it completes downloading to the user's computer. You can also choose Mouse Over, which plays the video when the user passes the mouse cursor over the video frame. In most cases, the File Open setting is best. For this tutorial, use FileOpen.

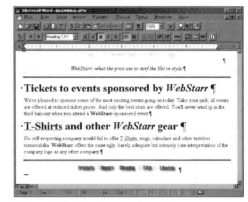

Figure 5-4: The text portion of the page.

Figure 5-5: The Picture dialog box.

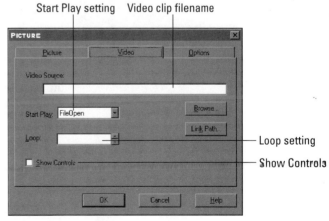

Figure 5-6: The Video version of the Picture dialog box.

Loop: This enables you to control the number of times the video plays. If you leave it blank, the video plays once and then stops. If you enter a number or click the up arrow to increase the number displayed, the video plays the specified number of times and then stops. If you click the down arrow while the Looping value is blank, it shows INFINITE, and the video clip plays over and over until the user goes on to another page. For this tutorial, use INFINITE.

Show Controls: If this checkbox is checked, the video has a simple control panel displayed beneath it, allowing the user to play, pause, or stop the video. For this tutorial, leave the box unchecked.

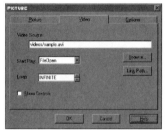

Figure 5-7: Video tab settings for the tutorial.

Set Alignment with Text here

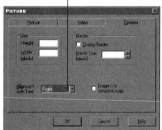

Figure 5-9: Setting Options for a video clip.

Figure 5-7 shows the values that should be set in the Video tab of the Picture dialog box.

The other two tabs of the Picture dialog box, Picture and Options, can also be used with a video clip. For example, you can add alternate text in the Picture tab (**Video for Internet Explorer**, for example). Click OK when finished.

TIP Internet Assistant treats a video clip just like a still picture. For each video clip, you can add the same options you use for a picture (height, width, alignment, and so on).

Figure 5-8 shows what the video looks like in a browser.

The default position for a picture isn't very attractive, however. Click the video image to select it, and then click on the Add Picture tool. In the Picture dialog box, click on the Options tab and set Alignment with Text to Right (see Figure 5-9).

Figure 5-10 shows the appearance of the video clip in Internet Explorer. Notice that the clip is now lined up at the right edge of the page, and that the text flows neatly around the video clip. If you prefer, you can use an Alignment with Text setting of Left and display the video to the left of the text. The Left and Right settings, unlike other alignment settings, allow the text to wrap around an image.

Video clip playing

Figure 5-8: Viewing the video clip in Internet Explorer.

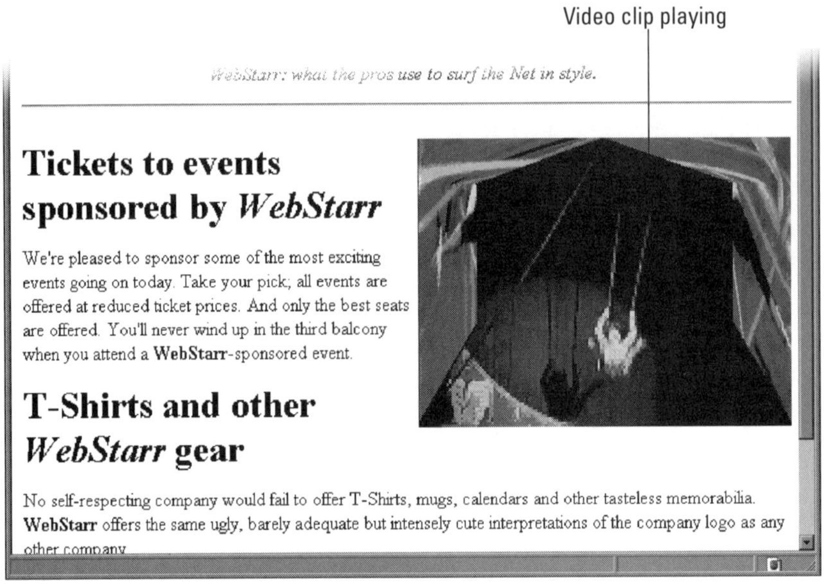

Video clip playing

Tickets to events
sponsored by *WebStarr*

We're pleased to sponsor some of the most exciting events going on today. Take your pick; all events are offered at reduced ticket prices. And only the best seats are offered. You'll never wind up in the third balcony when you attend a **WebStarr**-sponsored event.

T-Shirts and other
WebStarr gear

No self-respecting company would fail to offer T-Shirts, mugs, calendars and other tasteless memorabilia. **WebStarr** offers the same ugly, barely adequate but intensely cute interpretations of the company logo as any other company.

Figure 5-10: The video placed at the right of the page.

Now add the second video clip, `tshirt.avi`, using the same steps. You may want to experiment with a Left alignment for one video and a Right alignment for the other video, to see whether this improves the layout of the page. Figure 5-11 shows my finished layout.

Animations

Animations are not really very different from video clips. For best results, in fact, you should plan on storing your animations in video files (that is, files with the extension .avi). That way, adding an animation is no different than adding a video clip.

There are really three common video formats, each having originated on a specific platform. It's a good idea to provide a link to a site that contains the files needed to play whatever video type you use on a variety of platforms. For example, if you use QuickTime video clips, include a link to the Windows and Windows 95 versions of QuickTime (`http://quicktime.apple.com`) so that Windows users can view your videos.

Figure 5-11: Two video clips added to the page.

If you have animation files that aren't already stored as a Video for Windows (.avi) file or as a QuickTime for Windows (.mov) file, you can use software such as Adobe Premiere to convert those animation files. Most animations use either the .fli or .flc file formats, and Premiere can convert either format to .avi or .mov. If you get an animation file from the sales department's presentation software, for example, you might need to convert it before you can put it on the Web. See the sidebar "Video file formats" for more information.

After you have converted an animation to a video file format, you can add it to your Web pages in the same way you added the video clips earlier.

Video file formats

There are three major types of video file formats. Each has its advantages and disadvantages. Microsoft created the **Video for Windows** format, which is designed to work in Windows and Windows 95. However, these files can be converted to play on a Macintosh.

The **QuickTime** format was originally created for the Macintosh, but there is a version of QuickTime for Windows and Windows 95.

The **MPEG** (Motion Picture Experts Group) format wasn't designed for any particular computer platform, and there are MPEG players for most types of computers. If you want your video clips to be viewed on a wide range of platforms, MPEG offers the best results.

When you add video clips to your Web pages, you need to decide which format (or formats) to use. If you expect most visitors to use Windows browsers, Video for Windows is the obvious choice. Likewise, if most visitors are likely to use Macintosh browsers, then QuickTime is your best choice. If you want to include UNIX browsers, too, MPEG is the best choice.

You may also be limited by your equipment or software. MPEG, for example, requires expensive equipment to capture at high-quality levels. Because Web videos usually aim for small and quick rather than large and good-looking, a software MPEG encoder will be adequate. Xing (`http://www.xingtech.com/xingmpeg/index.html`) and Ulead (`http://www.seed.Net.tw/~ulead/mpeg.htm`) offer MPEG encoders.

Video to the max

To make effective use of video, you need to optimize various factors. As I mentioned earlier, the size of the video clip is important. That includes the overall file size, which determines how long it takes to download the video, and the frame size, which influences file size dramatically.

The two video clips you added to the `shopping.htm` Web page earlier, for example, use a large frame size: 320×240. This results in a file size of 1.25 MB for `sample.avi`, which takes about five to seven minutes to download with a typical 28.8 Kbps modem connection. Because these two videos are part of the actual page, they should download as quickly as possible. If six minutes each isn't fast enough for you, you could easily output a smaller frame size when you (or the art department) create the video. For example, using an image size of 160×120 results in a file size of 400K, with an approximate download time of 2 minutes. Using a smaller video frame size also changes the appearance of the page. Figure 5-12 shows what the `shopping.htm` page looks like using the smaller video frame size.

Figure 5-12: The Shopping page using smaller-sized video clips.

Another way to speed up downloading of page elements is to use a still picture as a stand-in for the video clip. Make the picture a hyperlink to the video clip so that the video starts to download when your visitors click on the still picture. The procedure for adding a still picture as a video hyperlink is summarized in the following steps. If you want to follow the steps, open the file \My Documents\My Web Pages\shopping2.htm in Word first.

1. Position the cursor where you want to add the picture. Use the Picture dialog box to locate the picture \My Documents\My Web Pages\ images\vid01.gif, and set Alignment with Text, Height, Width, and so on, as desired. Click on OK to save the changes. Note that the picture is a small version of a video frame, which you can create either by exporting a single frame or by capturing a single frame to the Clipboard (press Alt+Print Screen while the video playback window is active). To make it clear what clicking on the image does, I added the text Video clip to the picture by using an image editor (Adobe Photoshop).

2. Click on the picture to select it, and then click on the Add Hyperlink tool. In the File or URL text box, type the correct relative path for the video clip. For the first picture (tickets), that path is videos\sample.avi. For the second picture (vid02.gif, for the T-shirts), that path is videos\tshirt.avi. For each picture, click on OK to save.

That's all there is to it. If (and it's an important if!) your browser is set up to automatically play downloaded video clips, the video is downloaded and then played in a window of its own. If your browser does *not* automatically play the video clip, consult the browser documentation regarding **MIME** types, and add settings for video clips. If the browser does not suggest a program for playing video clips, use the built-in Windows Media Player. Add the **/play** parameter to force Media Player to play the video automatically. The entry for the program to play the video should look like the following (depending, of course, on the actual folder in which you installed Windows):

```
c:\Windows\mplayer.exe /play
```

You also can add a text hyperlink to play a video clip. Instead of selecting a picture in step 1 above, select the appropriate text and then add the hyperlink.

Small frame sizes reduce a file's size. To further reduce the time required for downloading, you also can reduce the frame rate of the clip by using software such as Premiere. For example, most video clips use a frame rate of 15 frames per second (fps). Changing to a frame rate of 12, 10, or even 8 fps dramatically reduces the file size. Keep in mind that smaller clips and lower frame rates reduce the quality of the video experience.

You also can use higher compression levels to keep file size down. If you compress too much, however, image quality can suffer dramatically. See the section "Creating Video Clips," later in this chapter, for more information about compression.

VDOLive is a newly released Web program that offers real-time video play-back. There is a significant cost in terms of image quality, but if real-time is important to you, VDOLive gives you an option. See the section "VDOLive Video," later in this chapter, for details.

Tutorial 5B: Adding Audio

Audio clips are much smaller than video clips, but they are still large enough to require special handling over the Internet. Download time is still an important factor for audio. For example, a two-second sound clip may take 5-10 seconds or more to download. Careful balancing of the various factors involved in creating digital audio is needed for best results.

As with video, there is a trade-off involved with audio on the Web. The better the audio quality you desire, the larger the file — and the longer the download times. You have to decide whether you want audio files that download quickly or audio files that have high quality. You can't have both at the same time.

In addition to creating audio files for downloading, there is a real-time audio feature that your Web server may or may not offer. It's called Real Audio. It offers no wait, real-time audio playback, but at a severe cost in terms of quality. See the section "Real Audio," in this chapter, for more information.

Clickable audio

Adding audio to a Web page is as simple as adding a hyperlink. You can make either text or an image into a hyperlink. Figure 5-13 shows the `shopping.htm` Web page with a bit of a twist: I've added an image shaped like an ear (`ear.gif`) which, when clicked on, causes a browser to download an audio file and play it. I have added one for each major topic. Although a sales pitch is appropriate, for this example, I'll use some dog barking for the sounds. We'll use some tricks to create a table that lays out the various elements shown in Figure 5-13. This is the most involved tutorial so far. If you get into trouble, simply back up and start over. If you want to save your work after every step, save it using the filename `shoppingnew.htm` so that you still have the original file.

Hyperlink image

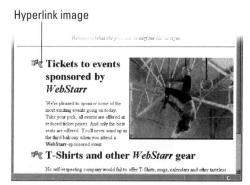

Figure 5-13: Adding audio hyperlinks to a Web page.

Open the file `\My Documents\My Web Pages\shopping.htm` that you modified earlier in Word. Our first task is to create the table. Begin by selecting four paragraphs: the two topic titles, and the text under each topic (see Figure 5-14). Select TABLE⇨INSERT TABLE to create a four-cell table (see Figure 5-15).

We really only need two cells, one for each major topic. To combine text from topic cells, select the text in the second cell (see Figure 5-16), being very,very careful not to select the end-of-cell marker, and cut it to the Clipboard (choose EDIT⇨CUT).

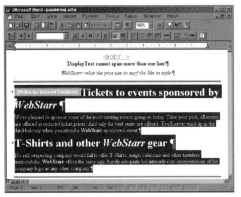

Position the cursor at the exact end of the title line in the first cell, and then press Enter to create a new paragraph. Make the new paragraph Normal,P style. Paste the text you cut in the last step into the new paragraph. The result should look like Figure 5-17. Select the empty row by clicking just to the left of it, and click on TABLE⇨DELETE ROWS to delete the row.

Repeat this same process for the second topic. Figure 5-18 shows the result.

Figure 5-14: Selecting text to make a table.

Figure 5-15: A table with four cells.

Figure 5-16: Selecting text.

Here is where things get a bit tricky, so we'll take it step by careful step. Select just the column of the table, not the little doohickeys to the right of each cell (see Figure 5-19). The easiest way to do this is to put the cursor anywhere in the table and select TABLE⇨SELECT COLUMN.

Text moved   Empty table cell

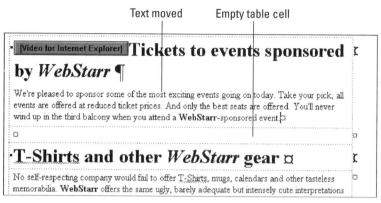

Figure 5-17: The text has been moved successfully.

Cell #1   Cell #2

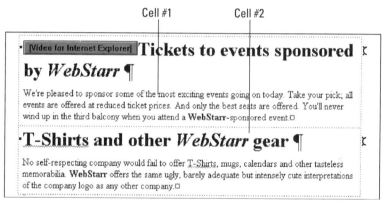

Figure 5-18: The table now has just two cells.

Doohickey

Choose TABLE⇨INSERT COLUMNS to add a column (see Figure 5-20). Don't panic — the column is simply too wide, and we can fix that.

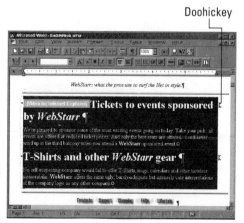

Figure 5-19: Select just the column.

Figure 5-20: The new column is too wide.

To adjust the column width, carefully position the cursor over the dotted-line boundary between the new column and the original column. The cursor changes to a pair of vertical lines with a side-pointing arrow. Drag the mouse to the left until the column is approximately half an inch wide (look in the ruler at the top of the Word window for reference). Figure 5-21 shows the result.

Narrow column   Column continues past

Figure 5-21: Narrowing the new column.

The original column may now be too wide. (That is, it may stretch beyond the confines of the Word window.) If it is, use the horizontal scroll bar at the bottom of the Word window to view the right edge of the table. Use the same technique to move the right edge back to the left so that the right edge of the original column is approximately at the right edge of the horizontal rules (see Figure 5-22).

Figure 5-22: Returning the original column to its original width.

The next task is to add the image to the two leftmost cells in the table and then make them hyperlinks to the audio files. Position the cursor in the first cell at the upper-left of the table and use the Add Picture tool to locate the image file `\My Documents\My Web Pages \images\ear.gif`. Figure 5-23 shows what the image looks like in the Insert Picture dialog box.

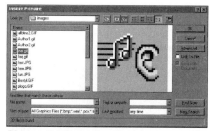

Figure 5-23: Adding the image ear.gif.

Click on OK to load the image and return to the Picture dialog box, then click on the Options tab. Add the following settings (see Figure 5-24) and click OK:

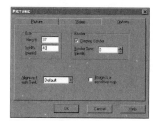

Figure 5-24: Adding options for the image.

Height	37
Width	40
Display Border	checked
Border Size	0

The border size setting removes the border that would normally be added for a hyperlink image. This image is so small that a border looks awkward at best. Figure 5-25 shows what the image looks like in Word. The image has a transparent background (I used SnapShot/32 to create transparency), but Word doesn't show such subtleties. Your browser shows the transparency, however.

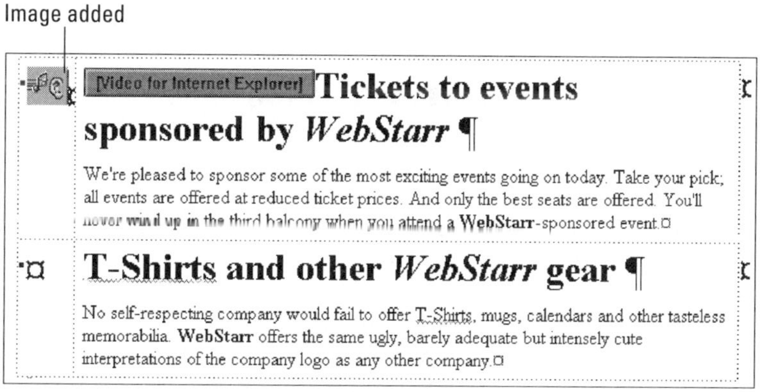

Image added

Figure 5-25: The ear image added to the page.

File or URL text box   Browse button

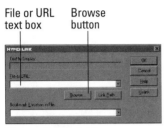

Figure 5-26: Adding a hyperlink.

Files of type drop-down list   Open button

Figure 5-27: Selecting the file type for viewing.

To add a hyperlink to the image, click on the image to select it (it reverses color when it is selected). Click on the Add Hyperlink tool to open the Hyperlink dialog box. Click on the Browse button below the File or URL text box (refer to Figure 5-26). This action opens the dialog box shown in Figure 5-27. If you started in the \My Documents\My Web Pages folder, click the audio folder to open it. You do not see any files — the Files of Type drop-down list is set for HTML and Word files. Click to select All Files (refer to Figure 5-27), and you will see several .wav files. Click on doggie.wav to select it, and then click on the Open button. This returns you to the Hyperlink dialog box, where the file path is now audio/ doggie.wav. Click on OK to save the changes.

The image of ear.gif may now be missing. If it is, it will be replaced by a few letters of text starting with Dis (see Figure 5-28). This simply means that there isn't enough room to display the image. If you could see the entire text, it would say Display text cannot span more than one line. This simply means that Word tried to display text that explained why the picture wasn't visible, but there wasn't enough room to do so on a single line. Arcane, yes, but now you know the inside story.

Missing image

Figure 5-28: A case of the missing image.

If we stop here, the image will appear at the vertical center of its cell, which is visually confusing. It belongs at the top of the cell. Make sure that the cursor is located in the leftmost cell of row 1 (just click in that cell if you are in doubt).

Select TABLE⇨ALIGN to display the Align dialog box (see Figure 5-29). In the section labeled Text in Table Cells, click on the Top radio button in the list of Vertical buttons, and then click on OK to save the change.

This completes the operation on the first image. Repeat this entire process to add another copy of the image in the first cell in the second row, using the same Options and other settings as you did the first time.

You can use the Clipboard to copy the image from the first row to the second row. When you copy the image, the Option settings are copied with it, as well as the hyperlink. The alignment setting is not copied, however; you must apply the alignment for the new cell manually.

Each document can have a title that appears in the window caption of your browser. To add a title to the document, click on FILE⇨HTML DOCUMENT INFO to display the dialog box shown in Figure 5-30. Simply type the appropriate title in the space provided. In this case, type **WebStarr Shopping**.

Figure 5-31 shows the final result; note that the title does, indeed, show up in the window caption of the browser.

Top radio button

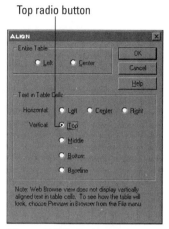

Figure 5-29: Setting cell alignment.

Put title here

Figure 5-30: Adding a title to the document.

Window caption

Figure 5-31: The completed Web page.

Background audio

Internet Explorer supports another kind of Web page audio: sounds that play in the background while the reader is viewing the page. At the time this book was being written, other browsers did not support this feature. You should test background audio with other browsers to see whether they do support it.

To add a background audio clip, choose FORMAT⇨BACKGROUND SOUND to display the dialog box shown in Figure 5-32. Use the Browse button to locate a .wav file, such as `doggie2.wav`, and use the Playback Loop to indicate how many times the sound should play. Click on the down arrow to get a setting of INFI-NITE, which makes the sound play over and over until the reader leaves the page.

Loop control   Sound filename

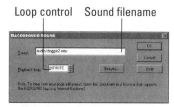

Figure 5-32: Adding a background sound.

 The sound does not start to play until it has completed download-ing. If it is a large file, it is possible that a visitor could hit the page, and leave it, without ever hearing the sound. It is also likely that the page will be less responsive to clicks while the sound file is downloading, so small is the order of the day.

"Woof! Woof!"

Figure 5-33: A page that uses a background sound.

To test this feature, I have in-cluded a fun file in the `\My Documents\My Web Pages` folder that uses a background sound (see Figure 5-33). Open the file `bgsound.htm` in Internet Explorer to hear the background sound. It uses an infinite loop, and I guar-antee that you won't be able to bear it for long! Just exit your browser to end the torture.

Real Audio

The examples of audio use discussed so far are based on downloading the file to a local computer and then playing it. Another option exists, and its called *Real Audio.* It plays low-quality audio clips in nearly real time. When a user clicks on a hyperlink to a Real Audio clip, the Real Audio player application starts up, then downloads a few seconds of audio into a buffer before it begins playing in real time.

Real Audio only works on your Web server if the Web server contains the files needed to make it work. Ask your Web administrator whether your server supports Real Audio, or a similar feature, before you attempt to work with it. Keep in mind that putting Real Audio on a server can be quite expensive — the licensing fee at the time this book was being written is from $2,000 to $10,000, depending on the number of simultaneous hits expected on the server.

To download the tools you need to convert your audio files to Real Audio format, visit the Real Audio Web site at http://www.realaudio.com (see Figure 5-34). You can also find complete instructions for your Web administrator on setting up Real Audio on a Web server.

Given the constraints of Real Audio — high cost, low quality — you may find yourself using it occasionally for downloading noncritical audio clips (sports quotes, for example) instead of using it to deliver audio clips on your own Web site. There is now a Real Audio personal server edition, but it allows just one outside person to listen to Real Audio files at a time. If more than one person logs in, the second person cannot access Real Audio until the first user is finished.

Figure 5-34: The Real Audio home page connects you to information and downloads about the product.

VDOLive video

VDOLive does for real-time video what Real Audio does for real-time audio: It enables you to deliver low-quality video clips in nearly real time over the Net. You can access the tools for working with VDOLive and get information about software and costs for installing it on your server at the VDOLive Web site: http://www.vdolive.com.

Figure 5-35 shows the first step in viewing a VDOLive video — the first few seconds of video are loaded to provide a buffer in case of interruptions in the data stream. This takes anywhere from 20 seconds to a minute — thus my reference to *nearly* real-time video. Figure 5-36 shows a clip while it is playing.

Load percentage

Animation plays during buffer loading

Figure 5-35: Loading a video clip into buffers before playing.

The clip was viewed over a typical 28.8 Kbps modem connection. Note (below the video image) that the player reports that 84% of the video frames are being skipped. This results in one video frame being displayed every second or two — there is, in fact, no semblance of motion at all except for the first few seconds of the video, which were downloaded and buffered. Note also that the image quality of the clip is very poor. If you cannot make it out, it shows three people, with the one on the left holding a guitar. A child is in the middle, and a woman on the right.

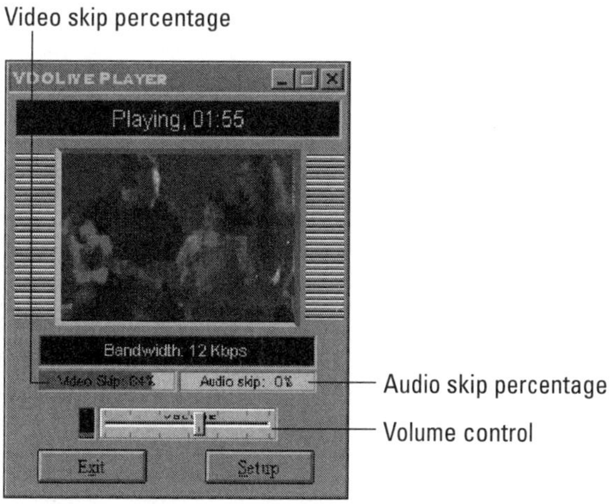

Video skip percentage

Audio skip percentage

Volume control

Figure 5-36: Playing a video clip with VDOLive.

The technology behind VDOLive gets a high cuteness score, but a low practicality score. It can be fun to be the first on your server to offer "real-time" video clips, but the cost in lost quality and dropped frames is high. Unless you know that your visitors will have at least an ISDN or faster connection to your Web site, you probably will want to offer video clips for downloading rather than real-time playback.

The Future of Web Multimedia

Video and audio clips are not the only possible ways to put multimedia on the Web. Rapid advances are occurring that will make it possible to put full-featured multimedia presentations on the Web. These technologies are available both as plug-ins for existing browsers and as free-standing applications that run along with your browser. Plug-ins are the most convenient — they enable you to view multimedia right on the Web page. Free-standing software isn't as convenient, but it gets the job done. With a free-standing program, the browser loads the program when it encounters the file type supported by the program.

Two key technologies that are likely to blossom in the near future are Virtual Reality Modeling Language (**VRML**) and Shockwave.

VRML

VRML is a language that enables you to specify 3-D objects, including animations and interaction with objects. It also allows you to specify hyperlinks and attach them to 3-D objects. Tools for creating VRML scenes are finally coming to market after several years of speculation about the direction this technology would take.

One such tool is Fountain Pro from Caligari, the makers of the 3-D modeling package trueSpace. Fountain looks a lot like trueSpace, in fact (see Figure 5-37). Fountain adds a host of VRML-specific features, however, and is designed for creating VRML worlds, not 3-D models for general use. Figure 5-37 shows a scene from a 3-D VRML world in Fountain Pro. The cube floating at center is a hyperlink that has just been clicked, and the Windows 95 dial-up connection to my Internet provider is attempting to make the connection.

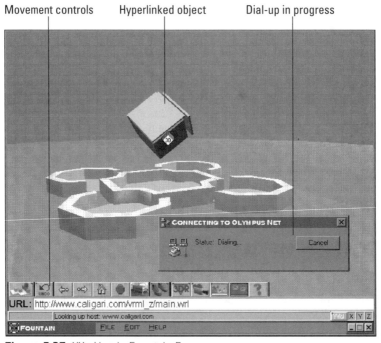

Figure 5-37: Working in Fountain Pro.

When the connection gets made, Fountain Pro downloads the VRML file for a new scene (see Figure 3-38). Note that the cursor over a new hyperlink shows that the object links to a 3-D VRML object on the Net.

You can use Fountain Pro both for creating models and for visiting VRML sites on the Web. As such, it is a free-standing program. If you click on a hyperlink to a 2-D Web site (that is, a standard Web site), Fountain Pro starts up your Web browser. The first time this happens, it asks you to locate your default browser (see Figure 5-39).

When used as an editor (see Figure 5-40), Fountain Pro provides a truly awesome set of 3-D tools. In Figure 5-40, a URL is being set for the cube object. You can create objects; paint surfaces; create child and parent relationships; distort shapes selectively to create complex, organic shapes; and much more. The full scope of Fountain Pro is impossible to cover here, but you can see for yourself by downloading a sample version from the Caligari Web page at http://www.caligari.com.

Viewing preferences   3-D hyperlink

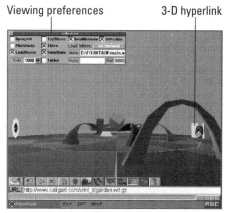

Figure 5-38: Jumping to a new VRML file.

Figure 5-39: Loading a browser to view a 2-D Web site.

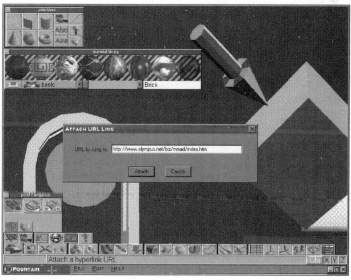

Figure 5-40: Creating a hyperlink while editing a scene in Fountain Pro.

As powerful as Fountain Pro is, if you don't plan to build VRML sites and only want to visit them, you can use a plug-in such as Web/FX. Whenever you visit a site with either an embedded VRML file or a VRML Web site, you'll see the site automatically in Netscape 2.0. Figure 5-41 shows an embedded VRML object in a page on my Web site (`http://www.olympus.Net/biz/mmad/vrx.htm`). You must have a VRML viewer such as Web/FX or VRScout installed to see the VRML content. The object was embedded by using Internet Assistant's capability to embed HTML commands that it doesn't support directly. See Chapter 7 for more information about **HTML Markup.** The command used to embed the scene shown in Figure 5-41 is the following:

VRML object

```
<embed src="vrml/mmad.wrl"
border=none align=center
width=150 height=150>
```

You learn how to use HTML markup to embed a simple VRML file in Chapter 7.

VRML is a new technology, and there is no telling how popular it will become. If your Web site has a message that can be delivered effectively with 3-D, however, VRML is the current standard. For more information on various VRML tools, visit sites such as `http://www.caligari.com`, `http://www.chaco.com/vrscout` and `http://www.paperinc.com`.

Figure 5-41: A VRML object embedded in a page on the author's Web site.

Shockwave

Shockwave is a plug-in for browsers that enables the browser to display Director files as part of a Web page. Director, from Macromedia, is a multimedia development tool with many capabilities. You can use Director to display animations, to create movies or interactive games, or to create multimedia presentations. Director is used for a wide variety of commercial products, such as the classic CD-ROM *From Alice to Ocean*.

It is beyond the scope of this book to teach you how to use Director to create multimedia products, because Director is both powerful and complex. If you are interested in learning more about Director, however, you can visit Macromedia's Web site at `http://www.macromedia.com` to get more information.

You can also download a copy of Shockwave from Macromedia's Web site. Figure 5-42 shows several frames from a Shockwave animation that you can view in a Shockwave gallery. Figure 5-43 shows a simple interactive game that you can play online by using the Shockwave plug-in. The game, called *Fireboy on Ice,* uses Director hotspots — the arrows at lower-left, for example, move the little man from square to square. He jumps by using a simple (but cute) animation, and sounds accompany all game actions. You can find the game on Macromedia's Web site.

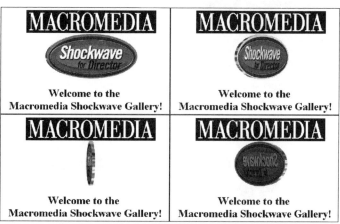

Figure 5-42: *An animation viewed with Shockwave.*

Shockwave is a technology with a lot of potential, but it also has certain limitations for use on the Web. It takes careful work to create Director files that accomplish the desired task and that are still quickly downloadable over the Web. File sizes of several hundred kilobytes are common, but a few are under 100K.

If you decide to work with Shockwave, give yourself several months to really learn the full range of tools and techniques involved in creating multimedia with Director. It is, first and foremost, a professional tool, and it will take some time and effort to learn how to use it well.

Jumping man

At the time this book was being written, the Shockwave plug-in was available only for Netscape 2.0. By the time you read this, Shockwave plug-ins should be available for most popular browsers, including Internet Explorer.

Figure 5-43: A game created with Macromedia Director and played on a Web page using the Shockwave plug-in.

CD Bonus: Creating Video clips with Adobe Premiere

Find it on the CD in the file `\Tutorial\bonus\make_video.htm`

CD Bonus: Creating Audio Files with Sound Forge

Find it on the CD in the file `\Tutorial\bonus\make_audio.htm`

Mastering the Internet: Forms and Feedback

In This Chapter

How to lay out a form effectively

The rules for each type of form element

How to get information back from forms

Integrating forms into your Web pages and your Web site

Customizing forms

Of all the Web features that put the *cool* in cool Web pages, forms are at the top of the list. Learning how to create forms can take your Web pages into another dimension. It takes some time and effort to master the art of creating good forms, but after you know how to create forms, an entire new world opens up to you. Using forms, you can take orders for products you sell, ask for feedback, or just have some fun interacting with your visitors.

Setting Up the Tutorial

In this chapter, you learn about every aspect of forms. This information includes how to build a form, how to output data from a form, and how to process that data afterwards. There are several tutorials, and you need a number of files on the CD-ROM to complete the tutorials. You can use automatic setup to copy files, or do the job manually.

Automatic setup

If you haven't already installed the software for automatic setup of the tutorials, turn to Appendix A and do so now. Otherwise, if you choose not to use automatic setup, see the next section, "Manual setup," which tells you how to copy the necessary files for this tutorial manually. If you didn't use automatic setup earlier, you can find complete instructions for starting, running, and using the automatic setup program in Chapter 1.

To run automatic setup, click the Start button, then Programs, and then click the Autopage icon, shown here.

This is the Chapter 6 tutorial, so click the Chapter 6 Files radio button to display the files for this chapter (see Figure 6-1).

Click here for Chapter 6 files

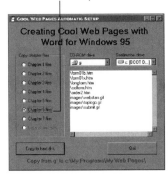

Figure 6-1: Automatic setup for Chapter 6 tutorial.

To copy the files for the tutorial to your hard disk, click the Copy to Hard Disk button. The files are copied to the My Web Pages subfolder of the My Documents folder. If you installed Microsoft Office to your C drive, the following is usually the folder:

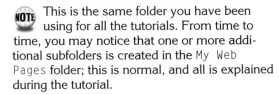

C:\My Documents\My Web Pages

NOTE This is the same folder you have been using for all the tutorials. From time to time, you may notice that one or more additional subfolders is created in the My Web Pages folder; this is normal, and all is explained during the tutorial.

After you have copied the necessary files, skip ahead to the start of the tutorial. If you choose not to use the automatic setup, read the next section to find out how to copy the necessary files manually.

Manual setup

Before you start the tutorial, open the folder called My Web Pages on your hard disk. If you already completed the tutorial in Chapter 1, you created it as a subfolder of the My Documents folder (usually **C:\My Documents**).

The tutorial in this chapter uses images and other kinds of files from the CD-ROM. They are located in the folder \tutorial\chap06. Copy the following image files

```
Webstars.gif

toplogo.gif

submit.gif
```

from the \tutorial\chap06 folder on the CD-ROM to the My Web Pages\images folder you created earlier on your hard disk (see Chapter 1 for complete details).

Copy the following document files

```
form01b.htm

form01x.htm

longform.htm

colform.htm

order2.htm
```

from the \tutorial\chap06 folder on the CD-ROM to the My Web Pages\video folder. If the My Web Pages\video folder doesn't already exist, create it now.

You are now ready to begin the tutorial.

What is a Form?

All the Web pages we have created so far contain just two kinds of elements on the page:

➠ Static elements, such as blocks of text and images, that are there simply to be read or viewed. They are not interactive.

➠ Dynamic elements, such as hyperlinks or video clips, that take the visitor to a new file or URL, or play a multimedia file.

Forms use a new kind of page element: controls. Controls for Web pages should be familiar to you — they are just like many of the standard features of Windows, such as text boxes, radio buttons, and checkboxes.

Submit button   Text box

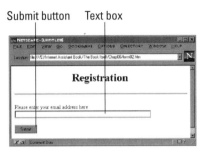

Figure 6-2: A simple Web-page form.

Forms can be simple or they can be complex. Figure 6-2 shows an example of a very simple form. There is one control — a text box — and a button to **submit** the form. The visitor to this page first types text into the text box, and then clicks the Submit button. Clicking the button causes some action to occur; you specify the action for each form. In this case, the action is to send e-mail to the owner of the page containing the text in the text box.

Figures 6-3 and 6-4 show the other extreme: a form so large and complex that it takes two figures to display all of it. Figure 6-3 shows the portion of the form that is used to collect information about a customer, and Figure 6-4 shows the portion that is used to collect information about a specific order. Each of these is a complete form, illustrating that you can have more than one form on a Web page.

This form is a template provided on the CD-ROM. The template is located with the Forms templates, and the filename is `Big Form.dot`.

Figure 6-3 shows several different kinds of controls. Most of the controls at the top of the form are text boxes, but there is also a checkbox and a multiline text box. There is a Submit button, but it uses an image instead of a plain gray button. There is also a Reset button, which clears the controls of text and resets them to their default values, if any.

Figure 6-4 shows how a table (with invisible borders) can be used to force alignment of controls on a page. It shows several groups of radio buttons, and it also includes Submit and Reset buttons.

Forms look complicated, but they are fairly easy to create. As you will recall, the secret to creating a Web page (see Chapter 3) is to start with a plan. A Web page with a form is no different. In fact, it's probably even more important to have a plan before you start creating a form — a form can easily be more complex than most Web pages. Figure 6-4 leaves little doubt about that!

Before we cover form planning, however, we are taking a side trip to talk about the various controls that you can place on a form. We'll create a form that contains one of each kind of control. It isn't an example of efficiency or beauty, but it shows you the tools you have to work with when creating a form. Then we do the fun stuff — creating forms that look good and perform specific tasks.

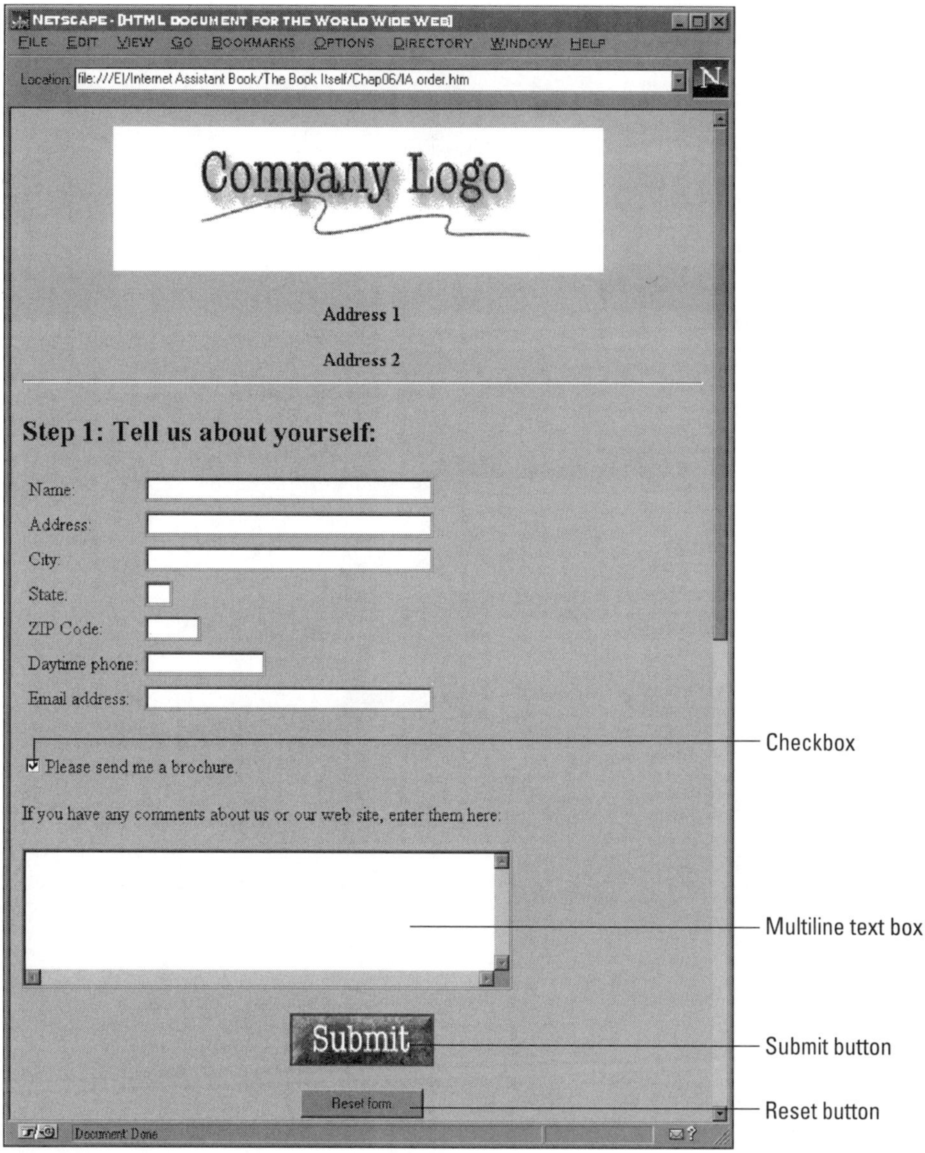

Figure 6-3: A form to collect information about a customer.

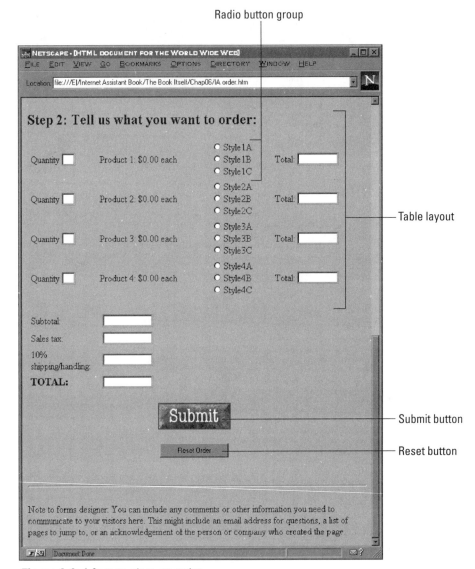

Figure 6-4: A form to place an order.

Creating a Sample Form

There is no button or menu selection in Word that says "Create a form." When you add the first form element to a Web page, Internet Assistant creates the form boundaries for you. For that reason, you should always add a control as the first step in creating a form. Don't put any text on the form until you have added the first control.

In this section, we are creating a form with each one of the different controls allowed on a Web page, as listed in Table 6-1.

Table 6-1	Form Controls
Control Type	**Description**
Text box	Allows users to enter a single line of text. You can set the width of the text box and the maximum number of characters the user can enter.
Hidden control	Hidden controls are used in processing a form. They can be used to identify the form by giving it a name, or to identify the destination for the output from the form.
List box	Provides a list of items from which the user selects. You can specify a single-selection list box, or a multi-selection list box.
Checkbox	A checkbox has two states: checked and unchecked. Unlike radio buttons, checkboxes are not grouped, so a user can check as many or as few as desired.
Group of radio buttons	Radio buttons also have two states, checked and unchecked, but they are grouped, and only one radio button in a group can be checked.
Multiline text box	Just like a normal text box, but allows entry of more than one line of text.
Password text box	Just like a normal text box, except the characters that the user types are replaced with an asterisk or similar character.
Submit button	Tells the Web browser to send the output of the form to a destination specified in the ACTION parameter of the form.
Reset button	Clears data entered by the user, and resets all controls to their default values (blank unless otherwise specified).

Defining form boundaries

Before we begin adding form elements, start by opening a new HTML file in Word (FILE⇨NEW; choose `html.dot` as the template). Save the file as `\My Documents\My Web Pages\form01.htm`.

During setup, the file `\My Documents\My Web Pages\form01x.htm` was copied from the CD-ROM. You can open this file at any time to see how the file `form01.htm` should look.

To create the form boundaries, simply position the cursor at the top of the file and click INSERT⇨FORM FIELD.

 Internet Assistant uses Word **fields** to simulate the appearance of controls on a form. It would be better if the menu selection were INSERT⇨FORM CONTROL, but it isn't.

Because form boundaries do not yet exist, you see the dialog box shown in Figure 6-5. The dialog box is warning you that you are about to create a form. If you already had a form on the page, and the cursor was outside the form, this dialog box would warn you that you had made a mistake. We want to create a new form, so this is not a mistake! Click the Continue button to create the form.

 If you don't see this dialog box, then you have turned off display of the dialog box previously. There is a checkbox at the bottom of the dialog box that enables you to prevent display of the dialog box in the future. Because this dialog box is intended simply to make sure you realize that you are creating a form, you can disable display if you want. If you do disable display, a new form is always created when you try to insert a control.

 If you turn off display of this dialog box, you must edit the Windows 95 Registry to turn it back on. Change the value for the key HKEY_LOCAL_MACHINE|HKEY_USERS|.Default|Software|Microsoft|Word|Internet Assistant|STOPNEWFORMDISP from 0 to 1. To edit the Registry, click START⇨RUN, type **REGEDIT** in the Open text box, and then click the OK button. See Chapter 2 for more details on working with Regedit and the Registry.

Click here to prevent future display of this dialog box   Continue button

NEW FORM

You are creating a new form in your current document

To complete the form, place text and form fields between the indicator lines.

If you wish to add to an existing form, cancel this dialog and move your cursor within the existing form before inserting the form field.

☐ Don't display this message again

Continue

Cancel

Help

Figure 6-5: You see this dialog box when you add the first control to a form.

Word goes through several gyrations to create the form, and the result is shown in Figure 6-6. The form is created, but the first control has not yet been added to the form. The Form Field dialog box at the center of Figure 6-6 enables you to select the type of control you want to add. The small tool panel to the right of the Form Field dialog box may appear anywhere within the Word window; it contains controls for creating and editing form controls.

TIP

We create controls in the same order they appear in this dialog box during the rest of this tutorial.

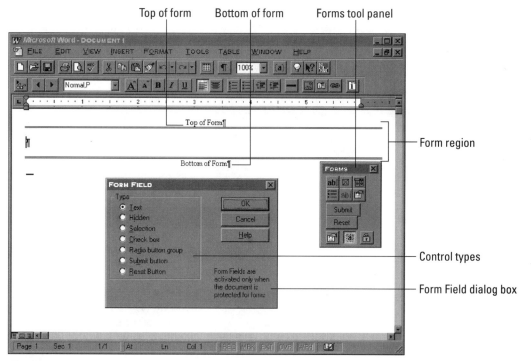

Figure 6-6: The view in Word after creating the form, before adding the first control.

Text box

To continue creating your first control, make sure the control name at the top of the dialog box (Text) is selected (to select it, click on it). Click the OK button, which displays the Text Form Field dialog box (see Figure 6-7).

The first task is to give the text box a name so that you can refer to it later. This text box is used to enter a visitor's name, so the name VisitorName is shown in Figure 6-7. Enter that value, and the other values shown in Figure 6-7, into the Text Form Field dialog box:

Item	Entry
Type of Text Field	Single line (default, already checked)
Maximum Number of Characters	40
Visible Size	25 Columns
Default Text	No entry (Could be used to display what-ever text you want as a default.)

Type of text box   Text box name

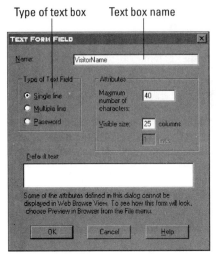

Figure 6-7: The Text Form Field dialog box enables you to set parameters for a text box control.

Text box control

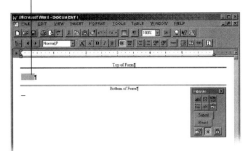

Figure 6-8: The newly created control.

Before you click the OK button to create the control, read the warning message at the bottom of the Text Form Field dialog box. It points out an important limitation of Internet Assistant. The text is as follows:

```
Some of the attributes defined in
this dialog cannot be displayed in
Web Browse View. To see how this
form will look, choose Preview in
Browser from the File menu.
```

This means that Word fields aren't flexible enough to show you what the form will look like in Word. For example, you specified a Visible size of 25 columns. Click OK to create the control, and note how wide the text box actually is (see Figure 6-8). Instead of 25 columns (characters) wide, the text box is about 5 columns wide. The width of the text box is one thing that Word cannot show accurately. As we create other controls, you will see other elements of controls that Word cannot display correctly. This is one instance where Word is not a WYSIWYG editor when it comes to Web pages. You will need to view your forms frequently in your browser to make sure that form layout works the way you intended it to.

A form control by itself means little or nothing. Position the cursor to the left of the control and add the following text: **Enter your first and last name here:** (see Figure 6-9). Figure 6-10 shows the result in the Netscape 2.0 browser. Note that the text box control has the proper width in the browser.

That's all it takes to create the form and the first control. We have not yet specified what will happen when the form is submitted, but we'll get to that after we create additional controls.

Added text

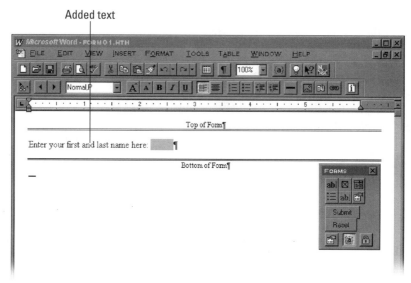

Figure 6-9: Adding text before a control.

Adding form controls

We will continue to add controls to the form, one of each type. To add the next control, press Enter and choose INSERT⇨FORM FIELD to display the Form Field dialog box. Click the second control type (Hidden), and then click the OK button. This displays the Hidden Form Field dialog box, shown in Figure 6-11.

Hidden control

You can use hidden form fields for various purposes, and their use depends on how the form will be handled after it is submitted. For example, you will probably want to create a hidden form field to give your form a name. On most Web servers, you also need to use a hidden form field to specify where the form data is to be sent after processing by a **script.**

Figure 6-10: The form control has the proper width when viewed in a browser.

Figure 6-11: The Hidden Form Field dialog box.

For example, my Internet provider uses a standard **CGI** script to process form data. This script requires two hidden fields: one to name the form, and one to identify where to send the data.

 CGI, which stands for Common Gateway Interface, is a method for moving data between Web pages and the rest of the server. This can involve scripts, programs, databases, and almost anything else you are likely to find on a computer. CGI scripting is outside the realm of this book, but there are several good books on the subject. If you are serious about using forms, consider the book *Creating Cool Web Pages with Perl* by Jerry Muelver, published by IDG Books Worldwide, Inc.

Let's use a hidden field to show how this is done. In the Name text box of the Hidden Form Field dialog box, enter the text **hide-FeedBkAdrs**. This name tells the CGI script that this particular hidden field will be used to provide the e-mail address to which the form data must be sent. In the Value text box, add the required e-mail address (see Figure 6-11). Click OK to create the hidden field.

 The Name and Value used here are specific to my Internet provider. Your Web server may have different requirements. Contact your Web administrator to find out how many hidden fields to use on your forms, and what names and values to use for those fields.

Figure 6-12 shows the appearance of a hidden field in Word. Note that the Value shows up as text inside the hidden form field. If you save your work and then view the result in your browser, you see that the field is really a hidden one. This is another example of how Word does not show you what a browser will display for your form.

Hidden control

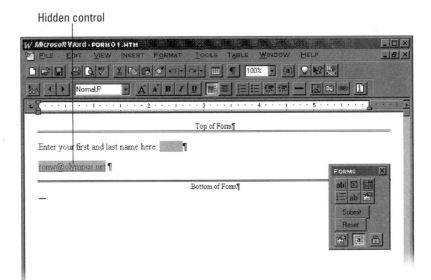

Figure 6-12: *A hidden field isn't hidden while viewed in Word.*

Selection list

To create the next control, select INSERT⇨FORM FIELD to display the Form
Field dialog box. Click the third type of control (Selection), and then click OK
to display the Selection Field dialog box (see Figure 6-13). Enter the name
Fruit for this control in the Name text box at the top of the dialog.

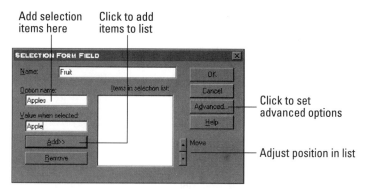

Add selection items here Click to add items to list

Click to set advanced options

Adjust position in list

Figure 6-13: *Adding a selection control.*

This dialog box is quite a bit different from the two we've seen so far. That's
because the Selection (often called a *list box*) control is quite a bit different.
This control displays a list of items to the user, and the user can select from the
list by clicking. You use this dialog box to add items to the list, and to rearrange
items if necessary. To add an item to the list, follow these steps:

1. Click in the Option Name text box, and type the text you want dis-
    played for that option. For this example, type **Apples**.

2. Now click the Value When Selected text box, and type the value that is
    to be sent when the form is submitted. For this example, type **Apple**.
    (We *could* type **Apples**, but I want to make the point that you are not
    required to type the same entry in both areas.)

    There are two important things to keep in mind regarding this situation:

    ➥ Always keep track of which text box is which, so that you are clear
       about which contains text to be displayed, and which contains the
       value sent upon form submission.

    ➥ The text displayed need not match the text sent at submission.
       For example, you might have a long display text (such as `Catalog
       of car parts for Chevies, 1983-1994`) and a short value for
       submission (such as "CHEV 83-94"). This means you can use lots
       of text for clarity at display time, and short text for concision at
       submission.

3. To add the item to the Items in Selection List box, click the Add
    button.

If you make a mistake, and only notice it after you Add the item, you can remove the item by selecting it in the Items in Selection List box, and then clicking the Remove button.

One item does not make a list. Add the following additional items to the list:

Option Name	Value When Selected
Oranges	Orange
Tangerines	Tangerine
Pears	Pear
Mangos	Mango
Bananas	Banana
Strawberries	Strawberry

To move the currently selected item in the list up or down, click the up and down arrows at the right of the list box.

You may have noticed that there is an Advanced button in the group of buttons at the right of the Selection Field dialog box. Clicking the Advanced button displays additional choices in the dialog box (see Figure 6-14). There are two additional choices. Multiple Selection enables the user to select more than one choice in the list. Selected Option Is Default means that the currently selected (highlighted) option in the list will be the automatic default choice, even if the user selects nothing at all. This is desirable for certain situations. For example, if the customer is ordering a catalog, you can make your general catalog the default selection. If you permit multiple selections, the user can select additional catalogs at the same time.

Figure 6-14: *Setting advanced options.*

NOTE The Advanced options do not display correctly in Word, but work correctly in your browser.

Click the OK button in the Selection Field dialog box to create the list. Add the text **Select your favorite kind of fruit:** to the left of the list. Figure 6-15 shows how the "list" appears in Word. As usual, the list will appear correctly in your browser, as a drop-down list control showing the first item in the list. To test it, save your work and use FILE⇨PREVIEW IN BROWSER.

To show more than one item, you must edit the HTML code for the selection list. (See Chapter 7 for information about editing HTML codes.) You have to edit the HTML file in Notepad to make this change. Find the HTML code for the selection list, and add the parameter **size=n** where *n* is the number of lines you want to display. Example: `<SELECT NAME="Fruit" SIZE="3">`

Selection list

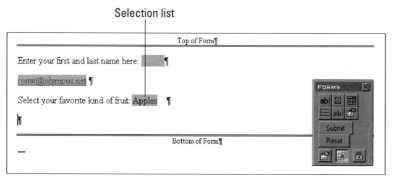

Figure 6-15: The appearance of a selection list in Word.

Checkbox

Checkboxes are simple to add and to use. Traditionally, the checkbox is placed to the left of the text that describes what the checkbox is for. A checkbox has two possible values: checked or not checked. If the checkbox is unchecked when the form is submitted, no data is sent for the control. If the checkbox is checked, the value you assign to the checkbox is sent.

To add a checkbox, position the cursor on a new, empty line below the line containing the selection list. Select INSERT⇨FORM FIELD. This displays the Form Field dialog box. Choose Checkbox and click OK to display the Checkbox Form Field dialog box (see Figure 6-16).

Figure 6-16: Adding a checkbox control.

Every control you add must be placed between the top of form/bottom of form markers. Otherwise, Word warns you that you are trying to create a new form.

Specify a Name (SendCatalog) and a Value (Catalog) in the areas provided. There is a checkbox (this is just the beginning of the confusion) below the Name and Value text boxes called Checked. If you check this checkbox, the checkbox you create will be checked by default when viewed in a browser. Click on OK. The urge to say "Check your work now and save it" is overwhelming, so there, I've said it, and we can move on. (If you have a better check joke than that one, e-mail it to jokes@olympus.net and I'll include the best one in the next edition of the book. Heck, I'll even send a WebStarr T-shirt to the winner!)

Whew! Figure 6-17 shows the result. I've added the text `send me one of your catalogs by mail` to indicate what the checkbox is for.

Checkbox control   Added text

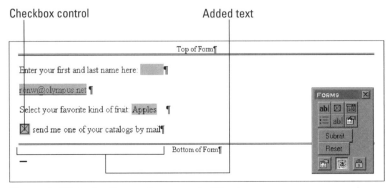

Figure 6-17: A checkbox as it appears in Word.

Radio Button Group

Radio buttons always should be used in a group. The behavior of radio buttons is specifically designed for a group of options, only one of which may be chosen. If you only have one option, or if more than one option can be chosen, use checkboxes. For example, a group of radio buttons is a good choice if you have a form that asks the user to specify the method of payment for a purchase: the user can choose only one of the available methods of payment for each purchase. Let's create a group of radio buttons that handles this task.

Put the cursor on a new, empty line. Click INSERT⇨FORM FIELD to display the Form Field dialog box, and select the fifth option: Radio Button Group. This displays the Radio Button Group Form Field dialog box (see Figure 6-18). Click OK.

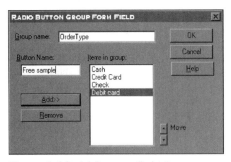

Figure 6-18: Adding a radio button group.

This dialog box is similar to the one you used to add a selection list. Type a name for the group (OrderType), and then add the following five items by typing each one into the Button name text box and clicking the Add button:

Cash

Credit Card

Check

Debit Card

Free sample

Click OK to add the radio button group to the form (see Figure 6-19). Notice that the items you entered into the list appear as individual buttons. The buttons appear as boxes (looking suspiciously like checkboxes), but they will appear as radio buttons in your browser. I also added a line of text above the radio buttons, Please indicate the method of payment, as shown in Figure 6-19.

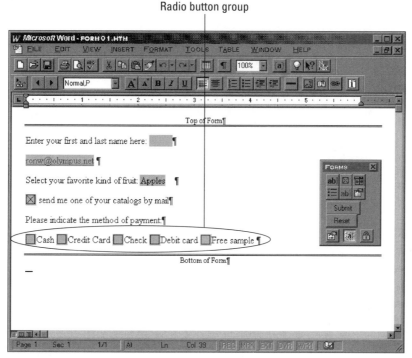

Figure 6-19: The appearance of a radio button group in Word.

Multiline Text Box

A **multiline text box** is added in the same manner as a standard text box. Begin in the usual manner: INSERT⇨FORM FIELD, choose Text in the Form Field dialog box, and then click OK. This displays the Text Form Field dialog box (see Figure 6-20). Click the Multiple Line radio button.

This enables you to access one additional entry in the Text Form Field dialog box: Lines. The Lines entry specifies the height of the multiple-line text box. Make the following entries in the Text Form Field dialog box:

Choose multiple line No entry necessary
(value ignored)

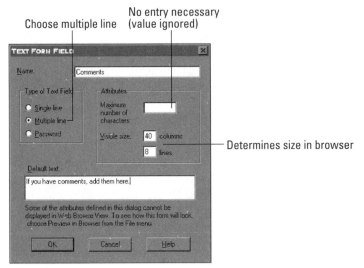

Determines size in browser

Figure 6-20: Adding a multiline text box control.

Item	Entry
Name	Comments
Type of Text Field	Multiple line
Maximum Number of Characters	No entry necessary
Visible Size: Columns	40
Visible Size: Lines	8
Default Text	If you have comments, add them here.

Click OK to create the multiline text box. Figure 6-21 shows the result in Word — it's not multiline at all. Don't worry; it will show up correctly in your browser. Because we used default text, it is not necessary to add any normal text to explain the use of this control to the user.

If you want to check the appearance of any of these controls in your browser, just save your work and select FILE⇨PREVIEW IN BROWSER to take a look.

Password control

A *password control* is almost exactly the same as a standard text box control. The only difference is that, when the user types text into a password control, the text shows up as a row of asterisks instead of as the text that is typed. You have probably encountered this type of control before if you log into a computer system (including all network versions of Windows). To add a password control, add a new line and type the text **To access special features, enter your password:** . Note that there is a space after the colon.

Multiline text box with default text

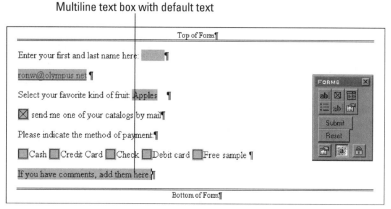

Figure 6-21: The appearance of a multiline text box in Word isn't multiline at all.

For all the other controls, we added the control first, and then added any text required. Except for adding the first control, it makes no difference at all whether you add accompanying text before or after you create the control. Just make sure that all text and all controls that are part of the form are placed between the top of form/bottom of form boundaries.

Position the cursor at the end of the line of text, and click the top-left icon in the floating Forms tool panel. This opens the Text Form Field dialog box (see Figure 6-22). Select Password as the Type of Text Field. Note that the Default Text Area becomes unavailable, and that the defaults for Maximum Number of Characters and Visible Size: Columns change from 25 to 10. (The typical password is from 5 – 8 characters.) Enter a Name (Password), and click OK to accept the other defaults. Figure 6-23 shows the result in Word. There is no visual difference from a normal text box control, but the Password control behaves differently when it appears in a browser.

Choose password

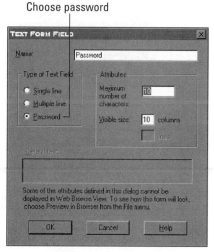

Figure 6-22: Adding a password control.

Password control

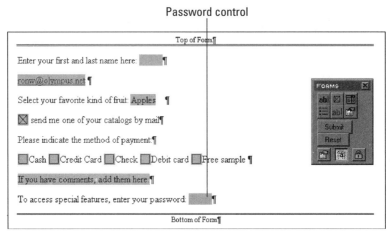

Figure 6-23: The appearance of a Password control in Word.

 You can create any of the control types using the Forms tool panel. Move the cursor over each of the icons to see what each tool on the panel will do for you. Figure 6-24 identifies each tool.

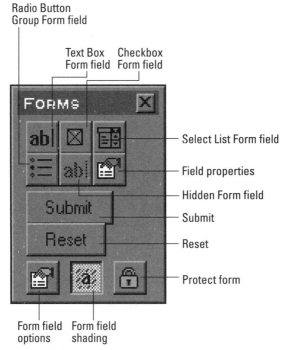

Figure 6-24: The tools on the Forms tool panel.

Submit button

Every form must have a submit button if the form is to actually do anything. The section "Submitting a Form," later in this chapter, tells you everything you ever wanted to know about submitting a form. Right now, you learn how to add the button that does the submitting.

Create a new line for the Submit button below all the other controls. It is most logical to put the Submit button after all the entries on a form, because the user must complete the entries before clicking the Submit button.

Choose INSERT⇨FORM FIELD, or click the Submit tool on the Forms tool panel, to open the Submit Button Form Field dialog box (see Figure 6-25). Like all other controls, the submit button needs a name; type **SendNow** in the Name text box.

The appearance area of the dialog box gives you two choices for button appearance. You can choose Text, in which case you supply text that will appear on the Submit button. Alternatively, you can choose Picture and specify an image file to use as a button. For this example, click the Text radio button, and type **Submit** as the Button Label.

If you do use a picture, make sure that you include some text or other cues in the picture that makes it clear that the picture is a Submit button.

Form encryption type (optional)   Form action   Form method

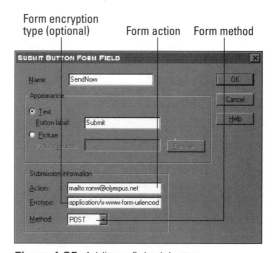

Figure 6-25: Adding a Submit button.

The bottom of the dialog box is very important. This information determines how the form's data will be submitted, and what the server does with the form data. For this example, we use the simplest example. The Action is `mailto:me@myaddress.com`. Accept the default for Enctype (Encryption type). The default Method, GET, is seldom used; select POST instead. Click OK to create the submit button. Figure 6-26 shows the appearance of the Web page with a Submit button added. The difference is not terribly dramatic, but it is important. Without a Submit button, the form has no meaning!

Submit button

Figure 6-26: The page with a Submit button.

Reset button

Adding a Reset button to your form is optional. The Reset button does just what its name implies: it resets all the controls on the form to their default state. If you supplied default text or a default selection in a list or for a checkbox, the default is applied when the Reset button is clicked. Text box controls without a default will be blank.

To add a Reset button, add a space after the Submit button so that the two buttons do not touch each other. Click the Reset tool on the Forms tool panel to open the dialog box shown in Figure 6-27. There is just one entry to make: the label (text) for the Reset button. Type **Reset** into the Button Label text box, and click OK to create the Reset button. Figure 6-28 shows the result.

Figure 6-27: Adding a Reset button.

Reset button

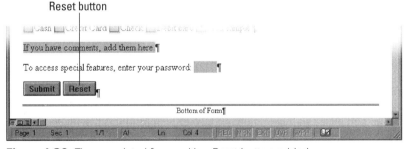

Figure 6-28: The completed form, with a Reset button added.

Save the HTML file, and select FILE⇨PREVIEW IN BROWSER to view the completed form in your browser. It should look similar to Figure 6-29.

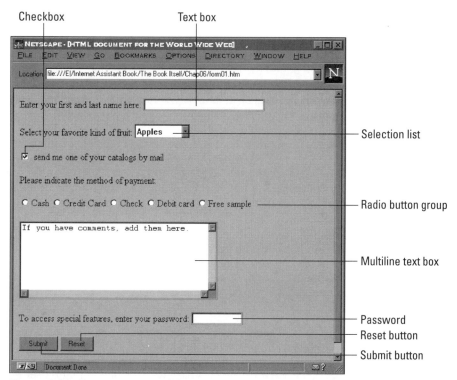

Figure 6-29: The appearance of the completed form in a browser.

Notice the following features of the various controls shown in Figure 6-29 (you might want to experiment with them in your browser):

➥ The first text control appears at its specified width. If you type more characters than can be displayed, the text scrolls (up to the maximum number of characters allowed).

➥ The selection list appears as a drop-down list, with a downward-pointing arrow to display the full list. (Try it and see!)

➥ The checkbox appears with a check in it.

➥ The radio buttons now have small circles. Clicking any radio button clears the black dot from the previous selection, allowing only one item to be selected at a time.

➥ The multiline text box has multiple lines. You can type beyond the right and bottom margins, and you can use the scroll bars to see what you type.

➥ Typing in the password control results in a row of asterisks. (Try it and see!)

Editing form elements

After you have added the form elements (controls and buttons) to your Web page, you can easily make changes. To edit a control on a form, highlight and double-click the control. You can also highlight the control and click the Form Field Properties tool on the Forms tool panel.

When you edit a control, you see the same dialog box that you used to create the control in the first place. If you highlight a text field and edit it, you see the Text Form Field dialog box. If you highlight a radio button group, you see the Radio Button Form Field dialog box, and so on. You can make whatever changes are required, and then click OK to save the changes when you are finished.

When you are finished with your form, click the Protect Form tool on the Forms tool panel. This prevents accidental changes to the form. If you do need to edit the form at a later time, position the cursor in the form and click Protect Form again.

Submitting a Form

The whole point of a form is collecting the information that a user types into it. When the user clicks the Submit button, the data is sent to — where? That's a good question, and it has several answers.

The easiest way to send the data from the form is with e-mail. The data from the form is collected together into an e-mail message, and is sent to a mail address that you specify. That's what we did with the Submit button in the previous tutorial (see Figure 6-25). The nice thing about using e-mail is that no special software or tricks are required to get the data to its destination. E-mail is e-mail, and it works.

E-mail, however, is limited as a way to move form data. As you'll see shortly, the data comes in just one highly compact and highly confusing format. In addition, when you use e-mail, you cannot generate any actions based on forms. You can't search a database. You can't run a program to call up the user's last form responses. You can't do anything but send the form data as e-mail.

The answer to this problem is CGI scripting. Scripts are placed on the server. The form points to the script. When the user clicks the Submit button, the form data is packaged just as it would be for e-mail, but it is sent to the script. A script is very much like a program. It can massage the data, it can call other programs on the server — it can do all kinds of wonderful things that we'll explore in just a bit.

The primary disadvantage of scripts is that someone has to write the script, and this takes time and skill to accomplish. Different servers might use different languages for scripts, although most servers will allow you to write scripts in a language called Perl.

A secondary disadvantage of scripts is that your particular Web server may not allow you to put your own scripts on the server! Many Web administrators are quite picky about the scripts they permit on the server — and for good reason. A script could, for example, cause a security breach on the server. That would allow a knowledgeable hacker to do things that make Web administrators shudder — files could be erased, data could be scrambled, or proprietary information could be compromised.

Check with your Web administrator to find out whether scripts are allowed on your server, and, if they are allowed, find out what languages can be used to write the scripts. If you have any kind of programming background, you can certainly learn to write scripts. Just use a search engine to find Web pages with information on the scripting language of your choice and give it a try. If you don't have programming experience, you should get your hands on a good book on scripting (I mentioned a good one earlier, *Creating Cool Web Pages with Perl*) before you dive in. If your Web server uses Windows NT, you might even be able to use Access Basic or Visual Basic for some of your scripting tasks.

Let's look at the details of working with e-mail and scripts for dealing with form data.

Mailto and Forms

I haven't pushed very much HTML code at you in the course of this book, on the theory that the main reason to use Internet Assistant is to *avoid* HTML as much as possible. But when it comes to forms, it's worth a little diversion to explore the HTML code behind forms. This information makes it easier to understand what forms are about and how they work.

At the top of each form, there is a line of HTML code that specifies what happens when a form is submitted. It is the line that defines the start of the form, and here is one taken from a form that I use on my own Web site:

```
<FORM ACTION="mailto:ronw@olympus.net" METHOD="POST">
```

The very first character (<) is the start of an HTML tag. The first part, FORM, is the tag itself. There are two **parameters** for this tag: ACTION and METHOD. You may recall them from the Submit Button dialog box (refer back to Figure 6-25). The ACTION parameter tells the browser how to submit the form — in this case, to bundle up the form data and mail it off to the address shown. The tag ends with that last character (>).

The METHOD parameter has two possible values, GET and POST. The difference between these two is very technical in its details, but there is only one thing you need to know in order to decide which one to use. The GET method is limited to about 1,000 characters (sometimes more, sometimes less; it depends on the server). The POST method is not as limited. The bottom line: Always use the POST method; you won't regret it.

Although the default value for a Submit button in Internet Assistant is GET, you should always use POST as the method for sending form data.

If you are the curious type, you may be interested to know that the GET method appends the form data to the URL of the page with the form and sends the data as a command line. That's the reason for the character limitation — command lines can only be so long. The POST method, on the other hand, is similar to putting the data into a file, and a file can be as large as it needs to be.

If you plan to use several forms, add a hidden control to the form that contains the name of the form. A hidden field has a Name and a Value. The Name of a hidden control could be "FormName", and the Value would be the name itself, such as "OrderForm" or "FeedbackForm".

When the data is mailed to you, you can immediately tell which form was the source of the data. Even better, if you write a program to process the data, the program can dump the data from one form into one file, and the data from another form into another file.

All these references to "form data" have no doubt whetted your appetite for some actual data. It's not a pretty sight. For example, I filled out the tutorial form as shown in Figure 6-30. I then submitted the data (remember, the ACTION is a mailto).

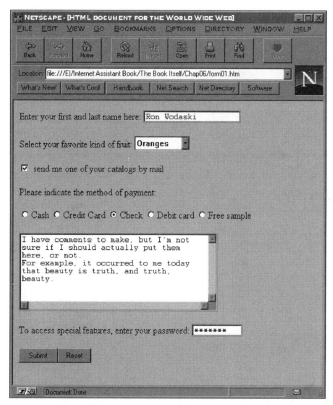

Figure 6-30: The form with values filled in.

Here is the clump of form data that arrived in my mail:

```
VisitorName=Ron+Wodaski&hideFeedBkAdrs=ronw@olympus.net&Fruit=Orange&Send
Catalog=Catalog&OrderType=Check&Comments=I+have+comments+to+make%2C+
but+I%27m+not%0D%0Asure+if+I+should+actually+put+them%0D%0Ahere%
2C+or+not.%0D%0AFor+example2C+it+occurred+to+me+today%0D%0Athat+beauty+
is+truth%2C+and+truth%2C%0D%0Abeauty.%0D%0A&Password=machine&
SendNow=Submit
```

What a mess! This is clearly not designed for human consumption. The data uses an equal sign between a control's name and the data, and the ampersand (&) separates different controls. Spaces are shown as plus signs, and hexadecimal codes are used for nonalphanumeric characters (such as %0D%0A for carriage return and line feed, or %27 for an apostrophe). Sorting this out on your own would be a tragic waste of time.

Fortunately, I have written a program (called a **parser**) that can sort out this mess. I've included it on the CD-ROM, and you can easily install it to your hard disk to aid in processing form data. See Appendix A for information on installation. Figure 6-31 shows the Parser program in action, with the data neatly converted to human-readable form.

Figure 6-31: The form data neatly parsed out.

 The parser is written in Visual Basic 4.0. I have included the complete source code if you want to create a custom version of the Parser for your own use. You will need Visual Basic 4.0 Professional Edition to modify the Parser, however.

To use the parser, you simply copy form data from your mail program to the Clipboard. Figure 6-32 shows a mail message in Netscape 2.0, selected and ready to be copied to the Clipboard. If you are using a different mail program, the appearance of the form data, and the appearance of the mail program, may differ.

Form data

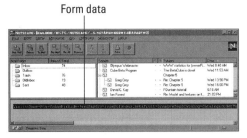

Figure 6-32: A message in a mail program containing form data.

To use the Parser to sort out your own form data, you simply click the buttons at the right of the Parser application window from top to bottom, starting with the Paste It button. Table 6-2 describes the various controls in the Parser application (refer to Figure 6-31 for the names of the controls).

Table 6-2	Parser Application Controls
Control	**Description**
Use columns	Determines how the data is displayed in the output text box. If Use Columns is checked, the data appears as shown in Figure 6-31. If unchecked, the data is displayed as shown in Figure 6-33. Data saved to a file is not affected by the Use Columns setting.
Overwrite/Append	Selects the method for writing data to a file. If Over-write is selected, the data for the current form over-writes any existing data, leaving just a single chunk of data in the file. If Append is selected, the current data is *added to* any data already in the file.
Configure	Allows you to set various parameters for operation of the parser. Figure 6-34 shows the appearance of the Configure dialog box. You can, if your mail program requires it, change the characters used for various functions in form data, or change the name of the output file.
Paste It	Copies the data from the Clipboard to the input text box at the top of the parser.
Parse It	Parses the form data. Parsing is just the process of converting all those symbols (=, +, &, %0D, and so on) into readable form. The result is displayed in the Output text box, with or without columns.
Copy	Copies the data from the Output text box to the Clip-board, where you can paste it into any Windows application you desire.
Save	Saves the data to the file specified in the Configuration dialog box (default is output.txt). Append and Overwrite radio buttons determine whether data is added to an existing file or overwrites an existing file. When you click the Save button, the dialog box shown in Figure 6-35 appears, enabling you to change the output filename at the last minute, if desired.
Quit	Quits the Parser program.

Figure 6-33: The data arranged without columns (compare to Figure 6-31).

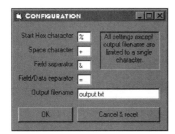

Figure 6-34: Configuring Parser options.

Output file name

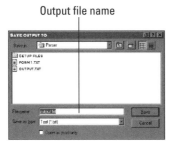

Figure 6-35: Saving parsed output to a file.

If you save the Parser output to a file, it looks like this:

```
"Ron Wodaski","ronw@olympus.net","Orange","Catalog","Check","I
have comments to make, but I'm not sure if I should actually put
them here, or not. For example, it occurred to me today that
beauty is truth, and truth, beauty.","machine","Submit"
```

Most database programs can read this kind of file (called a comma-delimited file) and add the form data to a database. Consult the documentation for your database software to find out how it's done. An alternative is to read the data into a spreadsheet. Programs such as Excel can read comma-delimited files, although they are referred to as "comma separated value" files (CSV files).

The primary purpose of the Parser program is to make it easier for you to work with e-mailed form data. Because many Web administrators will not let you put custom scripts on the server, you may wind up having to process your form data on your own. There are many different ways to work with form data, and no Web parser can anticipate every possibility. By providing the source code for the Parser program, I've given you a starting point to create custom solutions. If you are not comfortable programming in Visual Basic, someone who knows that language can modify the program for you.

I suggest that you experiment with the mailto option and learn how it works with your browser and your mail program. You don't have to put your forms on the server to test them. Just open the form in your browser while you are already on-line, and when you click the Submit button, the mail is sent automatically.

If you are not online when you click the Submit button, your browser will either act in a very confused fashion, or try to go online. Different browsers and mailers handle this situation differently.

A final word of warning: Not every browser supports the mailto option. The list of such browsers is getting shorter every day, however, as the mailto option becomes one of the most popular ways to send form data. If in doubt, just test a form with your browser/mailer combination to see whether it works properly.

Scripts and forms

I have taken pains to point out that many Web administrators will not allow you to put custom forms on their Web servers. In many cases, this does not totally prevent you from using scripts on the server — it only means you can't put *custom* scripts on the server. Many servers contain a library of standard scripts that enable you to do limited amounts of forms processing. The primary advantage of using a library script is that the data that comes to you won't be as scrambled as the earlier mailto examples.

To tell your form to use a script, you simply supply the path and filename of the script in the ACTION parameter of the form. When using Internet Assistant, this is done when you specify the options for the Submit button. Figure 6-36 shows an example of an Action entry in the Submit Button Form Field dialog box that specifies a script.

You can find a version of `form01.htm` on your hard disk that uses a script instead of mailto. The filename is `\My Documents\My Web Pages\ form01b.htm`. You can open the document in Word and examine the Submit button and hidden fields by double-clicking the button and the fields.

Script path and name (on server)

Figure 6-36: Specifying a script for a form.

The text entered in the Action text box is:

```
/cgi-bin/formGeneric
```

This is the script supplied by my Internet provider that processes data from any form and returns it in a somewhat human-readable form. The form name is `formGeneric`, and it is located in the `cgi-bin` directory on the server. The `formGeneric` script also requires two hidden fields (see the following list). These fields will almost certainly vary from one provider to the next; check with your Web administrator to find out which hidden fields, if any, are used by your server's library of scripts for generic forms processing.

Hidden Field Name	Hidden Field Value	What the Hidden Field Does
hide-Form	form	Specifies that the data comes from a form
hide-FeedBkAdrs	ronw@olympus.net	Tells the script where to send the output after processing the form data

The hidden fields, by the way, should not be added just anywhere on the form. In some cases, the hidden fields must be the first fields on the form. The only reason the hidden field was second in the tutorial is that the Hidden control is the second item in the Form Field dialog box, and we added controls in order of appearance.

I modified the form from the previous tutorial to make sure it included these two hidden fields, and I changed the Action so that it specifies the `formGeneric` script.

TIP If you are testing the form from your hard drive while you are online, you need to specify a complete path to the script. For example, for my provider, this is `http://www.olympus.net/cgi-bin/formGeneric`.

One of the nicest things about scripts is that they can output an HTML form to give the user feedback after submitting the form. For example, the formGeneric script displays a one-line Web page (see Figure 6-37). A script does not have to display a Web page at all, and the page can be as simple as the one shown in Figure 6-37, or as complex as it needs to be — it can even be another form!

Figure 6-37: The HTML page output by the script.

The script returned the following to my mailbox:

```
Origin URL:          file:///E|/Internet Assistant Book/The Book
Itself/Chap06/form01b.htm
Remote host:         ptpm017.olympus.net
Remote IP address: 198.133.237.47

Hidden Fields
 hide-Form***form
hide-FeedBkAdrs***ronw@olympus.net

End Of Hidden Fields

Form Fields
 VisitorName***Tom Thumb
 Fruit***Strawberry
 OrderType***Cash
 Comments***I'm short, so I guess that I don't have
a whole lot to say here.

 Password***shorty
 SendNow***Submit

End Of Form Fields
```

Of course, a generic form-processing script on your server may return form data in a completely different format. The entire point here is that most generic scripts return data that a human can read, instead of the computerese of the mailto option.

Scripts can be very powerful Web tools. Talk to your Web administrator to learn what library scripts are available to you. You may also find that there are pages on the server that explain what scripts are available and how to use them. You can also look at forms that already exist on the server to see whether they offer clues about how to work with the library scripts on the server.

If you are serious about scripts, however, you owe it to yourself to get a good book that describes how to use the appropriate scripting language to perform just those scripting tricks that you require. Some of the things that scripts can do for you include

➡ Create a guest book that registers visitors to your home page

➡ Display custom Web pages for each visitor

➡ Automatically generate Web pages from a database

➡ Generate Web pages that are updated daily, hourly, or any specified period

➡ Add comments from Web visitors to Web pages

➡ Manage a message board on your Web site

The list of possibilities for scripts is endless — limited only by the imagination of the programmer writing the scripts. If you want to create a Web site with flexibility and lots of custom features, scripts are the way to achieve that goal.

Creating Elegant Forms

The form we created earlier in this chapter showed the essentials of building a form, but it was hardly an elegant solution. Let's look at some forms that illustrate the techniques you can use to create useful forms on your Web pages. We'll create two forms: a feedback form for WebStarr and an order form for ordering online.

Creating a feedback form

Figure 6-38 shows a first attempt at a feedback form. This version already uses several techniques that often help arrange the elements of a form into logical order. These include

➡ Using a table to align the form controls (right column) and the text for the controls (left column)

➡ Using right alignment within a table to force the text in the left column next to the controls in the right column

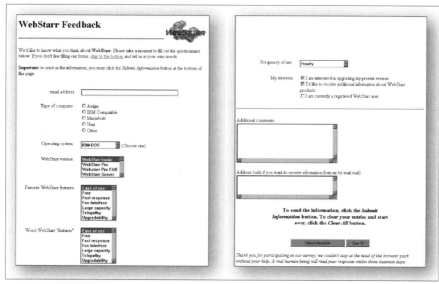

Figure 6-38: A first draft of a feedback form. See text for criticism.

➡ Using multiple-selection lists instead of a series of checkboxes

➡ Using cell spacing to add a bit of white space between the controls, making it easier to visually organize the form

Unfortunately, the result is a form that is very long. So long, in fact, that it takes four screens at 800 × 600 to show this form. There are several reasons for the length of the form. For example, the multiple-selection lists get expanded by the browser — to illustrate this, look at the choices for Favorite WebStarr features — the seven items take up seven vertical lines.

The first thing to notice about this form is that there is a large amount of white space available. If we could find another arrangement that would leave less white space, we could make the form shorter and more elegant.

As shown in Figure 6-38, the form uses two columns in a table. The left column contains text and a lot of white space. The right column contains the various controls. Most of the controls take up a lot of vertical space, but they aren't very wide. If we could find an arrangement that eliminated the vertical space between text entries, and used more of the horizontal space next to the control entries, we'd have a better layout.

One way to accomplish both tasks is to stack the text and controls vertically in multiple table columns. Figure 6-39 shows the form rearranged using two columns. This puts all of the information on one screen — granted, it is still too large to fit on an 800 × 600 screen, but the complete form fits easily on a standard 1,024 × 768 Windows desktop.

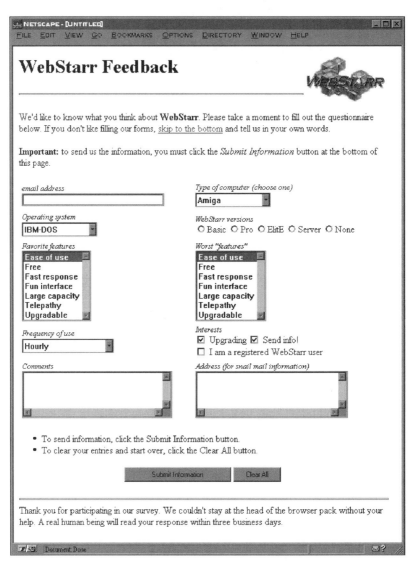

Figure 6-39: By using two columns, the information is presented more elegantly.

I have included the two files for these forms (the original layout and the two-column layout) on the CD-ROM, and they were copied to your hard disk during chapter setup. The file `\My Documents\My Web Pages\longform.htm` shows the original layout, and the file `\My Documents\My Web Pages\colform.htm` shows the two-column layout. To see how each layout was created, open the files and double-click each control. Here is the short version of how I created the two-column page:

1. The text control for E-mail Address is nothing special: 30 characters wide (to keep within the two-column arrangement), with a Name of "e-mail" to keep things simple and direct.

2. The Type of Computer control is a simple selection list. The Name is "ComputerType". Operating System is also a simple selection list, with a Name of "OS".

3. The WebStarr versions control is a radio button group. I used it only because it fits on one line, and still is able to show all the available choices at one time. The two selection lists have text entries that are too long to fit on a single line. The Name is "Version".

4. The Favorite Features and Worst "Features" controls are both selection lists with the Advanced option multiple selection turned on. This makes them large, multiline controls, but that's the price you pay to get the multiselection ability. The Names are "Best" and "Worst".

5. Frequency of Use is another simple selection list. The Name is "Frequency".

6. Interests consists of three checkboxes, with Names of "Upgrade", "Info", and "Registered".

7. The Comments control is a multiline text box (also called a text area, because the HTML code is <TEXTAREA>). The Name is "Comments". The Address control is another multiline text box, with a Name of Address.

8. The Submit Button has a Name of "SubmitIt"; Value is "Submit Information". The Reset Button has a Name of "Reset" and a Value of "Clear All".

9. Other points to ponder: All table cells were set for a vertical alignment of Top, and a horizontal alignment of Left. The table itself has the WYSIWYG setting (of the TABLE⇨CELL WIDTH AND SPACING dialog box) checked. And I added a few horizontal rules to make it clear what is, and is not, part of the form.

If you have trouble creating the multiline text controls in a table cell, you can either add them below the table, or you can modify the HTML file in Notepad (see Chapter 7 for discussions of such neat tricks).

This form is intended to be called from the WebStarr "Products" page you created in Chapter 3. To create the link, open the file `products.htm` in Word, and find the hyperlink for Feedback Central near the bottom of the form. Currently, this hyperlink points to:

```
feedback@Webstarr.com
```

To change the hyperlink, double-click it to open the Hyperlink dialog box. Change the File or URL text box from the preceding text to:

```
colform.htm
```

and click the OK button to save the change. Save the file, and then use your browser to check the hyperlink. It should jump to the two-column version of the form.

CAUTION To submit the form, you must be online. Some browsers will recognize that you are not online and attempt to make the connection for you. If you have not replaced the default ACTION for the form (see the end of this section), the form is submitted to a nonexisting e-mail address, which generates an error message several hours later, when your server determines that the mail cannot be delivered.

Earlier in this chapter, I emphasized that Word doesn't handle forms in a WYSIWYG manner, and this form is no exception. Figure 6-40 shows how the form in Figure 6-39 looked in Word. The most important thing to notice is that the multiple-selection lists look suspiciously like radio buttons. Don't worry — they look just like multiple selection lists in your browser.

There are many different ways to process the data from this form. Using a simple ACTION of `mailto:ronw@olympus.net`, I received the following from a sample use of the form:

```
hide-Form=form&hide-
FeedBkAdrs=ronw@olympus.net&email=me@myaddress.com&ComputerType=
IBM&OS=Windows+NT+3.x&Version=Pro&Best=Free&Best=Telepathy&
Frequency=Hour&Upgrade=Upgrade&Info=Want+info&Registered=Registered
&Comments=I+really+like+WebStarr%21%0D%0A&Address=4404+Lok
i+Drive%0D%0AWilliamsburg%2C+TK+38483%0D%0A&SubmitIt=
Submit+Information
```

A more readable version of the same data, from the Parser application:

Field name	Contents
hide-Form:	form
hide-FeedBkAdrs:	ronw@olympus.net
email:	me@myaddress.com
ComputerType:	IBM
OS:	Windows NT 3.x
Version:	Pro
Best:	Free
Best:	Telepathy

```
Frequency:          Hour
Upgrade:        |   Upgrade
Info:               Want info
Registered:         Registered
Comments:           I really like WebStarr!


Address:            4404 Loki Drive
                    Williamsburg, TK 38483


SubmitIt:           Submit Information
```

Figure 6-40: The form shown in Figure 6-39 looked different when it was being created in Word.

You could also use a generic forms processing script on your server. The output from such scripts varies from one Internet provider to the next. You could create a custom script, or you could send the information to a database as a comma-delimited string (again, from the Parser application):

```
"form","ronw@olympus.net","me@myaddress.com","IBM","Windows NT
3.x","Pro","Free","Telepathy","Hour","Upgrade","Want
info","Registered","I really like WebStarr! ","4404 Loki Drive
Williamsburg, TK 38483 ","Submit Information"
```

If you are unsure about how to handle forms data, the simplest method is probably the best way to get started — and that means the mailto ACTION. Simply substitute your own e-mail address for my address. The sample forms copied to your hard disk all use the ACTION of

```
mailto:me@myaddress.com
```

If your e-mail address were `billg@macrosoft.com`, you would simply use an ACTION of

```
mailto:billg@macrosoft.com
```

That's all there is to it!

Creating an order form

An order form represents a substantially more complex problem than the types of forms we have looked at so far. The feedback example dealt only with layout issues. An order form has the potential to add much more information. Careful layout becomes a major issue, and can make or break the form.

 Of course, order forms aren't the only kind of forms that can grow to high levels of complexity. They are, however, a perfect example of the breed.

Figure 6-41 shows an example of an order form. Pay particular attention to the center of the form (marked Step 2). It took some effort to find a way to arrange this much information so efficiently in a small space. You can find the complete form on your hard disk; it was copied as part of chapter setup. The filename is `\My Documents\My Web Pages\order2.htm`.

Figure 6-42 shows the form under construction in Word for Windows. Part of the effort to create the form results from the fact that it doesn't look the same in Word as it does in the browser view shown in Figure 6-41.

You may have guessed by now that tables are a key to organizing information on a form. The more complex the form, the more likely it is that you will have to resort to tables to sort out the various kinds of information needed on the form. This order form uses multiple tables to clearly present the various areas of the form.

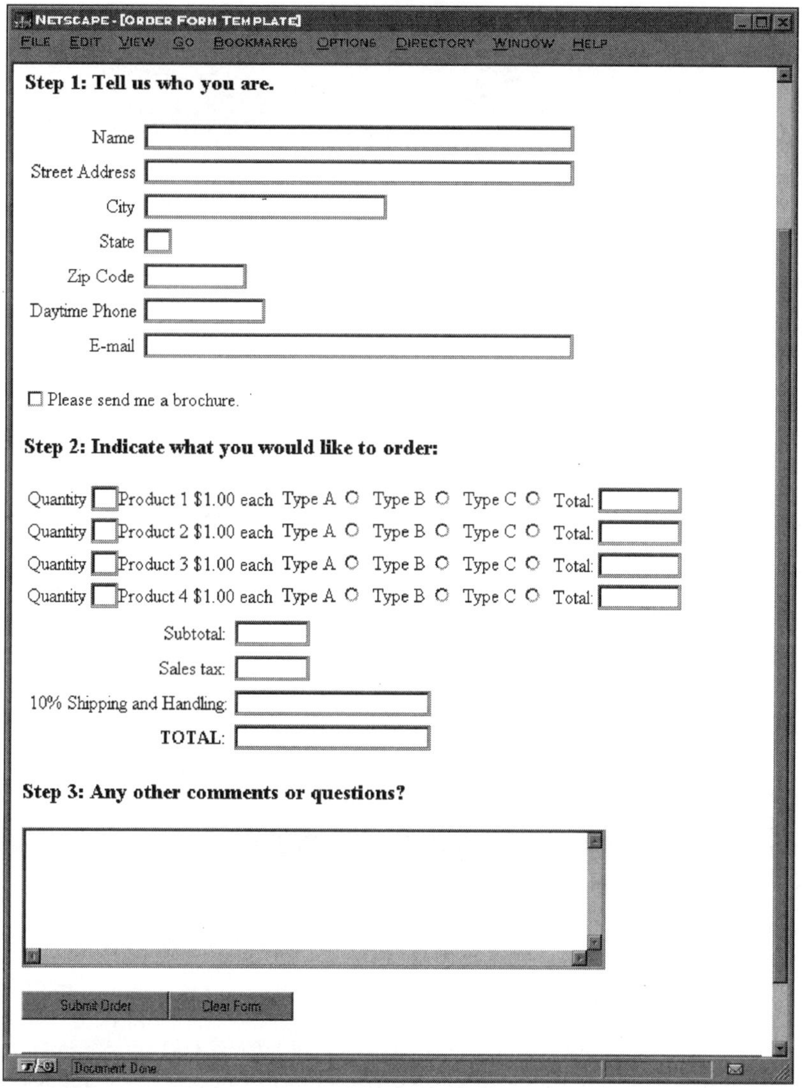

Figure 6-41: An order form, viewed in a browser.

The bad news about this form is that it requires the visitor to do math calculations. The fields below the products — subtotal, sales tax, and so forth — are not filled out automatically. There are ways to automate these calculations, but both methods currently available involve either a lot of money or a lot of work. The money would go toward server software that automates much more than just the calculations on an order form; such software usually offers a complete online shopping package, including shopping baskets, credit card encryption, and many other purchase-related features.

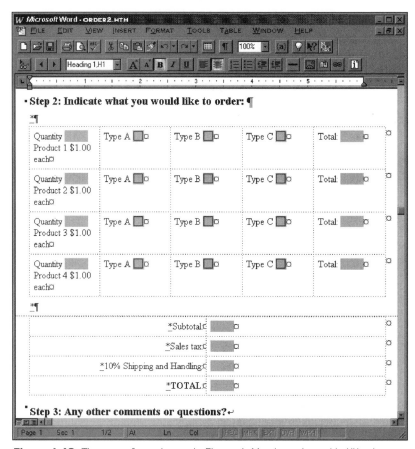

Figure 6-42: *The same form shown in Figure 6-41 when viewed in Word for Windows.*

To create your own automated calculations, you could break the form into parts and use scripts, or you could use a client-side (that is, browser-based) tool such as JavaScript. In fact, you'll find a form and scripts in Chapter 7 that do just that. See the section on JavaScript in Chapter 7 for details.

To see exactly how I built the order form, double-click the various controls on the form in Word. The dialog boxes reveal all. If you know some HTML, you will also find it rewarding to examine the HTML code behind this form, because it contains several custom modifications. Pay close attention to the code for the product area; that is where I did the most finagling.

Mastering the Internet: Advanced Web Tricks

In This Chapter

Adding your own HTML **markup**

Using HTML 3 alternatives to **image maps**

Embedding VRML and other objects in a page

Working with **JavaScript**

Server services you can use or ask for (working with your **provider**)

Last-minute tips for Web mastery

When it comes to creating a Web site, you need to have an edge to make sure that visitors will come back again and again. In this chapter, you learn how to add features that make your Web pages stand out.

Working together, Word and Internet Assistant give you access to most of the features supported by Web browsers. There are some features of **HTML**, however, that Internet Assistant cannot support directly, or that it supports only partially. This chapter shows you how to go beyond the limitations of Internet Assistant and into the magical world of HTML.

Setting Up the Tutorial

In this chapter, we once again jump from one tutorial to the next. Some of the tutorials build on what you created in earlier chapters, and some start from scratch. There is a lot to cover in this chapter, and the tutorials pick up speed as we go along. Hang onto your keyboard — this is where we kick into overdrive.

Automatic setup

If you haven't already installed the software for automatic setup of the tutorials, turn to Appendix A and do so now. Otherwise, if you choose not to use automatic setup, see the next section, "Manual setup," which tells you how to copy the necessary files for this tutorial manually. If you didn't use automatic setup earlier, you can find complete instructions for starting, running, and using the automatic setup program in Chapter 1.

To run automatic setup, click the Start button, then Programs, and then click the Autopage icon (shown here).

This is the Chapter 7 tutorial, so click the Chapter 7 Files radio button to display the files for this chapter (see Figure 7-1).

Click here for Chapter 7 files

Figure 7-1: Automatic setup for Chapter 7 tutorial.

To copy the files for the tutorial to your hard disk, click the Copy to Hard Disk button. The files are copied to the My Web Pages subfolder of the My Documents folder. If you installed Microsoft Office to your C drive, the following is usually the folder:

    C:\My Documents\My Web Pages

NOTE This is the same folder you have been using for all of the tutorials. From time to time, you may notice that one or more additional subfolders is created in the My Web Pages folder; this is normal, and all is explained during the tutorial.

After you have copied the necessary files, skip ahead to the start of the tutorial. If you choose not to use the automatic setup, read the next section to find out how to copy the necessary files manually.

Manual setup

Before you start the tutorial, open the folder called My Web Pages on your hard disk. If you already completed the tutorial in Chapter 1, you created it as a subfolder of the My Documents folder (usually **C:\ My Documents**).

The tutorial in this chapter uses image and other kinds of files from the CD-ROM. They are located in the folder \tutorial\chap07. Copy the image file

    htmlhide.jpg

from the `\tutorial\chap07` folder on the CD-ROM to the `My Web Pages\` `images` folder you created earlier on your hard disk (see Chapter 1 for complete details).

Copy the VRML file

```
sample.wrl
```

from the `\tutorial\chap07` folder on the CD-ROM to the `My Web Pages\vrml` folder you created earlier on your hard disk.

Copy the following document files

```
nobreak.htm

ordrjav.htm

ordrjav2.htm

plaintxt.htm

rule01.htm

rule02.htm

table2.htm

vrmlobj.htm

vrmlobj2.htm

vrmlobj3.htm

wbreak.htm
```

from the `\tutorial\chap07` folder on the CD-ROM to the `My Web Pages\video` folder. If the `My Web Pages\video` folder doesn't already exist, create it now.

You are now ready to begin the tutorials.

Tutorial 7A: Adding HTML Markup

Version 2.0 of Internet Assistant supports a large group of HTML commands, but there are a few that it does not support. Some nonsupported HTML commands, such as nested tables, cannot be supported at all in Internet Assistant. Other commands, such as NOBR (no break), can be added by using HTML markup.

What is markup?

Markup simply enables you to enter some nonsupported HTML commands directly. To understand how this works, it's useful to look at how Internet Assistant accomplishes its tasks. Figure 7-2 shows a typical Web page in Word (this is a form from Chapter 6). The shaded areas are actually Word fields that represent controls on a form. By clicking the HTML Hidden button (see Figure 7-3), you can look at what Internet Assistant does behind the scenes to store information about HTML commands in fields.

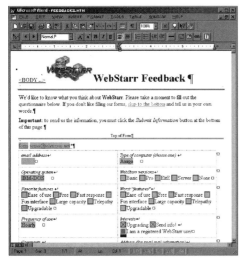

Figure 7-2: A typical Web page in Word.

Figure 7-3: The HTML Hidden button.

Figure 7-4 shows what the page from Figure 7-2 looks like after the HTML Hidden button is clicked. The first code, at the top of the page, is

```
{ {PRIVATE <BODY
BGCOLOR="#ffffff">}MACROBUTTON
HtmlDirect <BODY ...>}
```

This code tells Word that there is a body color. Note the use of private codes, such as HtmlDirect (which tells Word to output the following text as HTML code).

The second code embedded in the file, and revealed in Figure 7-4, is for the image at the top of the Web page:

```
{PRIVATE SCR="Webstar2.GIF"
ALIGN="RIGHT"} MACROBUTTON
HtmlResImg {INCLUDEPICTURE "C:/
WINDOWS/TEMP/wia3d8/Webstar2.bmp"
\*MERGEFORMAT }}
```

The first part, inside the first pair of curly braces, specifies the HTML-related information, whereas the second part specifies where the displayable copy of the image is kept (in a temporary file). I won't try to explain the full details of this coding, because to do so is well beyond the scope of this book. My point is that Internet Assistant is using a combination of HTML command language, Word fields, and **macros** to trick Word into outputting HTML files.

HTML hidden codes

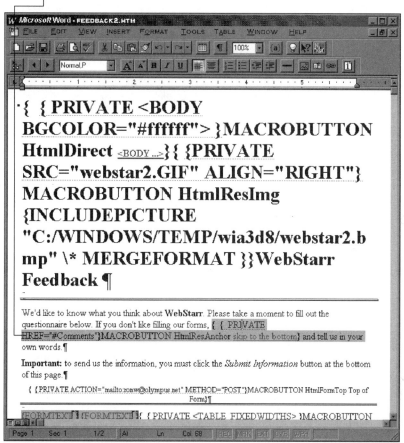

Figure 7-4: The same page as shown in Figure 7-2, but with HTML codes revealed.

When you add HTML markup, Internet Assistant simply adds an HtmlDirect code similar to the ones used for features supported by Internet Assistant. For example, if you insert the tag for No Break (<NOBR>), the following codes are added, and can be viewed with the HTML Hidden button:

```
{ {PRIVATE <NOBR>}MACROBUTTON HtmlDirect <NOBR>}
```

This sounds much more complicated than it is. The reason that I went to such great lengths to show you what is going on behind the scenes is that there are two kinds of HTML markup — markup that you add to normal text in your document, and markup that is hidden within Internet Assistant's own codes.

For example, the NOBR markup is a *free-standing markup* — it is isolated within normal text and is not part of an existing HTML command. The other kind of markup is called *embedded markup*. For example, if you want to use the LEFTMARGIN parameter for the BODY command, you need to use a special technique for making the change. You learn how to do embedded markup later in this chapter.

If you find this subject confusing, the following examples will clear up any questions that you may have.

Free-standing markup

There are a number of HTML commands that are not supported by Internet Assistant. You can easily add these commands to your document by using HTML markup. For example, Internet Assistant supports horizontal rules, but it does not directly support variations on the standard horizontal rule. By using markup, you can add rules that look like you want them to. Let's look at some examples.

Horizontal rules

Normally, you add a horizontal rule to a document by using the Horizontal Rule tool, or by choosing INSERT⇨HORIZONTAL RULE. Both methods simply add the default horizontal rule. However, HTML offers several variations on the rule, as discussed in the following sections.

Alignment

Horizontal rules can be aligned to the left, to the right, or centered. This feature is supported by HTML version 3, so not all browsers support it yet. Newer browsers, such as Internet Explorer 2, do support it. The HTML code for a center-aligned rule, for example, looks like this:

```
<HR ALIGN=CENTER>
```

ALIGN is called a parameter of the <HR> command.

Let's add a centered rule with a width of 50 percent (see "Width percentage," in this chapter). Open the file `\My Documents\My Web Pages\rule01.htm` in Word. This is a file with several paragraphs of text. Place the cursor at the start of the second paragraph (see Figure 7-5), and choose INSERT⇨HTML MARKUP to display the dialog box shown in Figure 7-6. There is a single text box in which to enter your markup. Add the following:

```
<HR ALIGN="CENTER"
WIDTH="50%">
```

Click OK to save the change. The HTML markup will show up as part of the second paragraph (see Figure 7-7), but when viewed in a browser (see Figure 7-8), it appears centered and 50 percent of the width of the page.

It's just that easy to add HTML markup. In the rest of this section, you can use the file `rule01.htm` to try inserting various HTML markups. Remember to save the file before you try to view the results in your browser. If you do not have a current browser, such as Internet Explorer 2.0 or Netscape Navigator 2.0, you may not see all of the examples displayed correctly.

Place cursor here

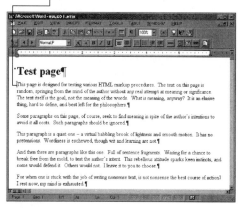

Figure 7-5: Place the cursor as shown before inserting HTML markup.

Type HTML markup here

Figure 7-6: The dialog box for adding HTML markup.

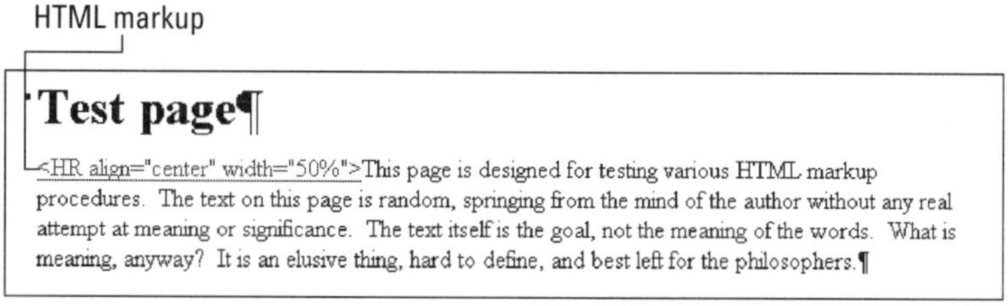

HTML markup

Test page¶

<HR align="center" width="50%">This page is designed for testing various HTML markup procedures. The text on this page is random, springing from the mind of the author without any real attempt at meaning or significance. The text itself is the goal, not the meaning of the words. What is meaning, anyway? It is an elusive thing, hard to define, and best left for the philosophers.¶

Figure 7-7: In Word, HTML markup shows up as blue, underlined text.

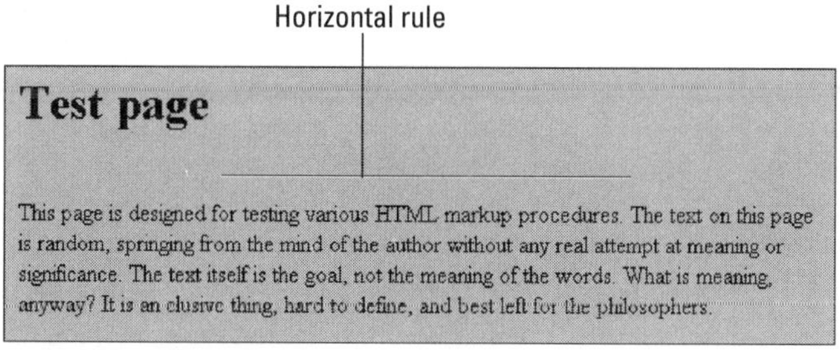

Horizontal rule

Test page

This page is designed for testing various HTML markup procedures. The text on this page is random, springing from the mind of the author without any real attempt at meaning or significance. The text itself is the goal, not the meaning of the words. What is meaning, anyway? It is an elusive thing, hard to define, and best left for the philosophers.

Figure 7-8: The 50 percent horizontal rule in a browser that supports HTML 3.

Shading

The NOSHADE parameter draws a rule without 3-D shading. To see this kind of rule, add the following markup

```
<HR NOSHADE>
```

at the beginning of a paragraph in the file rule01.htm. Figure 7-9 shows what such a rule looks like.

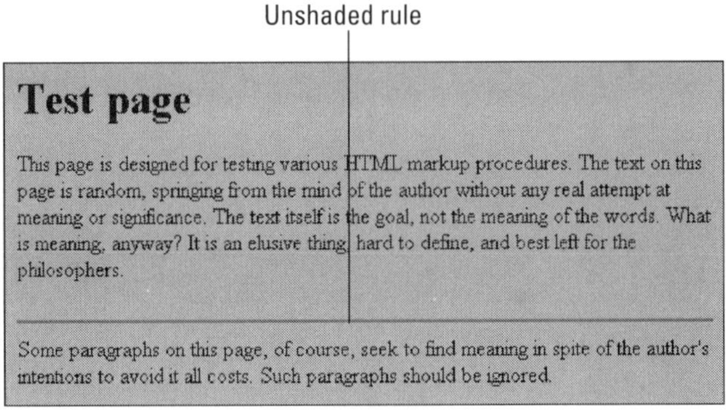

Unshaded rule

Figure 7-9: The appearance of a NOSHADE rule in a browser.

Size

The SIZE parameter sets the height of the rule in pixels. This parameter enables you to add thicker, more obvious rules to your pages; Figure 7-10 shows a size of 10. You can also use a markup such as

```
<HR SIZE=300
    width=5>
```

to create vertical lines (see Figure 7-11 and the file \My Documents\ My Web Pages\ rule02.htm). To get results like those in Figure 7-11, you use a three-column table with the TABLE⇨CELL WIDTH AND SPACING dialog box set to WYSIWYG.

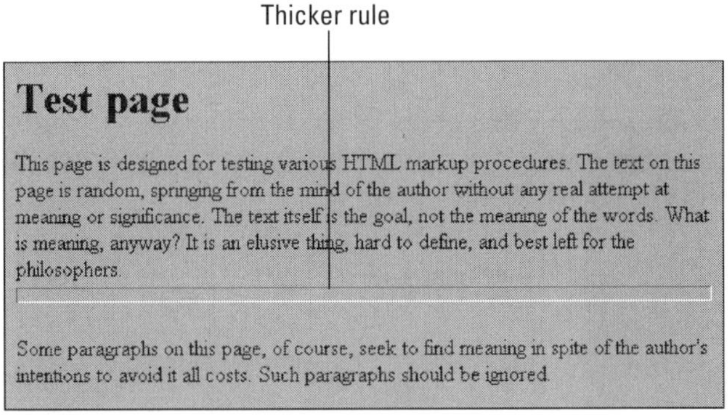

Thicker rule

Figure 7-10: Making thicker horizontal rules with markup such as <HR SIZE=10>.

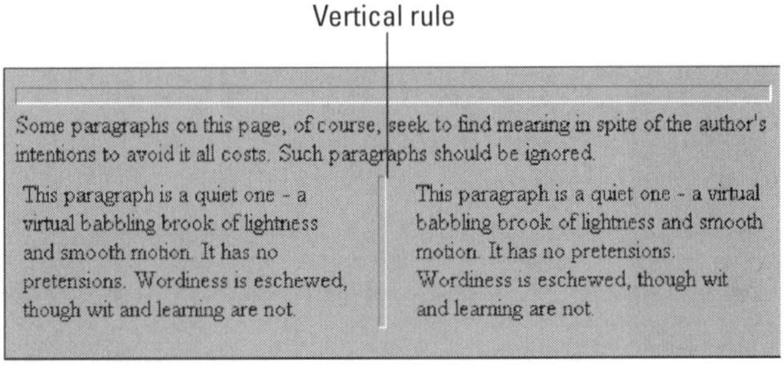

Vertical rule

Figure 7-11: Creating a vertical rule.

The middle column should be narrow — just wide enough to hold the vertical rule.

When you reopen a file with a horizontal rule that contains markup, Word displays a standard rule (see Figure 7-12), but the markup codes are still there. If you look carefully, you can see a bit of blue color at the left of the standard rule — double-click that blue color carefully to open the Insert Markup dialog box if you want to change the settings for your customized rule.

HTML markup barely visible

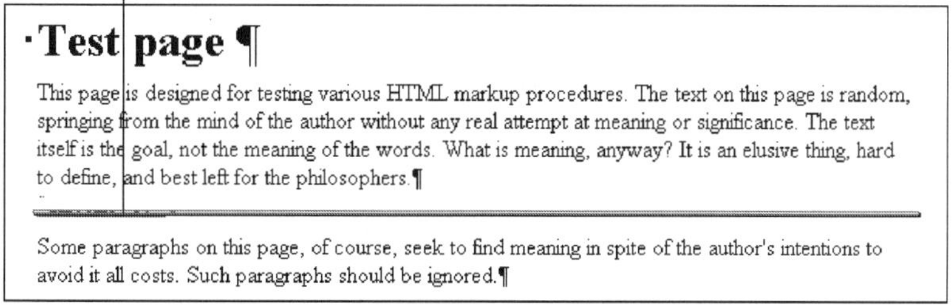

·Test page ¶

This page is designed for testing various HTML markup procedures. The text on this page is random, springing from the mind of the author without any real attempt at meaning or significance. The text itself is the goal, not the meaning of the words. What is meaning, anyway? It is an elusive thing, hard to define, and best left for the philosophers.¶

Some paragraphs on this page, of course, seek to find meaning in spite of the author's intentions to avoid it all costs. Such paragraphs should be ignored.¶

Figure 7-12: The appearance of a custom rule when you reopen the file in Word.

Width percentage

Use can use the WIDTH parameter to have the rule cover a certain percentage of the width of the page. If the user changes the width of the page while viewing it, the rule adjusts accordingly. For example, to create a left-aligned rule, three pixels high, that occupies just the left 25 percent of the page, use this markup:

```
<HR WIDTH=25% ALIGN=LEFT SIZE=3>
```

If you were to add such a rule after the Heading 1,H1 paragraph at the top of the page in the file rule01.htm, it would be far below the text, because the H1 style allows a large amount of space below the text. You can trick the browser into displaying your line near the text by moving the cursor to the end of the first paragraph (to the right of Test page), adding a soft carriage return (Shift+Enter), and then inserting the markup on the new line. Figure 7-13 shows the appearance in Word, and Figure 7-14 shows the result in a browser.

Width absolute

You can also set a width as a fixed number of pixels. Use markup like this

```
<HR WIDTH=250>
```

to create a rule that is 250 pixels wide. You can also add SIZE or ALIGN parameters to control the exact appearance of the rule.

Soft carriage return   A short rule using HTML markup

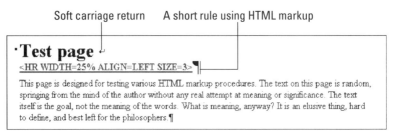

Figure 7-13: Adding a short rule below a heading.

Short rule

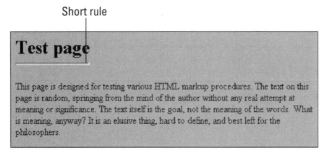

Figure 7-14: A left-aligned rule, three pixels thick, occupying 25 percent of the page width.

No Break

There may be times when you do not want a block of text to break when displayed in the browser. For example, if you are including some computer code on your page, it might be confusing if the lines break in the middle — in many languages, code must appear on a single line or it will cause problems. You can add the No Break tags before and after the text to indicate that it should not be broken if the browser window is narrower than the text.

Open the file \My Documents\My Web Pages\nobreak.htm to see an example of this (see Figure 7-15). There is one very long line, and I added a <NOBR> tag at the beginning, and a </NOBR> tag at the end. The first tag starts the No Break region, and the second tag ends it.

As a general rule, HTML commands end with the same tag that starts them. The only difference is that the ending tag has a forward slash in front of the command.

No Break tag

Figure 7-15: Using the No Break command.

Figure 7-16 shows what the file looks like in a browser. Notice that the long line of text does not wrap (break) at the right edge of the window; it extends to the right as a line of program code should. The visitor can use the scrollbar at the bottom of the browser to see the continuation of the line.

You may have noticed that the lines of program code in Figure 7-16 are indented to different levels. You may also recall that I stressed earlier that there is no way to indent without using lists. I didn't lie; those aren't indents. They are nonbreaking spaces. There are either none, four, or eight nonbreaking spaces at the beginning of each line. The combination of nonbreaking spaces and the No Break HTML command give you an alternative to the Preformatted style.

Noncreating spaces   The long line does not break

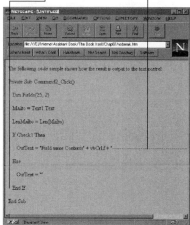

Figure 7-16: The appearance of the nonbreaking line in a browser.

To add nonbreaking spaces, use HTML markup. For each nonbreaking space, use the following markup:

```
 
```

There are no angle brackets at either end. This isn't a tag; only tags use angle brackets. This is an example of using the ampersand (&) as an **escape character**, and there are quite a few such characters that you can add to a Web page; see Appendix B for a complete list. An *escape character* is a character that tells the browser that the following characters are not text, but a special code that must be interpreted in a special way. The escape character, plus the special code, plus a character that ends the special code, taken together, are called an *escape sequence*. See the definition in the Glossary for more information.

To add four nonbreaking spaces, the markup would be as follows:

```
    
```

The ampersand acts as an escape character, telling the browser to interpret "nbsp" as a special code for "nonbreaking space", instead of just text. The semicolon (;) indicates the end of the escape sequence.

Soft line breaks

The command <WBR> inserts a soft line break in a block of No Break text. For an example, open the file \My Documents\My Web Pages\wbreak.htm (shown in Figure 7-17). It shows several lines of No Break text, with several <WBR> commands added to control exactly where the line can break. This might be useful for poetry, for example, in a situation where you have several long lines and want absolute control over how those lines break, no matter how wide or narrow the user's browser might be.

Figure 7-18 shows how the lines are broken in a narrow-windowed browser view of the page. Notice that the lines only break where the <WBR> command says they can be broken. I do hope that you will forgive the awful poetry!

Plain Text

The PLAINTEXT command renders text in fixed-width type without processing any HTML tags that might be present. If you ever have occasion to illustrate HTML code on your page, this is a quick way to do it. After it encounters a <PLAINTEXT> tag, the browser ignores any and all HTML commands, tags, and parameters until it encounters the </PLAINTEXT> tag.

Soft line break

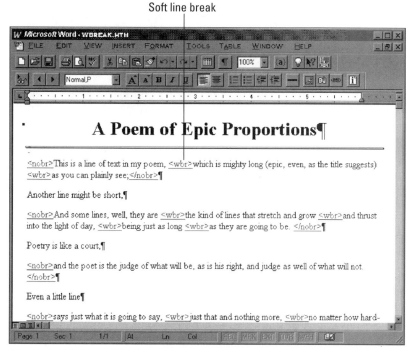

Figure 7-17: Controlling line breaks with the <WBR> command.

Never use the PLAINTEXT tags with Internet Assistant. They do not work, and they will cause unpredictable problems when the page is viewed in a browser. See the rest of this section for details.

However, this tag isn't necessary if you are working in Word with Internet Assistant. If you type HTML codes in normal text, they are converted for proper display in the browser (that is, codes force the browser to display such HTML commands as text, not as instructions to the browser about how to display text). Figure 7-19 shows such text displayed in a browser — note that the HTML codes appear as text, not as a hyperlink. The source file for Figure 7-19 is \My Documents\My Web Pages\plaintxt.htm.

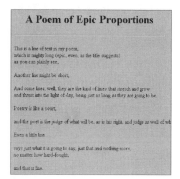

Figure 7-18: The text only breaks where there was a <WBR> tag.

If you use the Plain Text feature in your Web pages, however, Word becomes terribly confused — and so does your browser, as shown in the lower half of Figure 7-19. Avoid using the PLAINTEXT tag at all costs!

Other tags

As HTML evolves, other tags will appeal to you. Even if the current version of Internet Assistant doesn't support the new tags directly, you can always use HTML markup to experiment with any tags that seem interesting to you. The only caution with new tags is the same caution

This is an example of HTML code in normal text:

To link to a hyperlink, you would use HTML codes like this:

Visit the <A HREF="http://www.toyota.com">site of the day</A>.

_____

You cannot, however, use the PLAINTEXT tag to achieve the same result:

To link to a hyperlink, you would use HTML codes like this:

```
Visit the &lt;A HREF=&quot;http://www.toyota.com&quot;&gt;site
of the day&lt;/A&gt;.</PLAINTEXT>
<P>
Notice that the various codes created by Word are suddenly visible,
and destroy the effect that is intended when using Plain Text.
 Worse, Words encoding methods cause browsers to miss the closing
&lt;/PLAINTEXT&gt;, and that makes for a real mess!
<HR>

</BODY>

</HTML>
```

Figure 7-19: You do not need to use the PLAINTEXT tag to enclose HTML code in normal text.

that has appeared throughout the book: Make sure that the browsers your visitors are typically using to view your pages also support the new tags!

Embedded markup

At the beginning of this section on HTML markup, you saw some examples of the normally hidden codes that Internet Assistant uses to do its work. Not only can you view these codes when you click the HTML Hidden button, you can also edit them.

Editing the internal codes used by Internet Assistant should not be undertaken lightly! You can easily destroy a Web page if you make a mistake in the codes. Always — let me repeat that — *always* work on a backup copy of a file if you are going to edit the internal codes. That way, if you do make a mistake, you have the original copy to go back to. I suggest that you take advantage of Windows 95 long filenames to add a phrase such as **copy of** at the start of the filename for the copy you will be working on. For example, if your original Web page is called `table.htm`, you could make a copy and call it `Copy of table.htm`. Alternatively, you can just add a number, such as **2**, to the filename: `table2.htm`. Work only on the copy until you are absolutely certain that your changes are just what you want.

Now that you have been duly warned, we can proceed. Open the file `\My Documents\My Web Pages\table2.htm` in Word for Windows. Click the HTML Hidden button to display the hidden codes; you should see something like Figure 7-20. With all that hidden code in the small cell in the first table, you may have to scroll down a bit to view the area shown in Figure 7-20.

Hidden HTML codes

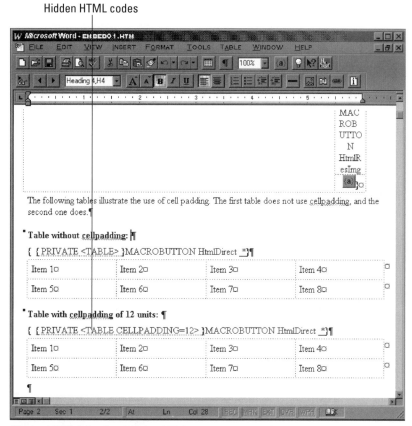

Figure 7-20: Viewing hidden HTML codes in Word.

This file contains two nearly identical versions of a table. The first table is a perfectly ordinary table created in Word with Internet Assistant. It is four columns wide and two rows high. The visible code for the first table, located just above the table, is

```
{ {PRIVATE <TABLE> }MACROBUTTON HtmlDirect_*}
```

The second table has undergone a modification. The visible code for the second table is

```
{ {PRIVATE <TABLE CELLPADDING=12> }MACROBUTTON HtmlDirect_*}
```

I added the text

```
CELLPADDING=12
```

to add space within each cell, which has the effect of spreading out the cells of a table. Figure 7-21 shows the page in a browser. Notice that the first table is squashed together, whereas the second table has cells that are nicely spread out for ease of reading.

How did I know to add CELLPADDING=12? That's the hard part of this technique: You have to know *exactly* the right HTML stuff to use when you edit the hidden codes. If you already have a working knowledge of HTML, you are ready to expand what you can do with Internet Assistant. If you don't yet know HTML, you can learn some tricks in Appendix B, but I would suggest that you also visit Web pages that cover proper usage of HTML. A good place to start is the Netscape Web site (try starting with http://www.netscape.com/people/hagan/ for some fun,

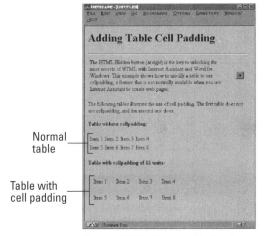

Normal table

Table with cell padding

Figure 7-21: The two kinds of tables viewed in a browser.

or http://home.netscape.com/people/hagan/html/top.html if you want to get straight down to business), where there are numerous helper pages that can teach you the details of HTML coding. An excellent book for learning more about HTML is *Creating Cool Web Pages with HTML* by Dave Taylor (IDG Books Worldwide, Inc.).

Not all HTML codes can be added using this technique. You have to experiment to discover exactly which of your own personal favorite HTML goodies work, and which don't. In most cases, if you can view the tag associated with the macro reference HtmlDirect among the hidden codes, you can add or revise parameters. If you need to add a tag itself, choose INSERT⇨HTML MARKUP instead. If you don't see the HTML code you are looking for when you click the HTML Hidden button to reveal the hidden codes, you probably can't add the feature you would like to add.

If you take the precaution of working only on a backup of your originals, you stand to gain a lot and you can't lose anything at all with embedded markup. The real key to success, however, is a good knowledge of HTML!

Tutorial 7B: Embedding Objects in a Page

The growth of **plug-ins** (add-on software for browsers) for the various Web browsers has created new opportunities for Web publishing. Plug-ins enable you to view Web content that doesn't involve (or goes beyond) HTML. Many plug-ins display the content right on a Web page — that's called *embedding*. HTML alone offers only the basics: hyperlinks with text and images. With plug-ins, you can create or view all kinds of Web goodies that were merely dreams a few short months ago: interactive games, for example, as well as multimedia presentations and 3-D worlds to explore.

Plug-ins enable you to create objects that are embedded in a Web page, and can be viewed by anyone who has the required plug-in.

What is embedding?

The technology for embedding objects is part of the current crop of Web browsers. The popularity of the Web made it reasonable to invest big bucks in the technology required to support a plug-in architecture: Third-party companies can follow a set of rules that enables their software to run as if it were a part of the browser itself. Typically, this enables you to view various file types from within the browser. You can view a presentation, for example, or play real-time audio, or chat over phone lines while browsing various Web sites.

For example, VRML technology enables you to view 3-D worlds within the context of your browser. You view the VRML world in a window within the browser, and that window has its own rules for navigation. In the following example, you build a simple VRML world, embed it as an object in a Web page, and then view the world as part of that Web page with a browser.

Embedding objects

Before you can embed an object, you have to create it. How you create it depends on what you are creating. If you want to create a Shockwave object, you must use Macromedia's Director (a multimedia development tool) to create the object. If you are creating a VRML object, you must use a 3-D modeling program to create the 3-D world, and then save it as a VRML object. For this example, I'll illustrate how to use Caligari's Fountain Pro to create a VRML object.

Embedding a VRML object

Creating the VRML object is the hard part; adding it to your Web page is comparatively easy. For Netscape 2.0's plug-in browsers, you use a Netscape enhancement to HTML, the <EMBED> command. This command enables you to specify the source VRML file, whether a border is used, alignment, and the width and height of the VRML window.

The sample.wrl file was copied to your hard disk during setup for this chapter, and I also copied a Word for Windows file that you can modify to include the EMBED statement. Open the file \My Documents\My Web Pages\ vrmlobj.htm in Word now. Add a new line below the existing text, and choose INSERT⇨HTML MARKUP to open the Insert HTML Markup dialog box (see Figure 7-22). Type the following into the text box:

Figure 7-22: Adding HTML markup for embedding a VRML file.

```
<embed src="vrml/sample.wrl" border=none align=center width=500
   height=450>
```

You can also open the file vrmlobj2.htm, which contains the markup and is ready to go. The markup tells the Netscape 2.0 browser the following information:

Markup	Description
src="vrml/sample.wrl"	The location of the VRML file relative to the HTML file. The VRML file was copied into the vrml subfolder during chapter setup.
border=none	Do not use a border around the VRML window.
align=center	Align the window in the center of the page.
width=500 height=450	The window is 500 pixels wide by 450 pixels high.

Viewing objects

Save the Word file, and then view it in your browser. Figure 7-23 shows two views of the world in Netscape, using the Web/FX plug-in. If you are using the Web/FX VRML plug-in, you can use your mouse to explore this simple world — click and drag to move your position. Dragging left of center moves to the left, dragging right moves right, dragging upward moves you forward, and dragging downward moves you backwards.

If you do not have the Web/FX plug-in, you can download it by clicking the hyperlink above the VRML window.

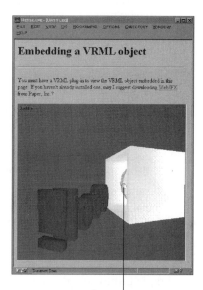

Cursor change
indicates hyperlink

Figure 7-23: Two views of the VRML world sample.wrl in Netscape, using the Web/FX plug-in.

If you are using Internet Explorer, use the following HTML Markup to embed the VRML window:

```
<IMG SRC="images/vrml.gif" VRML="vrml\sample.wrl" width=60%
  height=60%>
```

Netscape 2.0 also can handle this syntax, but it just shows the image file; you cannot view the VRML object. Alternatively, you can simply open the file vrmobj3.htm, which already contains the HTML markup for viewing the file.

If you haven't already downloaded the latest version of Microsoft's VRML plug-in for Internet Explorer, you can get it at `http://www.microsoft.com/windows/ie/iedl.htm`.

Embedding support on the Web

The key to offering embedded objects is to make it easy for visitors to your Web page to download whatever plug-in is required to view the object. Be sure to include download links for the required plug-ins in two places: on the page preceding the page that contains the object (so thoughtful sorts of users can go get the plug-in ahead of time) and on the page with the embedded object, for those who prefer to wait until the last minute.

Which plug-ins should you use? There are three classes of plug-ins:

➡ Those that are so hot everyone has already downloaded them. Shockwave is an example of a hot technology.

➡ Those that aren't well-known yet, but will be soon. The experts do their best to predict which plug-ins will be the most popular, but the reality is that usage on the Net is what really determines the winners and losers. If you start seeing a lot of support for a plug-in, you are looking at one of the winners. If you see folks *talking* about a plug-in, don't count on it succeeding!

➡ Those that are never going to be popular with masses of Web surfers. Some of these will be special-purpose plug-ins that are useful to a small group of people (for example, industry-specific plug-ins), and some will be of no use to anyone.

Choosing which plug-in to use involves risk — if you use some wonderful but off-the-beaten-path plug-in, your visitors may balk at having to download the plug-in just to enjoy your site. It's probably safest to stick with the most popular plug-ins — those that are in use on the sites you normally visit.

CD-ROM Bonus Techniques

The attached CD-ROM includes extra coverage of advanced web techniques:

"Building a VRML World" (Tutorial\bonus\make_vrml.htm);
"HTML 3.0 and You" (Tutorial\bonus\HTML3.htm);
"Server Services" (Tutorial\bonus\provider.htm);
"HTML Tidbits" (Tutorial\bonus\HTML_tips.htm);
"The Basics of JavaScript" (Tutorial\bonus\java_basics.htm).

A Catalog of
the CD-ROM

There are many goodies awaiting your attention on the CD-ROM. This appendix provides information about the contents of the CD-ROM and tells you how to install or otherwise access the materials on the CD-ROM.

Late-Breaking News

Software was still being added to the CD-ROM disc as we finished putting this appendix together. To find out what the latest additions were, load the CD-ROM and double-click the file readme.1st. It contains information about additional software, last-minute changes, and so forth.

Internet Assistant 2.0

Internet Assistant is an add-on to Microsoft Word for Windows 7.0 that enables you to create Web pages with Word. You can install it from the CD-ROM, or you can download the latest version of Internet Assistant from Microsoft's Web site and install that. If you do not already have access to the Internet, the CD-ROM version will enable you to get started right away. You may also choose the CD-ROM version if you prefer to avoid the hassles of downloading.

To get the very latest version of Internet Assistant, however, you should download from Microsoft's Web site and then perform the installation.

Installing Internet Assistant from the CD-ROM

If you elect to install Internet Assistant from the CD-ROM, proceed to Step 3 of the next section.

Detailed method for installing Internet Assistant via download

Use this method if you don't already have an Internet browser, or if you are unsure how to use it, or if you just want to see every tiny, little step in the process laid out in detail.

Step 1: Word for Windows 7.0 and Windows 95

If you haven't already upgraded to Windows 95, do it now. Word for Windows 7.0 and Internet Assistant 2.0 are built to take full advantage of the 32-bit features of Windows 95. You can upgrade your current copy of either Word for Windows or Windows 3.x for a fraction of the cost of the full package. Word 7.0 includes a few new features (my favorite is a much improved real-time spelling checker), and Windows 95 is much easier to use (after you get through the learning curve, that is).

Step 2: Download Internet Assistant 2.0

Here's the best part: Internet Assistant 2.0 is free. It costs nothing. You start with your Internet browser. I recommend using either Microsoft's Internet Explorer or Netscape Navigator. You'll want at least version 2.0 of either program. Netscape's software is more widely used, and Internet Explorer supports a few unique features also supported by Internet Assistant. If you are serious about publishing, you'll want both so that you can check your work in different browsers. Sadly, not all browsers work exactly the same way. You learn more about how to cope with this right off the bat in Chapter 1.

If you don't want to run out right now and get yourself an Internet browser, install the browser supplied on the CD-ROM that comes with this book. Instructions are included in this appendix.

If you don't want to bother with a browser right now — say, if you don't have an Internet access account yet — you can simply install the version of Internet Assistant that is on the CD-ROM. To install the version from the CD-ROM, skip to Step 3.

Here are the steps for downloading the latest version of Internet Assistant:

1. Start your browser by double-clicking its icon. You must have an active Internet account to use the browser on the Internet. If you aren't sure how to do this, see the Glossary entry *Provider*.

2.   Most browsers take you to some kind of home page. This might be your own home page, a home page for your company, or a home page for the company that sold you the browser. Figure A-1 shows the home page for the Microsoft Internet Explorer browser. Of course, that page will probably change by the time you read this book. Home pages change all the time — that's what's so cool about publishing on the Web.

Figure A-1: The Internet Explorer home page.

3.   Most browsers have a selection on the File menu that says something like "Open" or "Go to location." Click the File menu of your browser, and then click this selection. You see a dialog box similar to the one in Figure A-2. Type the following:

```
http://www.microsoft.com/freestuff/msword
```

Press the Enter key. Your browser now goes to this location. The result should be a Web page similar to the one shown in Figure A-3. Because Web pages tend to change over time, the exact appearance will vary.

Type URL here

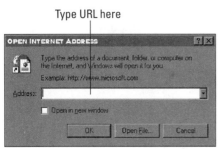

Figure A-2: Accessing a Web page with Internet Explorer.

Hyperlink to download Internet Assistant

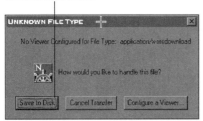

Figure A-3: Accessing the Microsoft Web site.

Save to Disk button

Figure A-4: Saving the downloaded file to disk.

Look on the page for a reference to downloading the latest version of Internet Assistant. You'll be looking for underlined text, which indicates a hyperlink. Click the text to go to the next step in downloading. Keep following the hyperlinks until you come to one that performs the actual download. When you click the link to download, you'll see a dialog box similar to the one shown in Figure A-4. If you are using a browser other than Internet Explorer to download, look for a button like the one marked Save to Disk, so that the file will be copied to your hard disk.

NOTE After clicking the button, you usually see a dialog box enabling you to specify where to save the file. You should save it right on your desktop (see Figure A-5).

Click here to indicate that the file should be saved to the desktop

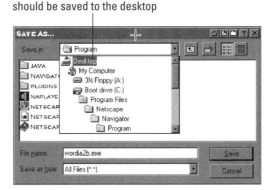

Figure A-5: Saving a file that you are downloading on your desktop is easy.

Step 3: Install Internet Assistant 2.0

To install Internet Assistant, just double-click the icon for the .exe file you downloaded in Step 2. You'll see the dialog box shown in Figure A-6, asking whether you want to install Internet Assistant. Click Yes.

Because software is often updated (especially software you can download from the Web), the screens you see during installation may not match exactly with what you see here. In most cases, the changes will be minor.

The setup program then decompresses the .exe file, displaying a progress meter as shown in Figure A-7.

Some possible detours can occur. Here's how to handle them:

➡ If you are already running Word for Windows, you see the dialog box shown in Figure A-8, asking you to close Word. After you close Word, click the OK button.

➡ You may see one or more messages, like the one shown in Figure A-9. These messages indicate that the installation program is performing a task that doesn't require your input. Just wait until the message goes away.

➡ If you, or someone else, already installed this version of Internet Assistant, you see a dialog box like the one in Figure A-10. If you see this dialog box, you will probably simply want to click the Exit Setup button and then head for Chapter 1. This dialog box also appears if you run the setup program to uninstall Internet Assistant.

Figure A-6: Verifying installation of Internet Assistant.

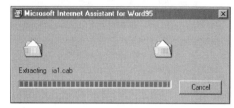

Figure A-7: A progress meter is displayed during decompression.

Figure A-8: You see this dialog box if Word is running during installation.

Figure A-9: A typical status message during installation.

Reinstall Internet Assistant

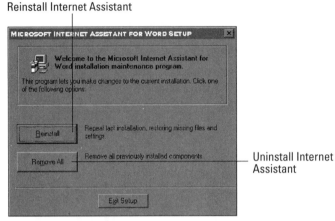

Uninstall Internet Assistant

Figure A-10: This dialog box indicates that you have already installed this version of Internet Assistant.

After the installation routine has settled down, you see the dialog box shown in Figure A-11. Click the Continue button.

This action displays the first dialog box that offers you any choice in the process (see Figure A-12). By default, Internet Assistant is installed in the following directory:

```
C:\Program Files\
Internet Assistant
```

Continue button

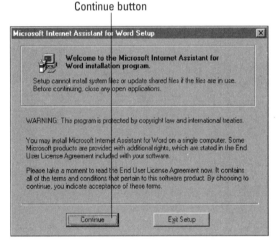

Figure A-11: Setup welcome message.

Click to change installation folder

Figure A-12: Choosing the installation directory.

Unless you have a reason to change this location (for example, if your C drive is already too full), accept the default by clicking the OK button. You see a rather large dialog box with a rather long license agreement. Presumably, it will meet your approval and you can click the Accept button to continue.

This action displays the dialog box shown in Figure A-13. Click the Complete button at left-center to begin the installation.

During installation, you see a progress meter (Figure A-14).

At the conclusion of the installation, you see a dialog box like the one shown in Figure A-15. I highly recommend that you click the Launch Word button, so that you can verify the installation of Internet Assistant. When Word starts, you see just one small change. Can you pick it out in Figure A-15? Look at the left of the Standard toolbar, where you'll see a new button. It has a small pair of glasses on it (see margin).

Complete button

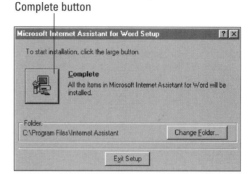

Figure A-13: Click the complete button to continue.

Figure A-14: The installation progress meter.

Internet Assistant Icon

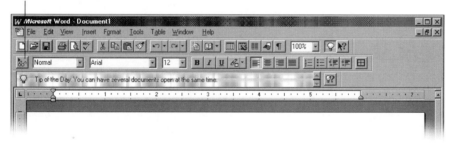

Figure A-15: Internet Assistant adds a new icon to the Formatting toolbar in Word.

There are lots of other changes to Word, but they are hidden until you open a new or existing Web page. You'll learn about those in the rest of the book.

That's it. You're finished. You're ready to start creating Web pages. What are you waiting for? Turn to Chapter 1 and get started!

Internet Explorer 2.0

There are two installation files for Internet Explorer on the CD-ROM. One is for Internet Explorer 2.0 itself, and the other is for a VRML extension to Internet Explorer. You can also visit Microsoft's Web site (http://www.microsoft.com) to download the latest and greatest versions of these programs. If you prefer to use the Netscape Navigator browser, you can download that from Netscape's Web site at http://www.netscape.com.

Click here to install
Internet Explorer

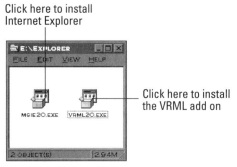

Click here to install
the VRML add on

Figure A-16: Installing
Internet Explorer and the
VRML add-on.

If you elect to install Internet Explorer 2.0 from the CD-ROM, you must have the CD-ROM that comes with this book inserted into your CD-ROM drive. Double-click the My Computer icon to display the available drives on your computer, and then double-click the CD-ROM drive icon. This displays a folder showing the contents of the CD-ROM. Double-click the explorer folder. You see the icons shown in Figure A-16. Double-click the Explorer icon to run the Explorer installation, and double-click the VRML icon to run the VRML installation. You must run the Explorer installation first, of course, because the VRML installation adds software to the Explorer installation.

Templates

The CD-ROM contains numerous templates that you can use to create Web pages with Microsoft Word and Internet Assistant. Chapter 1 of the book explains how to access the templates using features built into Microsoft Word for Windows 95 (Workgroup Templates). There is no way to access or use the templates outside of Word for Windows.

If you have lots of free hard disk space, you can copy the template folders from the CD-ROM to a hard disk. You can then set the Workgroup Templates directory to whatever directory you copy the templates into.

The template files are large, usually from 500K to 1 MB each. Copying them to your hard disk will eat up a lot of space! Copying all the files, for example, would eat up hundreds of megabytes of hard disk space. Only copy as many templates as you need at one time, unless you have lots and lots of free hard disk space.

To use the templates, you must have the CD-ROM that comes with this book inserted into your CD-ROM drive.

If you must use the Workgroup Templates feature for other purposes (such as company-wide templates), you can copy the templates from the CD-ROM to your hard disk. To copy a group of templates to your hard disk, follow these steps:

1. You must have the CD-ROM that comes with this book inserted into your CD-ROM drive. Double-click the My Computer icon to display the available drives on your computer, and then double-click the CD-ROM drive icon. This displays a folder showing the contents of the CD-ROM. Double-click the `Cool templates` folder to display the template subfolders.

2. Double-click the icon for the drive where you installed Word or Microsoft Office. Double-click the `MS Office` or `Winword` folder to open it. You should see a folder called `Templates`. If not, create it now.

3. You now see the various categories of templates available to you. Pick one or more template groups that you would like to copy to your hard disk. Click to select one or more (hold down the Ctrl key while you click to select more than one).

4. Simply drag the folders you selected in Step 3 to the `Templates` folder you identified in Step 2.

The copied templates will now be visible when you select FILE⇨NEW in Word for Windows. If you need to free up the hard disk space used by a template folder, simply drag the folder to the Recycle Bin. You can always recopy the templates later if you need them again.

Graphics

Several graphic vendors have provided sample graphics for your use on the CD-ROM. Each vendor has provided software for accessing its images. To make access as simple as possible, I have created a master access application and installed it to the CD-ROM.

To run the master access software, you must have the CD-ROM that comes with this book inserted into your CD-ROM drive. Double-click the My Computer icon to display the available drives on your computer, and then double-click the CD-ROM drive icon. This displays a folder showing the contents of the CD-ROM. Double-click the Graphics folder. You now see the icon shown in Figure A-17.

Master Access icon

Figure A-17: The icon for the Master Access program.

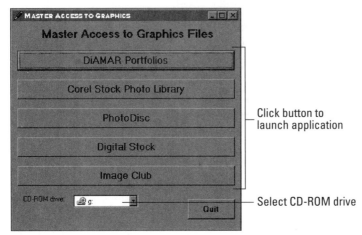

Double-click the icon to run the Master Access program (see Figure A-18). The Master Access program has buttons, one for each vendor who has supplied graphic images. To run the access program for a vendor, just click the vendor's button.

Figure A-18: Running the Master Access program.

The vendor names shown in Figure A-18 may change, depending on exactly which vendors supply material in time for pressing of the CD-ROM. We'll include as many different vendors as we can!

Software for the Book

I have written some programs for this book. They are the following:

➡ Automatic Setup software

➡ The Magic Parser

This section describes how to install the software. Refer to the chapters in which the software is used for details on its use.

Automatic Setup software

To install the Automatic Setup software, you must have the CD-ROM that comes with this book inserted into your CD-ROM drive. Double-click the My Computer icon to display the available drives on your computer, and then double-click the CD-ROM drive icon. This displays a folder showing the contents of the CD-ROM. Double-click the Autopage folder. You see the setup icon shown in Figure A-19. Double-click the Setup icon to run the setup program, and follow the on-screen prompts to complete installation.

Setup copies several files to a temporary directory, and then displays the Welcome banner shown in Figure A-20. Click OK to continue. This displays the dialog box shown in Figure A-21. Click the installation button to begin actual installation of the software. If you want to change the installation directory, click the Change Directory button.

After installation, you can run the Automatic Setup program by clicking the Start button, then Programs, and then the Autopage icon. The program window is shown in Figure A-22. To install all files for all chapters in one step, select the last radio button: Copy All Files Now. The software will attempt to identify the correct source and destination drives, but you can change the defaults if you prefer. To copy files, click the Copy to Hard Disk button.

Setup icon

Figure A-19: Running Autopage setup.

Figure A-20: The Welcome banner.

Installation button

Click to change installation folder

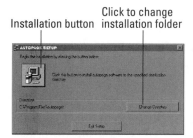

Figure A-21: The Installation dialog box.

Copies files for one chapter   Select destination drive

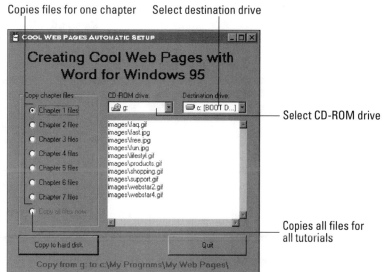

Select CD-ROM drive

Copies all files for all tutorials

Figure A-22: Running the Automatic Setup program.

After files are copied, for one or more chapters, or for all chapters, you can work with the various tutorials in each chapter.

Files for manual setup

If you elect not to install the Automatic Setup software, you have to copy the files for each tutorial manually. You'll find specific instructions on which files to copy at the beginning of each chapter. These files are located in various subfolders of the \tutorial folder on the CD-ROM.

The Magic Parser

Setup icon

Figure A-23: Running setup for the Parser.

Parser icon   Parser project file

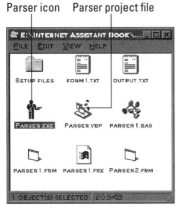

Figure A-24: The Parser software icon.

To install the Magic Parser software, you must have the CD-ROM that comes with this book inserted into your CD-ROM drive. Double-click the My Computer icon to display the available drives on your computer, and then double-click the CD-ROM drive icon. This displays a folder showing the contents of the CD-ROM. Double-click the Parser folder. You now see the setup icon shown in Figure A-23. Double-click the setup icon to run the setup program, and follow the on-screen prompts to complete installation. See the installation for the Automatic Setup program to see how to change the default installation directory — the dialog boxes for both installation routines are nearly identical.

After installing the Parser, you can run it by clicking the Start button, then Programs, and then the Autopage icon. The program icon is shown in Figure A-24. The program window is shown in Figure A-25. For complete instructions on using the Parser, see Chapter 6.

If you own Visual Basic 4.0, you can copy the entire Parser folder to your hard disk and view source code, modify the program, and so on. To load the source code into Visual Basic 4,0, double-click the Parser project icon (see Figure A-24). The source code shows how to manipulate dates from a form in Visual Basic. Suggestions for enhancing the code include the following:

➤ Modify the program to accept input from a file or series of files, instead of the Clipboard.

➤ Develop other formats for display of the data in the main Parser window.

➤ Output data in other formats, not just comma-delimited format.

Third-Party Software

Figure A-25: Running the Parser application.

I have included several third-party programs on the CD-ROM. The two programs listed here are discussed at length in the book. Programs other than those listed here may appear on the CD-ROM, too. All shareware, freeware, and demo programs are located in subfolders of the ThirdP folder.

To install any of the third-party programs, you must have the CD-ROM that comes with this book inserted into your CD-ROM drive. Double-click the My Computer icon to display the available drives on your computer, and then double-click the CD-ROM drive icon. This displays a folder showing the contents of the CD-ROM. Double-click the ThirdP folder to see the folders for the third-party programs.

Many of the third-party programs can also be downloaded from the Net. Where the location for downloading is known, I have included it.

SnapShot/32

SnapShot/32 is a program that does double duty. On the one hand, it is an excellent Windows 95 screen capture program. On the other hand, it saves GIF images with transparency and interlacing. I used it extensively in creating the screen captures for this book and I recommend it highly. See Chapter 4 for information on working with SnapShot/32.

SnapShot/32 is shareware. If you like it and use it, see the software's Help menu for information on registering the program.

To install ShapShot/32, double-click the snap32 folder to display the program files. Create a suitable folder on your hard disk (such as c:\Program Files\Snap32) and just drag and drop the SnapShot/32 files. To run the program, double-click the Snap32.exe icon (see Figure A-26). For additional information about SnapShot/32 and its installation, read the file readme.txt by double-clicking it (see Figure A-26).

Readme file   Snap Shot/32 icon

Figure A-26: The icons for SnapShot/32 version 2.55.

The version on the CD-ROM is 2.55. To check for or to download a more recent version of SnapShot/32, visit the author's Web site at

```
http://198.207.242.3/authors/gregko/
snap32.htm
```

MapTHIS!

MapTHIS! is a program for creating image map files. It creates CERN, NCSA, and client-side map files. See Chapter 4 for complete information on using MapTHIS!.

MapTHIS! is freeware; it costs you nothing.

Map THIS! icon

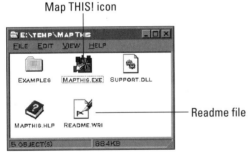

Readme file

Figure A-27: The icons for MapTHIS! version 1.2.

To install MapTHIS!, double-click the `mapthis` folder to display the program files and the `examples` subfolder. Create a suitable folder on your hard disk (such as `c:\Program Files\mapthis`) and just drag and drop the MapTHIS! files. To run the program, double-click the `Mapthis.exe` icon (see Figure A-27). For more information on MapTHIS! or its installation, read the `readme.wri` file by double-clicking it (see Figure A-27).

The version on the CD-ROM is 1.20. To check for, or to download, a more recent version of MapTHIS!, visit the author's Web site at:

```
http://galadriel.ecaetc.ohio-state.edu/tc/mt/#download
```

HTML and Internet Assistant

Appendix B

HTML and Microsoft Word for Windows have nothing in common. HTML is a purely text format that uses tags — such as <BODY>, <IMG>, and so on — to define a Web page. Word is a WYSIWYG word processing tool that uses an extremely sophisticated file format to store a much wider range of formatting information with each document. The bottom line is that they don't speak the same language.

Enter, stage right, Internet Assistant. Internet Assistant speaks both languages. It knows HTML, and it knows Word. It uses that knowledge to translate between the two. This gives you the advantage of working in an environment you already know — Word — to create Web pages with the standard language for Web pages — HTML.

The marriage between Word and HTML isn't perfect. HTML supports some features, such as nested tables, that Word does not. Word supports a huge number of features — annotations, footnotes, headers and footers, and so forth — that HTML does not.

This appendix is designed to help you work within the limits of the three-way alliance: Word, Internet Assistant, and HTML.

HTML Tags and Word for Windows/ Internet Assistant

Table B-1 shows the various HTML tags that are supported by Word, how to access them, and what they are typically used for.

 Many HTML tags have historical roots that indicate how they are used. You can usually recognize these tags because the description starts with "Traditionally used to identify…." Because Word for Windows and Internet Assistant hide HTML tags, you have complete freedom to use the tags in ways that work best for you. For example, nothing about HTML requires you to use the ADDRESS tag for your address — if you think that a centered paragraph of normal text with a font size one less than standard and italicized yields the best result, go ahead and use it.

Table B-1: HTML Tags and How to Use Them

HTML tag	Word Style, Command, or Tool	Description
<A HREF=...>	Add hyperlink tool	Creates an anchor that jumps to another document or file — called a *hyperlink*. The dialog box asks you for a complete URL or filename. See **hyperlink** and **URL** in the Glossary.
<A HREF="#...>	Add hyperlink tool INSERT⇨HYPERLINK⇨ BOOKMARK LOCATION IN FILE	Creates a hyperlink that jumps to another location within the same document (#location), or to a specific location in another file (otherfile.htm#location).
<A NAME=...>	Add Bookmark tool	Adds a bookmark to the current file at the current cursor location. A *bookmark* is a destination for hyperlinks to jump to.
<ADDRESS>	Address style	Used to format text information about a document's author, typically name and e-mail address. Most browsers represent the ADDRESS tag as *italic*. It is not required that you use the ADDRESS tag for address text.
<B>	Bold button on the Formatting toolbar	Formats text in bold type. To create bold text, select the text, and then click on the Bold button.

HTML tag	Word Style, Command, or Tool	Description
<BASE>	FILE⇨HTML DOCUMENT INFO⇨ADVANCED	Specifies a base URL. Browsers use the base to find files referenced in the document. It is usually the URL of the Web page itself, but it can refer to another URL. The BASE tag is not required, and Word does not create it unless you add a URL using the indicated menu selection.
<BGSOUND>	FORMAT⇨ BACKGROUND SOUND	Plays the specified sound when the document is opened. Note that the sound cannot play (nor the page be used) until the sound file completes downloading. This tag works best with small sound files that download quickly. Limited to .wav files.
<BLOCKQUOTE>	Blockquote style	Traditionally used to set off a block of text quoted from another source. This tag is most useful when you need to indent a paragraph without using a list, such as when you use a background image at the left of a page.
<BODY>	None	Defines the visible content of an HTML document. This tag is automatically inserted by Internet Assistant before the first text in the page. Attributes of the BODY tag, such as BACKGROUND (color) are set with the Background and Links command on the Format menu.
 	Shift+Enter	A standard Word soft carriage return. It forces a line break. Use it when you do not want white space (called leading) between lines. If you do want white space, use a normal line break by pressing Enter alone.

(continued)

Table B-1 *(continued):*

HTML tag	Word Style, Command, or Tool	Description
<CENTER>	Center text button on Formatting toolbar	Centers graphics or para-graphs. To center a table, select TABLE⇨ALIGN.
<CITE>	Cite style	Traditionally used to identify a citation, such as a book title. Most browsers display this tag as italic type.
<CODE>	Code style	Traditionally used to identify a line of programming code. Most browsers display this tag as a monospace font (such as Courier).
<DFN>	Definition style	Traditionally used to identify a term you are defining for the first time. Most browsers display this tag as bold type.
<DIR>	Directory List style	Creates a list of items. In most cases, items are quite short (fewer than 25 characters or so).
<DL>	Definition List style	Creates a two-column list of terms and definitions.
<DL COMPACT>	Definition Compact style	Creates a two-column list of terms and definitions (a defini-tion list) with no vertical space between entries, and using a smaller font.
<DT>...<DD>	Automatically applied only	These are styles that are automatically applied to the definitions of the terms in a definition list. These styles are automatically applied with the Definition List style; you do not create them directly.
<EM>	Emphasis style	Traditionally used to identify words you want to emphasize. Typically displayed in italic or bold type. In most cases, you can simply use bold or italic instead of using the Em-phasis style.

HTML tag	Word Style, Command, or Tool	Description
<FONT>	FORMAT⇨FONT	Changes the way text is displayed in your document. You can change the font used for text, the size, the color, and you can apply superscript and subscript styles.
<FORM>	INSERT⇨FORM FIELD	A form tag is created when you insert the first form field (also referred to as a *control*). Be sure to position the cursor within the form boundaries whenever you insert a new control. See **form** in the Glossary.
<H1> through <H6>	Heading 1 through Heading 6 styles	Headings are used on a Web page in the same manner you normally use headings in any document—to show the hierarchical structure of the document. Heading 1 is displayed in large bold type, and each succeeding level of heading uses smaller type.
<HEAD>	None	Similar to the BODY tag, in that it defines a segment of HTML document structure. The HEAD tag is automatically inserted by Internet Assistant.
<HR>	Horizontal rule button on the Formatting toolbar	Inserts a horizontal rule between paragraphs. Rules provide a visual break between sections of your document.
<I>	Italic button on the Formatting toolbar	Formats text in italic type.
<IMG>	Add Image tool	Inserts a picture at the current cursor location. In HTML-speak, a picture is called an *inline graphic.* You can specify many options for pictures; see Chapter 4 for information.

(continued)

Table B-1 *(continued):*

HTML tag	Word Style, Command, or Tool	Description
<ISINDEX>	FILE⇨HTML DOCUMENT INFO⇨ADVANCED	Indicates to browsers that your document is an indexed document, which can be searched using keywords. See your Web administrator for information about indexing methods supported on your server.
<KBD>	Keyboard	Traditionally used to identify text that you intend to be typed exactly as shown. Most browsers display KBD text in a monospace font, such as Courier.
<LI>	None	Traditionally used to identify an item in a list. This style is automatically applied with the List Bulleted and List Numbered styles. You do not create it yourself.
<MARQUEE>	INSERT⇨MARQUEE	Inserts a marquee, which consists of scrolling text when viewed in browsers that support marquees. There are many attributes for this tag; see Chapter 2.
<MENU>	Menu style	Creates a list of items, usually with one line per item. Traditionally, the list consists of hyperlinks. The MENU tag applies no text attributes, so you do not have to use it in this specific way, or at all, for that matter.
<META>	FILE⇨HTML DOCUMENT INFO⇨ADVANCED⇨META	Adds "meta-information" about your document. Such information is placed in the HEAD section of your document. A few <META> tags (Name attribute of Generator, Author, and Operator) are automatically inserted by Internet Assistant.

HTML tag	Word Style, Command, or Tool	Description
<OL>	List Numbered style	Creates a list of numbered items.
<P>	Normal style	Identifies the beginning of a new paragraph. This style is automatically applied whenever you create a new paragraph; you do not create it directly.
<PRE>	Preformatted style	Used to control layout of text on a page. Most browsers display PRE text in a monospaced font such as Courier. The PRE tag is used frequently for laying out tables without using the Table feature of Word (or the HTML TABLE tag), enabling browsers that do not support tables to display tabular data.
<PRE WIDTH=...>	Preformatted – Wide style	Used when you want to specify how many characters are to be displayed in one line of your <PRE> text. The default width is 80.
<STRIKE>	Strikethrough style	Creates "strike out" text, such as that used in a legal document.
<SAMP>	Sample style	Traditionally used to identify a literal sequence of characters, such as a word or phrase from a programming language. Most browsers display SAMP text in a monospaced font with single quotation marks added.
<STRONG>	Strong style	Traditionally used to identify words that you want to make more important than words with the emphasis tag. Most browsers display the STRONG tag in bold type.

(continued)

Table B-1 *(continued):*

HTML tag	Word Style, Command, or Tool	Description
<SUB>	FORMAT⇨FONT	Formats text as subscript.
<SUP>	FORMAT⇨FONT	Formats text as superscript.
<TABLE>	TABLE⇨INSERT TABLE	Inserts a table into your document. Tables are a major feature of Word, and there are numerous settings to play with. See Chapters 1-3 for information about working with tables. See also the PRE tag for creating simple tables that can be viewed with browsers that do not support the TABLE tag.
<TITLE>	Title button at right edge of Formatting toolbar	Gives your document a title. The title is usually displayed in the top bar of the browser window. Because most index systems emphasize titles when scanning the Web, you should make the title as clear and as related to page content as possible.
<TT>	Typewriter style	Formats text in a fixed-width font.
<U>	Underline button on Formatting toolbar	Formats text as underlined.
<UL>	Bulleted list button, or List Bulleted style	Creates a list of items that you want displayed as a bulleted list.
<VAR>	Variable	Traditionally used to identify text as a variable name. Most browsers display VAR text in italic type.

Form Tags and Word for Windows/ Internet Assistant

Forms tags are a different kind of beast than the standard HTML tags. For one thing, form tags are all connected to the INSERT⇨FORM FIELD menu selection — you do not use styles to create forms and form controls. You simply select the type of form control you want to add in the Form Field dialog box, and then type in or choose the appropriate values for the various parameters.

Most of the form tags start with INPUT. These tags specify controls on the form. The TYPE parameter defines the type of control that will actually appear on the form.

Most form tags include a NAME parameter. Assign a unique name to each control. Use names that will be easy to recognize when the form data is received — if a text control is for an e-mail address, a name such as *email* or *emailAddress* works well.

Most form tags also have a VALUE parameter. This is the value that will be returned, along with the NAME, when the form data is submitted. For some controls, the value you set is a default value, and the reader of the page can change it. For other controls, the value you set is the value returned when the form is submitted. For example, if the NAME of a text control is emailAddress, and the VALUE is set to none, then when the form is submitted, you will get something like this back in a mailto

```
emailAddress=none
```

if the reader does not type in an e-mail address, and something like this

```
emailAddress=pandrews@bigcollege.edu
```

if the reader enters an e-mail address. Radio button groups have one name for the entire group, whereas multiple-selection lists have a name and a value for each item in the group. For the most part, Internet Assistant guides you through the process of creating these controls, and you do not need to stop and think about what gets a name and what does not. The only reason to concern yourself with NAMEs and VALUEs and all the stuff shown in the following table is if you intend to edit HTML code directly, outside of Word (for example, with Notepad).

Table B-2 should help you get and keep your bearings as you wade through the morass of the HTML code for a typical form.

Table B-2: Form Tags and How to Use Them

Form Tag	Control Type	Parameters	Description
<INPUT>	TYPE=TEXT	NAME	Creates a text box on the form that accepts text input. You must supply text (usually placed before the control) that serves as a prompt for this input.
		VALUE	Optional. If included, specifies default text for the control.
		MAXLENGTH	Defines the maximum number of characters that can be input.
		SIZE	Defines the size of the control on the Web page, in character widths. For most browsers, "character width" means the width of an "m".
<INPUT>	TYPE= CHECKBOX	NAME	Creates a small box on the form. You must supply text (usually placed after the control) that defines what the user is checking off. Unlike radio buttons, the user can check more than one checkbox.
			When checked, the box has a small checkmark or "x" in it. When un-checked, the box is empty.
		VALUE	The value returned when the box is checked.
		CHECKED	Optional. When checked (see Chapter 6 regarding check jokes), indicates that the control will appear checked by default.

Form Tag	Control Type	Parameters	Description
<INPUT>	TYPE=RADIO		Creates a linked group of radio buttons on the page, as well as the text associated with each button.
		NAME	The name applies to the buttons as a group, not to the individual buttons.
		VALUE	Only the selected item returns a name/value pair when the form is submitted.
<INPUT>	TYPE=SUBMIT	VALUE	Creates a submit button on the form. When the submit button is clicked, the form contents are sent to the script or location defined in the ACTION parameter of the FORM tag. The VALUE specifies the text that will appear on the button.
<INPUT>	TYPE=IMAGE	SRC	Creates a Submit button in the form of a graphic that you specify with the SRC parameter. See Chapter 6 for an example.
<FORM>		ACTION	The FORM tag defines the beginning and end of the form. The ACTION parameter defines how the form is processed when the Submit button is clicked. The ACTION can refer to a script to which the data will be sent, or to an e-mail address via a mailto specification.

(continued)

Table B-2 *(continued):*

Form Tag	Control Type	Parameters	Description
		ENCTYPE	Optional. Used to specify the nature of the form contents. In most cases, you can simply accept the default.
		METHOD	Can be either GET or POST. GET is limited to about 1,000 characters and should be avoided. Make it a habit to choose POST unless you have a specific reason to use GET.
\<INPUT\>	TYPE=RESET	VALUE	Creates a Reset button on the form. The reset button causes all controls on the form to be reset to either blank or a default value, when specified. The VALUE specifies the text that appears on the button.
\<INPUT\>	TYPE= PASSWORD	NAME	Creates a text control on the form, but when text is typed into the control, asterisks appear instead of the text. Otherwise, behaves just like a text control.
		VALUE	Default text, which makes infrequent sense when you're using a password!
		MAXLENGTH	Maximum number of characters that can be input.
		SIZE	Width of the password control on the Web page.

Form Tag	Control Type	Parameters	Description
<INPUT>	TYPE=HIDDEN	NAME	Hidden controls are used to send information back to yourself that visitors to the page do not see. For example, you can specify a name for the form with NAME="form-name" and VALUE="SignUpForm".
		VALUE	The value returned when the form is submitted.
<TEXTAREA>		NAME	Creates a multiline text control on the form.
		ROWS	Specifies the height of the control in lines.
		COLS	Specifies the width of the control in characters.
<SELECT>		NAME	Creates a drop-down list on the form. The NAME applies to the entire list and is returned with the VALUE of the individual item selected.
<SELECT>	MULTIPLE	NAME	When MULTIPLE is used as a parameter, the user can select more than one item in the list.
<OPTION>		VALUE	This is the value that is returned to you when the form is submitted. You may have noticed that there is no parameter for the text for each item; Internet Assistant handles this for you in the Form Field dialog boxes.
		SELECTED	By default, the option with this attribute appears as selected in the drop-down list.

(continued)

Table B-2 (continued):

Form Tag	Control Type	Parameters	Description
<SELECT>	MULTIPLE	NAME	When MULTIPLE is used as a parameter, the user can select more than one item in the list.

Word versus HTML

The menus and toolbars in Word are modified a great deal when you are working on an HTML document. One reason for this is to prevent you from adding anything to the document that will be illegal on a Web page. However, Internet Assistant can't protect you from every possibility. There are still several ways to get into trouble, and possibly wind up with illegal characters or styles in your Web pages:

➥ If you add tabs to your document when the paragraph style is anything other than PRE, DL, or DIR, Word attempts to recover by turning the tab into a space. This will most likely alter the layout of the document, and the Web page will not appear as you expected it to look.

➥ Never use the shortcut menu to apply font or paragraph formatting. If you do, you can add formats and styles that are not Web-legal.

➥ Do not use paragraph indents for any style besides OL or UL.

➥ Be careful about running macros that were not designed specifically for HTML pages because they may invoke Word features that are not compatible with HTML.

To be completely safe, you can close your document and then reopen it to look for any changes. It is highly unlikely that you can find a way to add garbage text to an HTML file using Word's various menus, commands, and tools. However, because Word strips any illegal characters and formatting when it saves the file, you should look for paragraphs that are not where you meant them to be, that do not have indents you expected, and so on. Then save the file again, and all should be well.

File Woes, and How to Avoid Them

If you upload your Web pages to a server, and suddenly some or all of the images are missing, it is likely that the server is case-sensitive about filenames. On such a server, the filename *image.GIF* is not the same as the filename *image.gif.* If you automatically entered all lowercase names, but your image-editing software added uppercase extensions, your files will be on the server, but they can't be found.

There are two cures: Either change the filenames so that their case matches whatever you used in your HTML files, or change your HTML files so that the case matches the actual filenames. If the server is a UNIX server, your best choice is to use all lowercase names for all files.

Special Symbols

The appendix of nearly every book on HTML contains the tables that you find in this section. Such tables list the HTML codes to use for special symbols, such as the ampersand (&), less than (<), and many other symbols. However, you will find that, for the most part, you do not need to rely on these special symbols. Word and Internet Assistant work together on this — if you use an ampersand, Internet Assistant conveniently converts it to the HTML form of &.

At times, however, you will have to either add HTML markup of your own or edit a file originally created in Word in something like Notepad. At such times, it is convenient to have a table at hand that shows all the special symbols and their codes.

There are two methods for adding the special symbols to HTML files. One method is to use ASCII codes. The format is

```
&#n;
```

where &# are required characters, and *n* is the ASCII code for the character. For example,   is the code for a nonbreaking space. The other method is to use the HTML codes for specific characters, such as ý which stands for a small *y* with an acute accent mark (ý).

Figure B-1 shows the Netscape browser with the file ascii.htm loaded. You can find this file on the CD-ROM in the directory \treats\html. It shows the result of evaluating all possible ASCII expressions (that is, values from 129 to 256). Some numeric values have no ASCII equivalent and are shown with empty boxes (such as 129, 141).

Figure B-2 shows the Netscape browser with the file special.htm loaded. You can find this file on the CD-ROM in the directory \treats\html. It shows the result of evaluating all possible special codes. Different browsers support different special codes, so not all browsers will display all the codes shown.

Not all browsers support these features, but most up-to-date browsers do.

Numeric value   ASCII equivalent   Special Code   Result

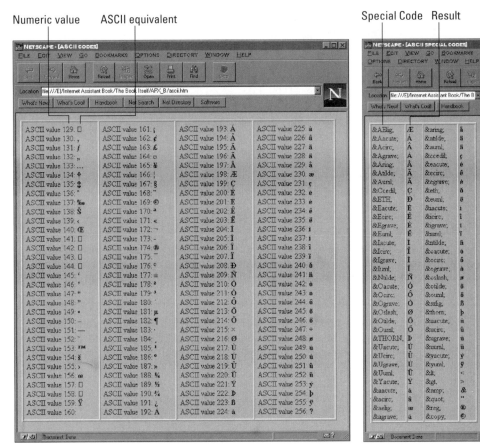

Figure B-1: Using ASCII codes.

Figure B-2: Special codes for HTML.

Glossary:
The Words
of the Web

3-D modeler	Software used to create 3-D objects and worlds. Often used to create VRML files for viewing on the Web. (See *VRML*.)
ACTION	The part of a form's definition that specifies what is to happen with the data on the form.
Add-on product	Software that is meant to work only with another product. For example, many programs, such as Web/FX, were created as add-ons for the Netscape Navigator Web browser.
Audio clip	Audio file that you can download over the Web or listen to in real time with products like Real Audio.
Background image	Graphic image that is repeated across a Web page. It is called a background image because text and other images on the page appear "over" it.
Bandwidth	The rate at which data can move across a given connection. Modems using phone lines are considered a low-bandwidth connection, whereas ISDN or T1 lines are considered high bandwidth. Truly high bandwidth is reserved for hardware in close proximity, such as hard drives on your local machine.
Banner	Can refer to two things: a line of text that scrolls on a page, or an image that serves as the identifier for a magazine or newspaper.
Baud	A unit for measuring modem transfer speeds.
Binary	A system of counting with just two digits: 0 and 1. To count from 0 to 10 in binary: 0, 1, 10, 11, 100, 101, 110, 111, 1000, 1001, 1010.
Bit	The ultimate unit of computing. A bit has two states: on and off. These states are usually represented by binary numbers: 1 for on, 0 for off. Everything a computer can do is ultimately handled as bits.

Bookmark	A point in a Web page that has a name. The HTML code for a bookmark is <A HREF="BookmarkName">. You can add bookmarks in Word by using the Add Bookmark tool.
Browser	A program for viewing Web pages.
Bytes	A unit of computing that contains 8 bits. A byte can contain 256 different values using binary notation. These values range from 00000000 to 11111111. (See *binary; bit.*)
Caption	A line of text at the top or bottom of a table, usually acting as a title for the table. (See *table.*)
Cell	A single unit of data in a table. (See *row, column, table.*)
CGI	Common Gateway Interface. It is a method by which Web-based files (usually Web pages) can interface with other files on the computer. For example, CGI can use environment variables on a UNIX server, or INI files on a Windows NT server.
CGI script	A script or program that uses CGI to process information related to Web pages. (See *CGI.*)
Channels	Refers to the number of channels in a sound file. There are just two choices: mono (one channel) and stereo (two channels — left and right).
Checkbox	A form control. When checked, the checkbox's value is true; when unchecked, it is false. A way to allow the user of the form to indicate yes or no kinds of information.
Codec	A video compression scheme, usually involving lossy compression, that greatly reduces the bandwidth of a video file during playback. (See *bandwidth, lossy compression*).
Column	A vertical group of cells in a table. (See *cell, row, table.*)
Compression	A method for reducing the file size of data. Normal compression involves using redundancies in the information to arrange the data more compactly. Lossy compression involves removing the least significant data to reduce size. (See *Lossy.*)
Control	A form element, such as text boxes and selection lists. (See *form.*)
Definition lists	An HTML list type represented in Word with the style Definition List,DL.
Directory	See *folder.*

Directory structure	The hierarchy of directories/folders and subdirectories/subfolders on a hard disk. (*Directory* and *folder* are synonyms.)
Domain name	The part of a URL that specifies a unique node on the Web. (See *URL; node.*)
Download	To copy a file from a server (on the Internet, from a Web server or ftp server) to your local computer.
Downloading	The act of copying a file from a server.
Embedding VRML	The act of adding a VRML object to a Web page. See *VRML.*
Escape character	Many scripting tools and languages (and this includes HTML) use certain characters for special jobs. For example, HTML uses the ampersand to mark special entities, such as the "<" symbol. The HTML code for this symbol is "<". When a Web browser encounters the ampersand character, it knows not to display it literally, but to "escape" from displaying text and to start decoding a special symbol. To actually display an ampersand, you would use the HTML code "&". When using Word, you seldom need to worry about escape characters — Internet Assistant handles them automatically.
Escape sequence	The escape character, plus the special code, plus a character that ends the special code, taken together, are called an escape sequence. (See *escape character.*)
FAQ	Frequently Asked Question. FAQ files are a good place to begin your quest for knowledge on any Web site.
Field	In Word, a special page element that contains variable information, with the content calculated at the time of printing or saving the file. Internet Assistant makes use of fields to store hidden HTML codes that are used to generate genuine HTML when the file is saved to disk. Fields are also used to represent form elements (controls). (See *form; control.*)
Filter	Used to convert from one graphic file format to another or to display an image on a Web page. Because Web pages mostly use images in the GIF and JPEG formats, Word must have those graphic filters installed to work properly with Internet Assistant. (See *GIF, JPEG.*)
Folder	A location on a hard drive that contains one or more files. Also referred to as a directory.
Form	An HTML device for Web pages that enables the user to enter data into controls on the page and to submit the data to a server for processing. See Chapter 6 for extensive coverage of forms. (See *control.*)

Frame rate   The rate at which video frames are presented. For Web video, the frame rate is usually much lower than for other media such as television, owing to the low bandwidth of the Web. (See *bandwidth.*)

FTP   File Transfer Protocol. Often used in lower case: ftp. Refers to a pre-Web method for copying files on the Internet. It is still used for file copying on many Web servers, and many ISP's with UNIX servers may ask you to use ftp to upload your Web pages. (See *ISP.*)

FTP client   Software that handles ftp connections for you. (See *FTP.*)

Full-motion video   Video that is presented at a full-frame rate (30 frames per second).

Function calls   A programming language concept. A function can contain one or more lines of programming code stored elsewhere, but you can refer to the function with just a single line of code. This leads to more readable, easier-to-maintain programs: If you need to change the code for a function, you only need to change it in one place, not every place where the function is called.

GIF   A non-lossy compression format used for many image files found on the Web. Stands for Graphic Interchange Format, reflecting the original intention of the format's developers that GIF files become the standard method for transferring image online. (See *lossy compression, JPEG.*)

High-bandwidth   A computer connection that offers relatively fast data transfer. (See *bandwidth.*)

Horizontal rule   A line, either 3-D or flat, that runs from side to side on a Web page.

Hot (text and graphics)   Another way to refer to a hyperlink. (See *hyperlink.*)

Hot spots   Another way to refer to a hyperlink. (See *hyperlink.*)

HTML   HyperText Markup Language. The language that is used to format Web pages.

HTML code   The tags, parameters, and other elements of HTML.

HTML Markup   The process of adding explicit HTML tags and parameters to a Web page in Word.

Hyperlink   A block of text or an image that, when clicked, jumps to or causes the download of a specific URL, file, or bookmark. (See *download, URL, bookmark.*)

Hypertext link A text hyperlink. (See *hyperlink*.)

HyperText Transfer Protocol HTML. (See *HTML*.)

Image map An image that, when clicked, sends coordinates of the click point to a map file. The map file then uses the coordinates to identify the correct hyperlink for the click. (See *map file, hyperlink*.)

Image program Software for creating or editing image files.

INI files A Windows file that contains information about some program. INI files are very diverse and can be used for a huge variety of information storage. Windows 95 no longer uses INI files; it uses a Registry to store this kind of information.

Inlining Said of VRML files. Inlining of a file allows the file to be viewed in your browser while the file is still being downloaded. (See *VRML*.)

Interlacing A method of video or image display that skips horizontal rows in the image to display the overall image more quickly.

Internet The collection of computers that constitutes the World Wide Web. Also, the method by which they are connected.

Internet Service Provider A company that provides access to the Internet, and may also provide a place (called a Web server) for your Web pages. (See *Web server*.)

Internet site A single location on the Web, consisting of one or more computers connected to the Internet.

ISDN A type of high-speed phone connection, offering data rates of up to 128 kilobytes per second. See *T-1*.

ISMAP The HTML code added to an IMG tag indicating that the image is an image map. (See *image map, HTML code*.)

ISP See *Internet Service Provider*.

Java A sophisticated programming language similar to C++ but even more object oriented and rigorous. (See *JavaScript*.)

JavaScript A scripting language loosely based on the Java programming language. (See *Visual Script, Java*.)

JPEG A lossy compression method often used for image files used on the Web. Stands for Joint Photographic Experts Group, the folks who created this standard. Pronounced "jay-peg." (See *lossy compression, GIF, MPEG*.)

Layout The art of arranging text, graphic, and other elements on a page.

Lists A method of grouping related items on a Web page. Word supports most of the different kinds of HTML lists. See *definition list, ordered list, unordered list.*

Logo A graphic that is used to represent a company or other entity.

Lossy compression A form of compression that involves loss of data, and is usually applied to image files. For example, if an image is compressed with JPEG (a form of lossy compression), the blue parts of the image will lose detail. Because the eye does not see detail in blue areas all that well, the apparent quality of the image suffers little because of the lost data, but the file size is greatly reduced. In addition to losing data in this fashion, lossy compression methods often also use sophisticated mathematical operations to further reduce the size of the image file.

Low-bandwidth A computer connection that offers relatively slow data transfer. (See *bandwidth.*)

Macro A computer "program" written in a language specific to a particular piece of software, such as a word processor or spreadsheet.

Mailto A Web technique for generating e-mail from a Web page. Two major uses for mailto are hyperlinks that autostart an e-mail program and sending forms data via e-mail. (See *hyperlink.*)

Map file A text file associated with an image map. The map file contains definitions of hot spots on the image that serve as hyperlinks. (See *image map, hyperlink, ISMAP.*)

Markup See *HTML markup.*

Marquee A moving block of text, first supported by the Internet Explorer browser. Not all browsers support the marquee.

Menu A list of selections. On a Web page, a menu is most likely to be a list of hyperlinks.

Method A programming concept; used when discussing object-oriented programming (OOP). Refers to actions made upon objects. (See *object-oriented programming.*)

MIME Multipurpose Internet Mail Extension. A method for identifying the type of content in a message, Web page, or hyperlink. For example, an Adobe Acrobat document would have a MIME type of `application/pdf`, and a JPG image has a MIME type of `image/jpg`.

Mixing console
A device that takes two or more audio inputs and mixes them into a single audio signal.

MPEG
A lossy compression format for video files. Stands for Motion Picture Experts Group, the folks who set this standard. (See *lossy compression, JPEG.*)

Multiline text box
A text box that has room for more than one line of text.

Multimedia
Probably the most overused term in computerese; your definition is probably as close to correct as mine. Generally refers to combining audio and video with text on the computer, but also taken to mean things like using phone lines to deliver video.

Nested tables
HTML enables you to place one table inside another table; this is called *nesting*. Word doesn't support nesting. If you try to load an HTML file with nested tables into Word, you'll get a real mess.

Node
Fancy word for an Internet site. (See *Internet site.*)

Object
Program code that uses properties and methods for interacting with other program code. Objects can be documents (Web page), selected text, and many other things. See Chapter 7 for details. (See *object-oriented programming.*)

Object-oriented
Uses objects instead of more traditional scripting or programming techniques. (See *object, object-oriented programming.*)

Object-oriented programming
A style of programming that restricts the manner in which program elements interact with each other. A lump of program code is called an object. Objects have properties, such as a Name or a Value. You can modify an object by using a method, such as Write or toUpperCase. (See *method, property, OOP, object.*)

OOP
See *object-oriented programming.*

Ordered list
An HTML list type, represented in Word by the style Ordered List,DL.

Paragraph Marks
The "reversed-P" symbol used by word to indicate a carriage return at the end of a paragraph. To view paragraph marks, select TOOLS⇨OPTIONS to display the Options dialog box. Click the View tab to access the checkbox for turning paragraph mark display on or off.

Parameters
In HTML, these are secondary pieces of information in a TAG. For example, in the HTML code <IMG SRC="myfile.gif">, the TAG is the text *IMG*, and the parameter is the text *SRC="myfile.gif"*.

Parser　　Software that interprets a string of characters or words.

Pathname　　A complete specification for a file. A filename is just the name of a file: `myfile.htm`. A pathname includes a full list of all the directories needed to locate the file, such as `c:\My Documents\My Web Pages\myfile.htm`. (See *relative path*.)

Placeholders　　Something that stands in for something else. In the templates included on the CD-ROM, I use placeholder images to indicate where you should place your own images when you create a Web page.

Plug-ins　　A kind of software that attaches itself to other software and will only work in the presence of the other software. (See *add-on product*.)

Property　　Refers to property of an object in an object-oriented programming language. You read or change the properties of an object. (See *object-oriented programming*.)

Protocol　　A method for communicating. A protocol specifies the nature of the communication. For example, a protocol between humans might consist of a smile and a handshake, indicating that communication was now okay. A protocol between two computers might specify that communication can begin after the two computers exchange the characters Ctrl+S and Ctrl+Q.

Provider　　See *Internet Service Provider*.

QuickTime　　A standard for video playback from Apple. Supports various video compression codecs that use lossy compression to reduce the bandwidth of video playback. QuickTime is available for both Macintosh and Windows computers. (See *codec, lossy compression, Video for Windows*.)

Radio button　　A form control that occurs in groups. When one radio button is clicked, it gets a little black mark that indicates it is the currently selected button; all other radio buttons are then unselected — only one radio button can be selected at a time.

Recalibration　　What many hard drives do to themselves from time to time to ensure that they can read their data correctly. If you do video or audio recording, you must use a hard drive that is capable of delaying recalibration until after you complete the recording. Such drives are often called A/V drives (audio/video drives).

Recording level　　The strength of the incoming audio signal. If the signal is too strong, it overloads the electronics involved in the recording and causes (usually extremely annoying) distortion. Similar to what happens to politicians in the heat of a political campaign.

Registry
What Windows 95 uses instead of INI files for storing information about itself and many programs.

Relative path
A pathname that does not specify the full list of folders/directories needed to locate a file. HTML files often use relative paths, and nearly always do so when referring to files located on the same server as the HTML file itself, such as images or other HTML files. (See *pathname*.)

Reset button
A button on a Web page form that causes the controls on the form to be reset to their default or blank values. (See *form, Submit button*.)

Resolution
Applies to sounds and images. For sounds, refers to whether the file uses one byte (8 bits) or two bytes (16 bits) to store information about the sound. For images, refers to the level of detail in an image. A low-resolution image contains relatively little detail, whereas a high-resolution image contains a great deal of detail. Resolution also refers to screen resolution: the more pixels, the higher the resolution.

Row
A horizontal group of cells in a table. See *cell, column, table*.

Sample rate
The rate at which a sound is sampled for conversion into a digital audio clip. Common sample rates are 11 kHz, 22 kHz, and 44 kHz. "kHz" stands for kilohertz, which translates as "thousands of times per second." Thus, 22 kHz simply means "22,000 times per second." Audio CDs use the highest rate, 44 kHz, which produces the best sound quality.

Script
The difference between a script and a computer program isn't very large — both a script and a program tell the computer to do something. In common usage, a script often uses a simple, word-rich programming language, so that the instructions to the computer are relatively easy to understand by a human being. A program, on the other hand, frequently uses a complex, arcane, and difficult-to-comprehend programming language, such as C. In reality, the line between script and programming languages is fuzzier than a woolly caterpillar before a really bad winter.

Server
A computer that is connected by a network to many other computers and acts as a common resource for the other computers. A Web server is a server dedicated to providing access via the Internet.

Shareware
Software that is sold by giving it away and then asking people to pay for the privilege of using it (with apologies to Ambrose Bierce and *The Devil's Dictionary*).

Software MPEG encoder   Software that applies the MPEG code to a video clip or animation, making the file smaller. Software encoders are much slower than hardware encoders, but hardware encoders cost tens of thousands of dollars, and software encoders are usually less than $500. (See *lossy compression, MPEG, codec.*)

StyleMap   You can create a StyleMap in the Windows 95 Registry to automate conversion of standard styles when saving .doc files as .htm files. (See *Registry.*)

Styles   Predefined fonts, font sizes, alignments, indentations, and so forth for a paragraph or text.

Submit button   A button on a Web page form that causes the data on the form to be sent to a destination defined by the ACTION for the form. (See *form, Reset button.*)

T-1   A type of ultra-high-speed phone line. Faster than an ISDN connection, but also much more expensive. Usually, a dedicated line between two points that is open (active) at all times. Commonly used to link Internet sites. (See *ISDN, Internet site.*)

Table   A key feature of HTML 3 standard that enables you to present information on rows and columns on a Web page. Tables are a great way to organize all kinds of data and images. See Chapter 3 for examples of using tables.

Table header   On a Web table, a table cell whose text appears bold and centered.

Tagline   A short (usually a single) line of text below a logo or banner; usually found at the top of a Web page. (See *logo, banner.*)

Templates   A file that specifies how a document should look, and what styles can be applied to the document. (See *style.*)

Transparency   Able to be seen through, as a politician: "His rhetoric was so transparent that even a programmer could have seen his real motives." (With no disrespect toward programmers, who simply have better things to do than assay the intentions of politicians.)

Unordered list   An HTML list type, represented in Word with the style Bulleted List,DL.

URL   Uniform Resource Locator. Defines the location of a Web page or other Web resource. Pronounced "you-are-**ell**," not "Earl." Example: `http://www.coolsite.com`.

Video clips	Video file that you can download over the Web or listen to in real time with products like VDOLive.
Video for Windows	A standard for video playback from Microsoft. Supports various video compression codecs that use lossy compression to reduce the bandwidth of video playback. Video for Windows video clips can be played back on both Macintosh and Windows computers. See *codec, lossy compression, QuickTime.*
Visual Script	A scripting language based on Visual Basic. (See *JavaScript.*)
VRML	Virtual Reality Markup Language. A text-based language used to define 3-D worlds for the Web. Many 3-D modeling programs, such as Fountain, enable you to create 3-D worlds and save them as VRML files. (See *3-D modeler.*)
Watermark	Originally, an impression on a sheet of paper that identifies its maker. On a Web page, a watermark is simply a nonscrolling background image. (See *background image.*)
Waveform	The visual representation of the data in an audio clip. (See *audio clip.*)
Web	Short term for World Wide Web. The Internet. A place to lose your mind, your money, and your time.
Web administrator	See *Webmaster.*
Web-legal	Refers to styles that can be used on Web pages. (See *styles, Web page.*)
Web page	What you find on the Web.
Web server	See *server.*
Webmaster	A person foolish enough to think that he or she is smart enough to manage a Web site.
World Wide Web (WWW)	See *Web.*
WYSIWYG	Pronounced "**wizz**-ee-wig." Short for "What you see is what you get." It refers to software that enables you to work on-screen with a visual representation of the final result. Word for Windows, for example, is a WYSIWYG word processor — especially if you select VIEW⇨PAGE LAYOUT.

Symbols & Numbers

(pound sign), URLs, 119
& (ampersand), 272
* (asterisks), passwords, 242
3-D modeler, 311
3-D objects, 214–216
; (semicolon), escape sequence, 272

A

Add Bookmark tool, 119
Add Horizontal Rule tool, 111
Add Hyperlink tool, 32, 44, 114, 208
Add Picture tool, 109, 111, 115, 118, 164, 195
Address style, 70, 89
Adobe Photoshop, 147
  Blend tool, 151
  image transparency creation with, 168
  Lasso tool, 150, 151
  saving GIF file in, 166
  tile creation in, 149–151
Adobe Premiere, 199, 218
Align dialog box, 136
  illustrated, 209
  Text in Table Cells section, 209
alignment
  controls, 222
  horizontal rule, 266–267
  image, 111, 112
    examples, 164
    with text options, 163
  text in cells, 136–137, 209
alternate text, 33
ampersand (&), 272
animations, 198–199
  file conversion, 199
  See also video

annotations, 61
Art Materials palette (Painter), 153
ASCII codes, 310
asterisks (*) in passwords, 242
audio, 189, 202–213
  adding, 202–213
  background, 210–211
  CD-ROM bonus, 218
  clickable, 203–210
  clips, 311
  downloading, 203
  file size, 203
  files, 192
  hyperlinks, 203, 208
  Real Audio, 203, 211–212
  See also multimedia; video
automatic setup
  Chapter 1 tutorial, 23–24
  Chapter 2 tutorial, 56
  Chapter 3 tutorial, 104
  Chapter 4 tutorial, 140
  Chapter 5 tutorial, 190
  Chapter 6 tutorial, 220
  Chapter 7 tutorial, 262
  Copy to Hard Disk button, 24, 56, 104, 140, 190, 220, 262
  illustrated, 24
  options, selecting, 24
  running, 23, 56, 104, 140, 190, 220, 262
  software installation, 290–292
  See also automatic setup
Autopage Setup program, 23, 291
AVI files, 199

B

Background and Links dialog box, 28–29, 79
  Color drop-down box, 126
  illustrated, 126

background audio, 210–211
  adding, 211
  defined, 210
  support for, 211
  testing, 211
  See also audio
Background Color dialog box, 135
background colors, 143–145
  in browser, 126
  cell, 134–135
  changing, 28
  clashing, 142
  custom, 143–145
  marquee, 74
  Products page, 113, 126
  setting, 143
  setting after conversion, 79–80
  See also colors
background images, 142–162
  colors and, 143–145
  defined, 311
  nonscrolling, 161
  seamless tiles, 148
  watermarks, 161
  ways of working with, 142
  See also images
background textures, 143
bandwidth, 192, 311
blank lines, adding, 76
Blend tool (Photoshop), 151
blending, 151–152
  illustrated, 152
  tiles, 151–152

Blockquote style, 71, 90, 158–159
blur filter, 147
blurring, 147
BMP files, 165
bold, 131
Bookmark dialog box, 120
Bookmark tool, 32
bookmarks, 122
  creating, 119–120
  defined, 119, 312
  linking to, 121
  managing, 120–121
  naming, 120
  number in a Web page, 120
  pound sign (#) and, 119
  Products page, 122
  sorting, 120–121
    by location, 121
    by name, 120
  specifying, 121
  using, 120
borders, 61
  adding, 40
  bottom, 61
  cell, 134, 136
  image, 38
  removing, 207
  table, 50, 51
Borders dialog box, 51
browsers. *See* Web browsers
Brushes palette (Painter), 153
bulleted lists. *See* unordered lists
buttons
  adding, 41
  Hidden, 264, 265
  hot spot, 177
  images as, 38
  MapTHIS! and, 178
  radio, 225, 234–235
  Reset, 222, 225, 240–241
  Submit, 222, 225, 239–240

captions, 61
  defined, 312
  table, 137–138
  in Word, 137
CD-ROM, 281–294
  audio files bonus, 218
  Automatic Setup software, 290–292
  graphics, 289–290
  Internet Assistant, 281–287
  Internet Explorer, 288
  latest additions to, 281
  loading, 22
  MapTHIS!, 173–185, 294
  Parser program, 246–249, 292–293
  programs, this book, 290
  SnapShot/32, 166, 293–294
  techniques, 280
  templates, 3, 9, 288–289
    accessing, 21–22
    usage methods, 21
  third-party software, 293–294
  video clips bonus, 218
  Web browser, 8
CD-ROM drive, selecting, 23
Cell Type dialog box, 129
Cell Width and Spacing dialog box, 82–83
  Cell Spacing option, 135
  illustrated, 135
cells, 131–138
  borders for, 134, 136
  color in, 134–135
  defined, 312
  header, 130
  lists in, 132
  multiline text control in, 255
  setting type of, 129
  space between, 135–136

text alignment, 136–137
  width, setting, 133–134
  See also table(s)
Center Text tool, 110
Center tool, 124
CERN, 180, 182–183
  defined, 180
  hot spot format, 182
  MAP file version, 182
  See also hot spots
CGI (Common Gateway Interface), 230
  defined, 312
  scripting, 243, 312
character styles
  basic, 69–70
  exotic, 72
  font size and, 70
  illustrated, 70
  See also styles
Check Box Form Field dialog box, 233
checkbox, 233–234
  adding, 233–234
  defined, 225, 312
  features, 241
  illustrated, 234, 241
  placement, 233
  values, 233
  See also controls
CITE style, 90
Client-Side Image Map. *See* CSIM
clip art, 29
  collections, 185–187
  Corel and, 186
  DiAMAR and, 186
  Digital Stock and, 187
  illustrated examples, 31
  PhotoDisc and, 187
  Publisher's Toolbox and, 186
  Screen Caffeine Pro and, 187
CODE style, 90
ColorHEX, 144

colors
  background
    in browser, 126
    changing, 28
    marquee, 74
    Products page, 113, 126
    setting after conversion,
      79–80
  body text, 29, 143
  in cells, 134–135
  HTML code, 145
  hyperlink, 29, 143
column widths, 82–83, 312
  adjusting, 206
  returning to original, 206
  setting, 133–134
  See also cells; table(s)
combination lists, 68–69
compact definition lists,
  67, 90
compression, 312, 316
Configuration dialog box,
  248
context menus, 53
controls
  adding, 229–242
  alignment of, 222
  changing, 238
  checkbox, 225, 233–234
  defined, 221, 312
  display of, 228
  hidden controls, 225,
    229–230
  multiline text box, 225,
    235–236
  Parser program, 247
  password text box, 225,
    236–238
  radio buttons, 225,
    234–235
  Reset button, 222, 225,
    240–241
  selection, 231–233
  stacking, 253
  Submit button, 222, 225,
    239–240
  text, 228–229

text box, 222, 225,
    227–229
  types of, 223
  See also forms
conventions
  CERN, 180, 182–183
  choosing, 180
  CSIM, 180, 183–185
  image map, 173, 180
  MapTHIS! and, 180
  NCSA, 180, 181–182
  this book, 5–6
conversion, document,
    57–74
  automatic, 59–62
  automating, 88–102
  fonts in, 75, 76
  HTML layout support
    and, 59
  key points about, 59
  rules, 75–76
  starting, 59–62
  tabs in, 75
  text and, 75
Cool Templates. See
  templates
Corel, 186
Corporate Looks templates,
  27, 53
Create Guides dialog box
  (MapTHIS!), 178–179
Creating Cool Web Pages
  with HTML, 17, 276
Creating Cool Web Pages with
  Word for Windows 95
  conventions, 5–6
  feedback, 8
  icons, 6
  organization of, 5
  software for, 290–293
CSIM, 180, 183–185
  default URL, 184
  defined, 180
  hot spot format, 184
  MAP file, 183–184
  See also hot spots
cursors
  crosshair, 170
  pointing hand, 41, 42

definition lists, 65–67, 90
  compact, 67
  creating, 65–66
  defined, 312
  illustrated, 65
  in Netscape, 67
  soft carriage return in, 66
  uses, 66
  in Word, 67
  See also lists
DiAMAR, 186
Digital Stock, 187
Director, 216–218
  defined, 217
  uses, 216
  See also Shockwave
directories. See folders
Directory style, 68, 90
DL (definition list). See
  definition lists
DOC file extension, 10
documents
  converting to Web pages,
    4, 55–102
  creating, 26–28
  customizing, 28–29
  saving, 37
  Word file extension, 10
domain name, 20
  defined, 313
  edu, 115
DOT file extension, 10
downloading, 113
  audio, 203
  defined, 313
  Internet Assistant 2.0,
    282–284
  multimedia, 189
  video, 193–194
drawing layer elements, 61

editing
  forms, 242
  hot spots, 179
  Internet Assistant internal
    codes, 274
  text, 46–47
e-mail addresses
  adding, 48
  hyperlinks, 44
e-mail, in sending forms,
    242
embedded markup,
    274–277
  See also HTML markup
embedding, 277–280
  defined, 277, 313
  objects, 61, 278–280
    viewing and, 279–280
  VRML, 278
  technology, 277
  Web support, 280
Emphasis (EM) style, 90
endnotes, 61
escape character, 272, 313
escape sequence, 272, 313
European Laboratory for
    Particle Physics. *See*
    CERN
Export Registry File dialog
    box, 98

fancy tables tutorial,
    126–138
FAQs page, 36, 124
  See also WebStarr Web
    page
feedback, author, 8
feedback forms, 252–258
  columns on, 254
  creating, 252–258

creation process, 255
first draft of, 253
illustrated layout, 254
Parser program version,
    256–257
stacking on, 253
white space, 253
See also forms
fields, 61, 313
file extensions
  AVI, 199
  DOC, 10
  DOT, 10
  MAP, 177
  MOV, 199
File menu
  Close command, 34
  HTML Document Info
    command, 209
  Load command, 166
  New command, 26, 109,
    128, 225, 289
  Open command, 34, 146
  Preview in Browser com-
    mand, 34, 41, 45, 48
  Save As command, 60,
    166, 170, 177
  Save command, 36
files
  audio, 192
  case sensitivity and,
    308–309
  copying, 23, 56, 104, 190
  filenames, 308–309
  GIF, 25
  HTML, 141, 143
  image, 141
  JPEG, 25
  manual setup, 292
  MAP, 169–185
  map-related, 142
  unsaved, 34
  video, 191
  video formats, 200
filters, 147
  blur, 147
  defined, 313

folders
  Cool Templates, 50, 53
  copying to hard drive, 54
  Corporate Looks, 53
  creating, 24
  defined, 21, 313
  map file, 173
  My Web Pages, 24, 25, 56,
    57, 104, 140, 190–191,
    220, 262
  setup for tutorial, 25
  template, 22, 53
  Templates, 50, 53
  tutorials, 24
fonts
  in conversion process, 75,
    76
  sizing, 70
footers, 61
footnotes, 61
Form Field dialog box,
    226–227, 229
Format dialog box, 92
Format menu
  Background and Links
    command, 28, 79, 126,
    143, 145
  Background Sound com-
    mand, 211
  Decrease Indent
    command, 69
  Increase Indent command,
    69
  Style command, 91, 92
formatting styles, 70–72
Formatting toolbar, 28
  Add Bookmark tool, 119
  Add Horizontal Rule tool,
    111
  Add Hyperlink tool, 32, 44,
    85, 114, 208
  Add Picture tool, 109, 111,
    115, 118, 164, 195
  Bookmark tool, 32
  Center Text tool, 110
  Center tool, 124
  Internet Assistant icon, 287

Picture tool, 32, 36, 46, 76
Styles drop-down box, 64
forms, 219–260
  boundaries, defining,
    225–229
  completed illustration, 241
  complex, 223, 224
  creating, 224–242
    elegant, 252–260
    feedback, 252–258
    order, 258–260
  data, handling, 258
  defined, 221–222, 313
  editing, 242
  HTML code and, 244–245
  illustrated, 222, 227
  length of, 253
  mailto and, 243–249
  scripts and, 249–252
  simple, 222
  submitting, 242–252
    with CGI scripting, 243
    with e-mail, 242
    online, 256
  tables and, 258–259
  tags, 303–308
  template, 222
  white space on, 253
  in Word, 227
  WYSIWYG and, 256
  See also controls
Forms tool panel, 227
  defined, 227
  icons, 238
  illustrated, 238
  Protect Form tool, 242
  Reset tool, 240
  Submit tool, 239
  See also forms
Fountain Pro, 214–216
  defined, 214
  uses, 215
  working in, 214
  See also VRML
Fractal Design Painter, 31,
  109, 153–157
  Art Materials palette, 153

Brushes palette, 153
Grabber tool, 156
image transparency cre-
  ation with, 168–170
masks, 169
Objects palette, 169
opening file in, 153
tile creation with, 153–156
Tools palette, 156
frames, 16
free-standing markup,
  266–274
  alignment, 266–267
  horizontal rules, 266–270
  inserting, 267
  no break, 270–272
  plain text, 272–273
  shading, 268
  size, 268–269
  soft line breaks, 272
  width absolute, 269–270
  width percentage, 269
  See also HTML markup
freeware, 294
FTP (File Transfer Protocol),
  14–15, 117
  client, 314
  defined, 314
  servers, 117
  sites, 117

GIF graphic files, 25
  defined, 314
  interlacing, 165–167
  properties, setting, 170
  saving as, 151
  saving in Photoshop, 166
  saving in SnapShot/32,
    166
  transparency and, 165,
    167–170
Grabber tool (Painter), 156
graphics, CD-ROM,
  289–290

headers (page), 61
headers (table), 129–130
  cell, 130
  defined, 320
  illustrated, 130
  specifying, 129
  See also table(s)
headings, 62–63, 90
  applying, 84
  HTML codes for, 62–63
  in Netscape browser, 63
  See also Web-legal styles
HEX strings, creating, 145
hidden controls, 225,
  229–230
  adding, 229–230
  defined, 225
  illustrated, 230
  location for, 250
  uses, 229–230
  See also controls
Hidden Form Field dialog
  box, 229
hidden HTML codes, 264,
  265, 275
Horizontal Rule (HR) style,
  61, 90
Horizontal Rule tool, 266
horizontal rules, 61, 124
  alignment, 266
  custom, 269
  defined, 314
  left-aligned, 270
  shading, 268
  size, 268–269
  width absolute, 269–270
  width percentage, 269
hot spots
  CERN format, 182
  changing, 175
  checking accuracy of, 176
  creating, 174–175
  CSIM format, 184
  data, displaying, 179

hot spots *(continued)*
  defined, 314
  editing, 179
  hyperlinks for, 176–177
  NCSA format, 181
  rectangle, 174
  viewing, 177
  See also image maps
HTML (HyperText Markup
      Language), 1
  defined, 13, 314
  features, 15
  Hidden button, 264, 265
  hyperlinks, 16
  Internet Assistant and,
      295–210
  layout support and, 59
  Registry entry styles,
      100–101
  saving documents as, 60
  standard, 15
  support, 15
  wars, 15
  Web browsers and, 16
  Web page illustration, 14
  Word support for, 14
  Word vs., 308
  See also HTML codes;
      HTML markup; HTML
      tags
HTML codes, 1
  autoformatting of, 146
  blue text and, 79
  browser interpretation of,
      34
  colors, 145
  defined, 314
  forms and, 243–244
  heading, 63
  hidden, 264, 265, 275
  identifying, 79
  illustrated, 2, 13
  removing, consequences
      of, 79
  special, 310
  text alignment options, 163
  viewing, 144

in Word-created page, 1, 3
  See also HTML (HyperText
      Markup Language);
      HTML markup
HTML files, 141, 143
HTML markup, 216
  adding, 263–277
  defined, 83, 264, 314, 316
  embedded, 274–277
  for embedding VRML file,
      278
  free-standing, 266–267
  inserting, 267
  types of, 265
  in Word, 267
  See also HTML codes;
      HTML tags
HTML parameters
  ACTION, 244, 249, 305
  ALIGN, 266–267
  CELLPADDING, 127
  CHECKED, 304
  COLS, 307
  defined, 317
  ENCTYPE, 306
  MAXLENGTH, 304, 306
  METHOD, 244, 306
  NAME, 304, 305, 306,
      307, 308
  NOSHADE, 268
  ROWS, 307
  SELECTED, 307
  SIZE, 268–269, 304, 306
  SRC, 305
  VALUE, 304, 305, 306,
      307
  WIDTH, 269–270
  See also HTML codes;
      HTML tags
HTML tags, 244, 272
  <A HREF='#...>, 296
  <A HREF=...>, 296
  <A NAME=...>, 296
  <ADDRESS>, 296
  <B>, 296
  <BASE>, 297
  <BGSOUND>, 297

<BLOCKQUOTE>, 297
<BODY>, 297

, 78, 297
<CENTER>, 298
<CITE>, 298
<CODE>, 298
<DD>, 298
<DFN>, 298
<DIR>, 298
<DL>, 298
<DL COMPACT>, 298
<DT>, 298
<EM>, 298
<FONT>, 299
<FORM>, 299, 305–306
<H1> through <H6>, 299
<HEAD>, 299
<HR>, 266, 299
<I>, 299
<IMG>, 299
<INPUT>, 304–305,
      306–307
<ISINDEX>, 300
<KBD>, 300
<LI>, 300
<MARQUEE>, 300
<MENU>, 300
<META>, 300
<NOBR>, 263, 265,
      270–272
<OL>, 301
<OPTION>, 307
<P>, 78, 301
<PLAINTEXT>, 272–273
<PRE>, 301
<PRE WIDTH>, 301
<SAMP>, 302
<SELECT>, 307, 308
<STRIKE>, 301
<STRONG>, 301
<SUB>, 302
<SUP>, 302
<TABLE>, 302
<TEXTAREA>, 307
<TITLE>, 302
<TT>, 302
<U>, 302

<UL>, 302
<VAR>, 302
<WBR>, 272
form, 303–308
information about, 264
Internet Assistant and, 295–302
unsupported, 263
See also HTML codes
HtmlDirect code, 264, 265, 276
HTTP (HyperText Transfer Protocol), 15, 117
Hyperlink dialog box, 38–39, 45
  Bookmark Location in File option, 122
  Browse button, 121, 208
  illustrated, 86, 115
hyperlinks, 16
  adding, 49, 85–88
    to picture, 39
    in products page tutorial, 114–122
    steps for, 114
  audio, 203, 208
  bookmark, 121
  button image, 45
  colors for, 29, 143
  cursor and, 41
  defined, 314
  e-mail address, 44
  hot spot, 176–177
  to image files, 172
  locations for, 116–117
  for mailto addresses, 86
  for playing videos, 202
  press release tutorial, 87–88
  punctuation and, 44
  relative, 37
  selecting text for, 44
  underlining, 43
  to URLs, 87
  viewing contents of, 86
  in Word, 87
  See also HTML

icons
  Autopage, 23, 56, 104, 140, 190, 220, 262
  Forms tool panel, 238
  Internet Assistant, 7–8, 26
  MapTHIS!, 294
  Master Access, 289
  My Computer, 50, 52
  SnapShot/32, 294
  this book, 6
  Windows 95, 52
image editors, 17, 167
image files, 141
image.GIF, 308–309
image maps, 173–185
  client-based, 183–185
  conventions, 173, 180
  creating, steps for, 173
  defined, 173, 315
  functioning of, 185
  hot spots, 174–176
  images for, 173
  implementing, 185
  server-based, 174–180
  See also MAP files; MapTHIS!
Image menu (Photoshop)
  Flip Horizontal command, 151
  Flip Vertical command, 150
  See also Adobe Photoshop
image-editable programs, 147
images
  adding, 109–110
    hyperlinks to, 39
    in press release tutorial, 76–78
  alignment, 111, 112
    examples, 164
    with text options, 163
  background, 142–162

blurring, 147
border, 38
  as buttons, 38
  changing to pattern, 154–156
  clip art, 29, 31
  column, 158–160
  cutting/pasting, 150
  graduated fill, 158
  hyperlinks to, 172
  for image maps, 173
  inserted, 35
  interlacing, 165–167
  lightening, 147
  line, 158–160
  loading, 112
  options for, 36–38, 112
  on the page, 163–165
  photo, 30, 31
  replacing, 29–42
  row of pixels as, 158, 159
  rules for working with, 31
  scanned, 30
  selecting, 32
  size of, 36, 38
    displaying in other than actual, 172
    Web page with data, 171
    Web page without data, 171
  sizing, 171–172
  sources, 29–30
  tips and tricks, 165–172
  transparency, 165, 167–170
  viewing, 35
  wire, 146–147
  World Wide Web and, 139
indentation, lists and, 68–69, 134
indented paragraphs, 61
index entries, 61
Info About This Mapfile dialog box (MapTHIS!), 180
Insert HTML Markup dialog box, 267

Insert menu
  Form Field command,
    229, 231, 233, 234,
    235, 239
  Horizontal Rule command,
    111, 266
  HTML Markup command,
    266, 277
  Marquee command, 73
  Picture command, 25, 166
Insert Picture dialog box, 33,
  124
installation
  Automatic Setup software,
    290–292
  Internet Assistant, 1, 7–8,
    285–287
  Internet Explorer, 288
  MapTHIS!, 174, 294
  Parser program, 292
  SnapShot/32, 166, 293
  templates to hard disk,
    50–53
  Web browser, 8
interlacing, 165–167
  defined, 165, 315
  effect of, 166
  illustrated, 165
  See also GIF graphic files;
    images
Internet, 14
  bandwidth and, 192
  defined, 315
Internet Assistant, 1,
    281–288
  advantage of, 14
  automatic conversion, 13
  Browse Mode icon, 7–8
  defined, 13, 281
  downloading, 6–7,
    282–284
  feature categories, 13
  features, 9
  Formatting toolbar icon,
    287
  HTML and, 295–310
  HTML tags and, 295–302

icon, 26
installation, 1, 285–287
  detours, 285
  directory, 286
  process meter, 287
  setup, 286
  steps for, 6–8
  verifying, 287
  via downloading,
    282–287
  with Web browser, 7–8
  internal codes, 274
  nested tables and,
    126–127
  Registry entries, 96, 97
  reinstalling, 286
  tools, 13
  unsupported HTML com-
    mands, 263
  version of, 5, 281
  Word styles and, 89–92
  See also Word for
    Windows 95
    (version 7.0)
Internet Explorer, 17, 288
  access Web page with, 284
  bulleted list in, 85
  home page, 283
  installation, 288
  press release in, 82
  sending mail with, 46
  table borders in, 52
  video in, 197
  See also Web browsers
Internet providers, 17
  defined, 315
  Web pages and, 20–21
ISDN connections, 16
  defined, 315
  video and, 193
italics, 131

JavaScript, 260, 315
JPEG graphic files, 25, 315

Lasso tool (Photoshop),
  150, 151
layouts
  additional pages and, 108
  changing, 81–83
  defined, 316
  details and, 106
  sketching, 106, 107
  Web page created from,
    107
line breaks
  controlling, 272, 273
  soft, 272
links. *See* hyperlinks
lists, 63–69
  adding, 84–85
  in cells, 132
  combination, 68–69
  compact definition, 67
  defined, 316
  definition, 65–67
  Directory, 68, 90
  indentation and, 68–69,
    134
  Menu, 67–68, 91
  nested, 68–69
  ordered, 64, 317
  in tables, 134
  unordered, 64, 320
  Web-legal, 63
  See also Web-legal styles
logos, creating, 109

Macromedia. *See* Director;
  Shockwave
macros, 101–102, 264
  asterisks removal,
    101–102
  defined, 316

Registry and, 101
using, 101
mailto
addresses, 86
defined, 316
forms and, 243–249
manual setup
Chapter 1 tutorial, 24–25
Chapter 2 tutorial, 57
Chapter 3 tutorial,
104–105
Chapter 4 tutorial,
141–142
Chapter 5 tutorial,
190–192
Chapter 6 tutorial,
220–221
Chapter 7 tutorial,
262–263
files, 292
See also automatic setup
MAP files, 169
adding information to,
179–180
CERN, 182
closing, 178
conventions, 173
creating, 178–180
CSIM, 183–184
defined, 316
file extension, 177
functioning of, 185
managing, 173
name of, 173, 177
NCSA, 181
starting, 178
uses, 178
See also image maps
map-related files, 142
MapTHIS!, 173–185, 294
buttons and, 178
conventions and, 180
creating map file with,
178–180
defined, 294
features, 177
icons, 294

installing, 174, 294
loading image into, 175
opening window, 174
Rectangle tool, 174
versions, 294
See also image maps
markup. *See* HTML markup
marquee, 72–74
creating, 73
defined, 72–73, 316
properties, 73–74
Marquee dialog box, 73–74
masks (Painter), 169
Master Access program,
289–290
icon, 289
running, 290
Media Player, 202
menu selections, 13
Menu style, 67–68, 91
Microsoft Internet Explorer.
See Internet Explorer
Microsoft Word
knowledge of, 4
required version, 5
See also Word for
Windows 95
(version 7.0)
MIME types, 202, 316
MOV files, 199
MPEG (Motion Picture
Experts Group), 200,
317
multiline text box, 235–236
adding, 235–236
defined, 225, 317
features, 242
illustrated, 237, 241
in table cell, 255
See also controls
multimedia, 189–218
defined, 317
downloading, 189
plug-in technology, 213
Shockwave, 216–218
VRML, 213–216
Web future, 213–218

See also audio; video
My Computer icon, 50, 52
My Web Pages folder, 24,
25, 56, 57, 104, 140,
190–191, 220, 262

National Center for
Supercomputing
Applications. *See* NCSA
NCSA, 180, 181–182
defined, 180
hot spot format, 181
MAP file version, 181
See also hot spots
nested lists, 68–69
nested tables, 126–127, 317
Netscape Navigator 2.0, 17
completed page illustration
in, 49
definition lists in, 67
headings in, 63
page appearance in, 35
sending mail with, 45
See also Web browsers
New dialog box
Corporate Look tab, 26
General tab, 109
New Form dialog box, 226
nonbreaking lines, 271
nonbreaking spaces, 272
numbered lists. *See* ordered
lists

objects, embedded,
277–280
viewing, 279–280
VRML, 278
Objects palette (Painter),
169

Options dialog box
  File Locations tab, 22
  View tab, 41
order forms, 258–260
  automated calculations,
      259–260
  browser view, 269
  building of, 260
  illustrated layout, 259, 260
  layout, 258
  Word view, 260
  See also forms
ordered lists, 64, 317
organization, this book, 5

page breaks, 61
Page Layout mode, 59
Paint Shop Pro, 147
paragraph marks
  defined, 317
  displaying, 42
  turned on, 76
paragraphs
  adding, 81
  indented, 61
  spacing, adjusting, 78
  white space after, 78
Parser program, 246–249
  code enhancement sug-
      gestions, 292–293
  controls, 247
  defined, 318
  feedback form data,
      256–257
  installation, 292
  language, 246
  options, configuring, 248
  output, saving to file, 248
  running, 293
  using, 246–247
password text box control,
      236–238
  adding, 236–238

asterisks and, 242
  defined, 225, 236–237
  illustrated, 238, 241
  See also controls
patterns
  3-D version, 157
  changing images to,
      154–156
  lighter version, 157
Photo CD, 30
photo images, 30
  illustrated example, 31
  See also images
PhotoDisc, 187
Picture dialog box, 33
  Browse button, 111, 115,
      118
  Options tab, 36–38, 46,
      77, 112, 115, 118,
      196, 207
  Picture tab, 196
  Video tab, 195–196
Picture tool, 32, 36, 46, 76
planning, 105–106
plug-ins, 277
  choosing, 280
  classes of, 280
  defined, 318
  growth of, 277
  multimedia, 213
pointing hand cursor, 41, 42
pound sign (#), URLs, 119
PRE (preformatted) style,
      61, 71, 91
PRE WIDE style, 71, 72, 91
press release tutorial, 57–74
  after HTML saved, 60
  background color, 79–80
  conversion changes,
      60–61
  conversion points, 59
  converted, 58
  converted in Word for
      Windows, 75
  graphic, 76–78
  hyperlinks, 87–88
  in Internet Explorer, 82

layout, 81–83
  non-convertible Word
      features, 61
  original, 58
  paragraph spacing, 78
  in Word for Windows, 60
previews
  template, 27
  transparency, 170
  unsaved file, 34
private codes, 264
Products page, 35, 38–40,
      108–126
  adding hyperlinks to,
      114–121
  areas of focus, 109
  background color, 113,
      126
  bookmarks, 122
  in browser, 114
  company memo, 108
  creating Web page,
      109–126
  end of page, 124–126
  as gateway to other pages,
      124
  minor topics, 123–124
  See also WebStarr Web
      page
Protect Form tool, 242
Publisher's Toolbox, 186

QuickTime for Windows,
      198, 199, 200, 318

radio button group, 234–235
  adding, 234–235
  defined, 225, 318
  features, 241

illustrated, 235, 241
See also controls
Real Audio, 211–212
  constraints, 212
  defined, 203, 211
  files needed for, 212
  format conversion, 212
  home page, 212
  See also audio
Rectangle tool (MapTHIS!),
  174
Registry, 55
  accessing, 93
  defined, 89, 319
  editing. *See* Registry Editor
  entries, 96–98
    adding, 99–101
    Internet Assistant, 96, 97
    Microsoft, 96
    names, 99
    styles, 99–100
    values, 100
  function of, 89
  macros and, 101
  navigating in, 94–96
  saving, 89
  saving branch of, 98
  StyleMap entry, 96
  working in, 93–101
Registry Editor
  defined, 93
  hierarchy, opening, 95
  illustrated, 94
  plus sign (+), 94, 95
  right-side window, 96
  working in, 94–96
  See also Registry
Registry menu
  Export Registry File
    command, 96
  Import Registry File
    command, 98
relative links, 37
relative paths, 37, 109, 319
repeating textures, 148, 152
Reset button, 240–241
  adding, 240–241

defined, 222, 225, 319
  illustrated, 240, 241
  See also controls
Reset Button Form Field
  dialog box, 240
Reset tool, 240
revision marks, 61
rows
  defined, 319
  deleting, 204
  See also table(s)

Save As dialog box, 33, 60
saving
  before viewing, 80
  documents, 37
  downloaded file, 284
  forget warning, 37
  as GIF files, 151
  Photoshop selections, 149
  Registry, 89
  Registry branch, 98
scanned images, 30
scanners, 186
Screen Caffeine Pro, 187
scripts, 243
  advantages/disadvantages
    of, 243
  custom, 249
  defined, 319
  forms and, 249–252
  forms processing, 250
  library, 249, 252
  output, 251, 257
  servers and, 243
  specifying, 250
  uses for, 252
  visual, 321
seamless tiles, 148
section breaks, 61
Select menu (Photoshop)
  All command, 149

Load Selection command,
  150
None command, 151
Save Selection command,
  149
Selection Form Field dialog
  box, 231–232
selection list control,
  231–233
  adding items to, 231
  defined, 225
  features, 241
  illustrated, 233, 241
  moving items in, 232
  removing items from, 232
  See also controls
semicolon (;), escape
  sequence, 272
setup. *See* automatic setup;
  manual setup
Setup program, 290–291
shading, 268
shareware, 115, 294, 319
Shockwave, 216–218
  animation viewed with,
    217
  browsers, 218
  defined, 216
  downloading, 217
  limitations, 217
  See also Director;
    multimedia
Shopping page, 35,
  194–198
  topics, 194
  video file size, 200–201
  video frame size, 200–201
  See also WebStarr Web
    page
sizing
  fonts, 70
  horizontal rule, 268–269
  images, 171–172
SnapShot/32, 293–294
  defined, 293
  icons, 294

SnapShot/32 *(continued)*
  image transparency
    creation with, 170
  installing, 166, 293
  interlace option, setting,
    167
  saving GIF file as inter-
    laced in, 166
  versions, 294
soft line breaks, 272
Sound Forge, 218
space
  after paragraphs, 78
  between cells, 135–136
  on forms, 253
  nonbreaking, 272
special symbols, 309–310
  ASCII codes, 309, 310
  methods for adding, 309
  special codes, 309, 310
Standard toolbar, 28, 77
styles
  Address, 70, 89
  Blockquote, 71, 90,
    158–159
  character, 69–70, 72
  CITE, 90
  CODE, 90
  defined, 320
  Directory, 68, 90
  displaying, 91–92
  Emphasis (EM), 90
  formatting, 70–72
  heading, 62–63, 90
  Horizontal Rule (HR), 61,
    90
  list, 63–69
  marquee, 72–74
  Menu, 67–68, 91
  non-convertible, 61
  PRE, 61, 71, 91
  PRE WIDE, 71, 72, 91
  Registry entry, 99–100,
    99–101
  selecting, 64
  Web-legal, 62–74, 89–91
  z, 91

Submit button, 222,
  239–240
  adding, 239–240
  defined, 225, 320
  illustrated, 240, 241
  importance of, 239
  See also controls
Submit Button Form Field
  dialog box, 239,
  249–250
Submit tool, 239
Support page, 35, 124
  See also WebStarr Web
  page

table(s)
  adding text to, 131–132
  borders
    adding, 50
    illustrated, 51, 52
    in Internet Explorer, 52
    in Word, 51
  captions, 137–138
  cells, 131–138
  columns
    inserting, 205
    returning to original, 206
    selecting, 204
    widths of, 82–83,
      133–134, 206
  creating, 128
  defined, 320
  empty, 128
  enhancements, 133–138
  fancy, 126–138
  forms and, 258–259
  headers, 129–130
  lists in, 134
  nested, 126–127, 317
  rows, 204, 319
  selecting, 50
  text converted to, 82

  text placement control and,
    160
  view from browser, 138
  Web-legal, 126
Table menu
  Align command, 209
  Background Color com-
    mand, 134
  Borders command, 50,
    134, 136
  Caption command, 137
  Cell Type command, 129,
    130
  Cell Width and Spacing
    command, 82, 133,
    135, 158
  Delete Rows command,
    204
  Insert Columns command,
    205
  Insert command, 82
  Insert Table command,
    203
  Select Column command,
    204
Table of Contents entries, 61
tabs, 61, 75
taglines, 111
  adding, 110
  defined, 320
  illustrated, 111
templates, 9–54
  accessing, 21–22
  colors, changing, 28
  contents of, 3, 10
  copying, 21, 288–289
  Corporate Looks, 27
  defined, 10, 320
  file extension, 10
  file size, 288
  folders, 22
  forms, 222
  illustrated, 11
  image replacement, 29–42
  installing to hard disk,
    50–53

previews, 27
suggestions, 10
text
  importance of, 43
  replacing, 43–45
  selecting, 43
tutorial, 26–54
usage methods, 21
using, 26–54, 288–289
Web page creation with, 3, 12
working with, 10
text
  adding, 44
  alignment options, 163
  alternate, 33
  color, 143–144
  control, 228–229
  converted to table, 82
  converting to bulleted list, 84–85
  deleting, 44
  in document conversion, 75
  editing, 46–47
  in HTML files, 143
  placement control with tables, 160
  plain, 272–273
  selecting for hyperlink, 44
  table, 131–132
  template
    importance of, 43
    replacing, 43–45
    selecting, 43
    underlining and, 43
text box, 222
  creating, 227–229
  defined, 225
  features, 241
  illustrated, 228, 241
  multiline, 225, 235–236
  password, 225, 236–238
  values, 227
  See also controls

Text Form Field dialog box, 227–228, 235–236, 237
  illustrated, 228, 236
  Multiple Line radio button, 235
  Password radio button, 237
  values, 227
  warning, 228
textures
  background, 143
  repeating, 148
  with repeating boundaries, 148
  wire bundle, 148
  without boundaries, 148
tiles
  blended, 152
  creation, 149–151
  seamless, 148
  software for creating, 153–157
Tools menu, Options command, 22, 41
Tools palette (Painter), 156
transparency, 165, 167–170
  creating, 167
    with Painter, 168–170
    with Photoshop, 168
    with SnapShot/32, 170
  defined, 167, 320
  illustrated, 167
  previewing, 170
  Web page demonstration, 170
  See also GIF graphic files; images
true-color image editor, 167
trueSpace, 214
tutorials
  audio, 202–213
  automatic setup for. *See* automatic setup
  background image, 142–162

copying files for, 23, 56, 104, 140, 190, 220, 262
embedding objects, 277–280
folder, 24
forms, 224–260
HTML markup, 263–277
image maps, 173–185
images on the page, 163–165
manual setup for. *See* manual setup
pages from scratch, 105–126
templates, 26–54
video, 192–202
Word document conversion, 57–74

underlining, hyperlinks, 43
unordered lists, 64
  converting text to, 84–85
  defined, 320
  in Internet Explorer, 85
  See also lists
URLs (Uniform Resource Locator), 16
  components, 18
  defined, 18, 320
  domain name, 20
  hot spot button, 177
  hyperlinks to, 86
  pound sign (#) and, 119
  using, 19
  See also hyperlinks; Web pages

VDOLive, 212–213
  constraints, 213
  defined, 202, 212
  playing video with, 213
  tools, 212
  See also multimedia; video
video, 189
  adding, 192–202
  adding clips, 194–198
  animations, 198–199
  appearance of, 196–198
  bandwidth and, 192
  CD-ROM bonus, 218
  clips, 321
  controls, 196
  downloading, 193–194
  file formats, 200
  file size, 200
  files, 191
  frame rate and, 193, 202,
    314
  frame size, 192, 200, 202
  full-motion, 314
  in Internet Explorer, 197
  ISDN and, 193
  looping, 196
  MIME types and, 202
  MPEG, 200
  optimizing, 200–202
  playing with hyperlinks,
    202
  QuickTime, 198, 199, 200
  starting, 195
  still pictures and, 201
  variations, 194–198
  VDOLive, 202, 212–213
  Video for Windows, 199,
    200
  See also audio; multimedia
Video for Windows, 199,
    200, 321
View HTML Source mode,
    144–145

View menu
  HTML Source command,
    144
  Page Layout command, 59
  Toolbars command, 28
VRML, 213–216
  defined, 214, 321
  embedding, objects, 279
  file embedding, 216
  viewers, 216
  See also multimedia
VRScout, 216

watermarks, 161
  defined, 161, 321
  illustrated, 161
  See also background
    images
Web browsers
  cell spacing in, 136
  choosing, 17
  collecting, 19
  defined, 312
  function of, 15
  HTML and, 16
  installing Internet Assistant
    and, 7–8
  nonbreaking line in, 271
  order form view, 259
  recommended, 17
  saving before using, 80
  Shockwave and, 218
  table in, 138
  Web page look in, 34
  See also Internet Explorer;
    Netscape Navigator 2.0
Web pages
  custom, 4
  defined, 321
  existing documents as, 4,
    55–102

information about yourself
  on, 125
  keys to, 4
  look in different browsers,
    34
  placing, 19–21
    on company Web server,
      19–20
    on Internet provider
      server, 20–21
    on Web server provider,
      21
    on your Web server, 19
  planning, 105–106
  positioning, 46
  requirements for creating,
    17–19
  from scratch, 103–138
    creating, 109–126
    planning and, 105–106
    strategy and, 106–108
  specifying options for, 46
  from templates, 3, 9
  transparency demonstra-
    tion, 170
  uses for, 19–21
  WebStarr, 32
  See also World Wide Web
Web servers
  company, 19–20
  defined, 319
  no access to, 21
  owning, 19
  scripts and, 243
Web/FX, 216, 279
Web-legal styles, 62–74
  Address, 70, 89
  Blockquote, 71, 90,
    158–159
  bottom borders and, 61
  character
    basic, 69–70
    exotic, 72
  CITE, 90
  CODE, 90
  combination lists, 68–69

compact definition lists,
67, 90
definition lists, 65–67, 90
Directory, 68, 90
Emphasis, 90
formatting, 70–72
headings, 62–63, 90
Horizontal Rule, 61, 90
listing of, 89–91
lists, 63–69
marquee, 72–74
Menu, 67–68, 91
nested lists, 69
ordered lists, 64
PRE, 61, 71
PRE WIDE, 71, 72, 91
type, 89
unordered lists, 64
z, 91
See also styles
Web-legal tables, 126
cell padding and, 127
nested, 126–127
See also table(s)
Webmaster, 19, 117, 321
WebStarr, Inc., 32
press release, 58
WebStarr Pro, 115–116
WebStarr Server Edition,
118, 123
See also WebStarr Web
page
WebStarr Web page, 32
FAQs page, 36, 124
illustrated, 42
Lifestyle page, 36
Products page, 35, 38–40,
108–126
Shopping page, 35,
194–198
Support page, 35, 124
Windows 95
icons, 52
knowledge of, 4
Media Player, 202
Registry, 55, 89, 93–101
upgrading to, 282

wire images, 146–147
Word for Windows 95
(version 7.0), 5
captions in, 137
converted press release in,
75
definition lists in, 67
document conversion
tutorial, 57–74
forms in, 227
graphic filters, 25
hidden HTML codes in,
275
HTML feature support, 14
HTML markup in, 267
HTML vs., 308
hyperlinks in, 86
nested tables and,
126–127
opening screen, 26
order form view, 260
press release in, 60
table borders in, 51
upgrading to, 282
See also Internet Assistant
World Wide Web, 139
defined, 14–16, 321
embedding support, 280
images and, 139
requirements for surfing,
16–17
See also Web pages
WYSIWYG (what you see is
what you get), 13, 83
defined, 321
forms and, 256
for setting table columns,
133–134

z styles, 91

IDG BOOKS WORLDWIDE, INC.
END-USER LICENSE AGREEMENT

<u>Read This</u>. You should carefully read these terms and conditions before opening the software packet(s) included with this book ("Book"). This is a license agreement ("Agreement") between you and IDG Books Worldwide, Inc. ("IDGB"). By opening the accompanying software packet(s), you acknowledge that you have read and accept the following terms and conditions. If you do not agree and do not want to be bound by such terms and conditions, promptly return the Book and the unopened software packet(s) to the place you obtained them for a full refund.

<u>License Grant</u>. IDGB grants to you (either an individual or entity) a nonexclusive license to use one copy of the enclosed software program(s) (collectively, the "Software") solely for your own personal or business purposes on a single computer (whether a standard computer or a workstation component of a multi-user network). The Software is in use on a computer when it is loaded into temporary memory (i.e., RAM) or installed into permanent memory (e.g., hard disk, CD-ROM, or other storage device). IDGB reserves all rights not expressly granted herein.

<u>Ownership</u>. IDGB is the owner of all rights, titles, and interest, including copyright, in and to the compilation of the Software recorded on the CD-ROM. Copyright to the individual programs on the CD-ROM is owned by the author or other authorized copyright owner of each program. Ownership of the Software and all proprietary rights relating thereto remain with IDGB and its licensors.

<u>Restrictions on Use and Transfer</u>. You may only (i) make one copy of the Software for backup or archival purposes, or (ii) transfer the Software to a single hard disk, provided that you keep the original for backup or archival purposes. You may not (i) rent or lease the Software, (ii) copy or reproduce the Software through a LAN or other network system or through any computer subscriber system or bulletin-board system, or (iii) modify, adapt, or create derivative works based on the Software.

You may not reverse engineer, decompile, or disassemble the Software. You may transfer the Software and user documentation on a permanent basis, provided that the transferee agrees to accept the terms and conditions of this Agreement and you retain no copies. If the Software is an update or has been updated, any transfer must include the most recent update and all prior versions.

<u>Restrictions on Use of Individual Programs</u>. You must follow the individual requirements and restrictions detailed for each individual program in Appendix E of this Book. These limitations are contained in the individual license agreements recorded on the CD-ROM. These restrictions include a requirement that after using the program for the period of time specified in its text, the user must pay a registration fee or discontinue use. By opening the Software packet(s), you will be agreeing to abide by the licenses and restrictions for these individual programs. None of the material on this CD-ROM or listed in this Book may ever be distributed, in original or modified form, for commercial purposes.

Limited Warranty. IDGB warrants that the Software and CD-ROM are free from defects in materials and workmanship under normal use for a period of sixty (60) days from the date of purchase of this Book. If IDGB receives notification within the warranty period of defects in materials or workmanship, IDGB will replace the defective CD-ROM.

IDGB AND THE AUTHOR OF THE BOOK DISCLAIM ALL OTHER WARRANTIES, EXPRESS OR IMPLIED, INCLUDING WITHOUT LIMITATION IMPLIED WARRANTIES OF MERCHANTABILITY AND FITNESS FOR A PARTICULAR PURPOSE, WITH RESPECT TO THE SOFTWARE, THE PROGRAMS, THE SOURCE CODE CONTAINED THEREIN, AND/OR THE TECHNIQUES DESCRIBED IN THIS BOOK. IDGB DOES NOT WARRANT THAT THE FUNCTIONS CONTAINED IN THE SOFTWARE WILL MEET YOUR REQUIREMENTS OR THAT THE OPERATION OF THE SOFTWARE WILL BE ERROR FREE.

This limited warranty gives you specific legal rights, and you may have other rights which vary from jurisdiction to jurisdiction.

Remedies. IDGB's entire liability and your exclusive remedy for defects in materials and workmanship shall be limited to replacement of the Software, which is returned to IDGB at the address set forth below with a copy of your receipt. This Limited Warranty is void if failure of the Software has resulted from accident, abuse, or misapplication. Any replacement Software will be warranted for the remainder of the original warranty period or thirty (30) days, whichever is longer.

In no event shall IDGB or the author be liable for any damages whatsoever (including without limitation damages for loss of business profits, business interruption, loss of business information, or any other pecuniary loss) arising out of the use of or inability to use the Book or the Software, even if IDGB has been advised of the possibility of such damages.

Because some jurisdictions do not allow the exclusion or limitation of liability for consequential or incidental damages, the above limitation or exclusion may not apply to you.

U.S. Government Restricted Rights. Use, duplication, or disclosure of the Software by the U.S. Government is subject to restrictions stated in paragraph (c) (1) (ii) of the Rights in Technical Data and Computer Software clause of DFARS 252.227-7013, and in subparagraphs (a) through (d) of the Commercial Computer—Restricted Rights clause at FAR 52.227-19, and in similar clauses in the NASA FAR supplement, when applicable.

General. This Agreement constitutes the entire understanding of the parties, and revokes and supersedes all prior agreements, oral or written, between them and may not be modified or amended except in a writing signed by both parties hereto which specifically refers to this Agreement. This Agreement shall take precedence over any other documents that may be in conflict herewith. If any one or more provisions contained in this Agreement are held by any court or tribunal to be invalid, illegal or otherwise unenforceable, each and every other provision shall remain in full force and effect.

Using the CD-ROM

Automatic Setup software

To install the Automatic Setup software, you must have the CD-ROM that comes with this book inserted into your CD-ROM drive. Double-click the My Computer icon to display the available drives on your computer, and then double-click the CD-ROM drive icon. This displays a folder showing the contents of the CD-ROM. Double-click the Autopage folder. Double-click the Setup icon to run the setup program and follow the on-screen prompts to complete installation.

Setup copies several files to a temporary directory and then displays the Welcome banner. Click OK to continue, then click the installation button to begin actual installation of the software. If you want to change the installation directory, click the Change Directory button.

After installation, you can run the Automatic Setup program by clicking the Start button, then Programs, and then Autopage. To install all files for all chapters in one step, select the last radio button, Copy All Files Now. The software will attempt to identify the correct source and destination drives, but you can change the defaults if you prefer. To copy files, click the Copy to Hard Disk button.

Templates

To begin installing templates from the CD-ROM, double-click the My Computer icon on your Windows 95 desktop. Double-click the icon for the drive where you installed Word for Windows or Microsoft Office. (The usual location is your C drive.) This action displays the folders on your drive; double-click the MS Office folder, and then double-click the Templates folder to open it. Double-click the icon for your CD-ROM drive. Double-click the folder icon for the Cool Templates folder of the CD-ROM. Rearrange your desktop so that you can clearly see the contents of the Templates and Cool Templates folders. To install any folder from Cool Templates, right-click on the folder you want to install and then drag it into the MS Office Templates folder. When you release the mouse button, you see the pop-up menu; select the Copy option. This copies the folder, and the templates and graphics it contains, to your hard drive.

Graphics

Several graphics vendors have provided sample graphics on the CD-ROM for your use. To run the master access software, you must have the CD-ROM that comes with this book inserted into your CD-ROM drive. Double-click the My Computer icon to display the available drives on your computer, and then double-click the CD-ROM drive icon. This displays a folder showing the contents of the CD-ROM. Double-click the Graphics folder. Double-click the Mastaccs.exe icon to run the Master Access program. The Master Access program has a button for each vendor who has supplied graphic images. To run the access program for a vendor, just click the vendor's button.

Third-Party Software

To install any of the third-party programs, you must have the CD-ROM that comes with this book inserted into your CD-ROM drive. Double-click the My Computer icon to display the available drives on your computer, and then double-click the CD-ROM drive icon. This displays a folder showing the contents of the CD-ROM. Double-click the ThirdP folder to see the folders for the third-party programs.